AMONG
THOSE
PRESENT

A Reporter's View
of Twenty-five Years
in Washington

RANDOM HOUSE / NEW YORK

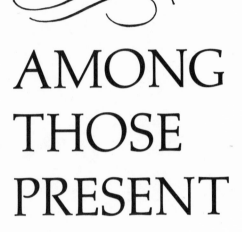

AMONG
THOSE
PRESENT

NANCY
DICKERSON

Library of Congress Cataloging in Publication Data
Dickerson, Nancy.
Among those present.
1. Dickerson, Nancy. 2. Journalists—United
States—Correspondence, reminiscences, etc.
3. United States—Politics and government—
1945–   I. Title.
PN4874.D44A33   070′.92′4 [B]   76–14164
ISBN 0–394–49876–3

Manufactured in the United States of America
3 4 5 6 7 8 9

As requested by Michael and John Dickerson,
this book is dedicated to them—and to all
of their relatives, especially their sisters, with love

AUTHOR'S NOTE

Shortly after Nixon's resignation I met Jill Volner, the incisive Deputy Assistant Prosecutor of the Watergate trials. She had done a masterly job, was highly acclaimed and deserved it. I introduced myself as a fan of hers, and then was both surprised and delighted when she said, "I wouldn't be here if it weren't for you."

She explained that when she was a student at the University of Illinois she had heard me lecture there, and as a result had entered journalism school and later came to Washington.

Naturally, I was pleased to have been an influence in her life, and I was doubly pleased because through her role as a vigorous prosecutor she helped terminate the dreadful tragedy that was Watergate.

There have been many young women who have written to me and asked, "How did you get there?" or "What's it like?" or "Please tell me about the people you interview and what they are really like." In this book I answer some—though by no means all—of their questions. I make no pretense at anything more. I thank those young women for their interest and I thank even more the women who came before them and took the time to be interested in me.

ACKNOWLEDGMENTS

No book can be written without help from many people, and I am grateful to those who helped me, especially Carl Marcy, whose invaluable suggestions, though few in number, were readily accepted; Ruth McCawley, who not only typed every draft ahead of schedule but acted as a sounding board; Mary Margaret Valenti, for her sensitive comments, even though she disagrees with some of my conclusions; Ann Dickerson Harrower, who read the original draft and whose pungent comments were a delight and some—but not all—of whose suggestions have been included; and C. Wyatt Dickerson, without whom there would be no book.

Of course, none of those mentioned above are responsible for anything I have written.

N.H.D.
Merrywood
McLean, Virginia
June, 1976

AMONG
THOSE
PRESENT

CHAPTER 1 ⟿

I come from Wauwatosa, Wisconsin, which is part of Eisenhower's "heartland" and the backbone of Richard Nixon's Middle America. In the summer we played kick the can in the street, and put up a lemonade stand. A Methodist minister lived on the corner, and up the block there was a deaf-mute family. It was a lazy, happy childhood, confined mostly to Cedar Street. But as far as I was concerned, nothing ever happened there.

After graduation from Wauwatosa High School I went to Clarke College, a Catholic girls' school in Dubuque, Iowa, where I got a little more religion and a healthy attitude toward sex. The lovely little nuns taught us that sex was a physical manifestation of love, and that since love was good, so too was sex; this was fairly progressive thinking in that time and place. There were religious retreats with grave stock-taking sermons, and we were not supposed to talk for three days. During these retreats, the nuns often served raw celery, never realizing its effect. When a hundred blue-uniformed girls were silent except for the crunching of raw celery, it made a funny sound that always pierced the dining-room piety.

There was an aura of mystery about nuns then. We were told that they all shaved their heads, and maybe some of them did. We were

3

fascinated by Sister Mary Cafeteria, the name we gave to the nun who ran the dining room. She ran away with the ice man. When she took off her habit her hair wasn't shaved at all; it was red and hung to her waist. The episode was forbidden conversation by the nuns, who were scandalized by the event.

I majored in piano, which was a joke, because although I had given lessons on it when I was twelve and had studied it all my life in the proper middle-class way, it should have been clear that Nancy Hanschman had no musical talent. I was tone-deaf, but persevering nevertheless. For a spring recital I chose a piece played entirely with the left hand. When I practiced so much that polyps appeared on my left wrist and I couldn't move my hand, I interpreted it as a clear sign from Heaven to change my major to something less strenuous.

After two insulated years in Dubuque, I transferred to the University of Wisconsin and applied to the medical school. A foolish admission clerk tried to dissuade me, arguing that it wouldn't be right to usurp the place of a man. That was typical of the advice given to girls in the forties and I ignored it, but I did decide not to be a doctor because it took too long. Instead I entered the School of Education, majoring in Spanish and Portuguese, and took part in every extracurricular activity possible. As a result, after graduation I was chosen to be a United Nations student delegate to Europe. Lord, was I excited! I got a passport and withdrew all the money I had: $900, saved from summer jobs.

It was 1948, the year of the New Look, meaning long skirts, and my entire traveling wardrobe went down to my ankles. If length alone determined it, I was extremely chic, or so I thought. I had never been downtown alone in Milwaukee at night, and I was going off to Europe all by myself. And I was like a wild horse trying to break loose.

I sailed on the *Volendam,* one of those Dutch ships used for troop transport during the war and later reconditioned to take U.S. Army wives and student groups such as ours to Europe. I was on it for seven days and never could see what was reconditioned about it. I shared a cabin with 350 other women and we were all seasick the whole time. I had my first encounter with aquavit, which the ship's old captain kept giving to me, swearing it would help. He gave me enough to make me roaring drunk, but it never stayed down long enough for that.

I was supposed to get off in England, but it was Bastille Day and

4

I decided to help the French celebrate, so I threw away my travel plans and got off at Le Havre. I could hardly believe what I saw: the rubble from the bombings still piled high in the streets was a sobering sight. We had all seen movies of the bombings and the devastation of the war, but to walk through a leveled city not via a camera's lens but with one's own eyes was a shock that I can recall in minutest detail even now. That sight and the summer that followed changed my life and set the pattern for what came after.

Somehow, speaking only the French I taught myself from a pocket guide, I managed to get on a train which arrived in Paris just before dusk. My French sounded good enough, so when I asked the question *"Où est un hôtel?"* I'd get a proper French answer. The trouble was that I couldn't understand the answer, but I knew enough to go to the Left Bank. Even my insular education had introduced me to Jean-Paul Sartre. I found a pension unpatronized by any other Americans and began a summer in Europe, savoring my independence and envisioning myself as a latter-day Cornelia Otis Skinner.

Postwar Paris was vibrating with excitement, and so was I. Walking down the streets of the Left Bank, all alone, knowing no one, I suddenly heard someone call. It was Sammy Hope from Wauwatosa, who kissed me on both cheeks, French fashion, and offered me a cigarette, declaring that here it was permissible to smoke in the street. It was July 14, the first time since the war that Paris, the City of Light, had lit up. I had never seen anything as spectacular. We danced in the streets that night, and I've often wondered who those nameless French partners were. Was a Mitterrand or Giscard d'Estaing among them, and were they thinking, as we were, about brotherhood and a new world? Intoxicated by the wine and the city, I decided, like a host of other young Americans of a previous generation, to live in Paris, perhaps forever.

But I had brought some added baggage: a mission. Simplistically, I thought that if forty of us UN student delegates from over thirty different countries could go to seminars and travel all over Europe together, sometimes in a boxcar, always crowded, always in the lowest class—which was fairly grim in those post–World War II days—and learn to get along individually (even though our group at times included two former Nazi SS troopers and two Jews from the new state of Israel), nations could do the same thing. Simplistic, perhaps, but we were no gin-ridden, jazz-mad generation; while we were naïve

5

and inexperienced, we also were products of that peculiar mixture of plain talk and Midwestern geography which have done their part to keep the national psyche in balance.

The international companionship and camaraderie, together with the shock at the devastation we encountered, convinced me that I was going to do something to see that this never happened again. I met an old Jewish rabbi from Brooklyn, and with the fire in my belly that most of us college graduates of the late forties had, I told him that my generation was going to change it all. He wasn't convinced, saying he had heard the same thing after World War I. With great passion I told him we were different and that we would make a world free from holocausts. That's how the summer ended. Firm conviction.

When the international student seminars and youth conferences were over, I returned to Paris and got two jobs, one as a model at Nina Ricci and one as a typist at the Economic Cooperation Administration. But my parents objected strongly and sent a stern wire reminding me that I had signed a contract to teach school. I was exasperated by the thought, but dutifully returned home to become a Milwaukee schoolteacher. It was a restless two years, punctuated by Harvard graduate school in the summer to study government, and in the winter enough dates to know that there weren't any eligible bachelors in Milwaukee who were thinking about changing the world the way I was.

The next stop was New York, which is the first place a Midwesterner goes to when leaving the Midwest. I wanted a job that had to do with foreign affairs or education or one of those more esoteric professions—at least to the unsophisticated Midwestern ear—like public relations. In desperation I even applied for a job as a guide in Rockefeller Center. Years later when I broadcast the NBC news from New York and the guides brought the tours by to watch, I often thought of my rejected job application.

Systematically, I went through the "Help Wanted" ads and was often lost as I groped around the city, job hunting with no encouragement and no luck. It was an exhausting process, and at night I stayed at one of those dreadful, lonely women's hotels. I knew no one and no one wanted to hire me. I was pathetic, but too young to realize it; mostly I was outraged that I couldn't find a job. Some family friends persuaded their daughter to see me to give me a few tips.

With the arrogance of a new New Yorker, she said that if I were to get a job in New York—which was highly unlikely—I'd have to get a whole new wardrobe. It took her less than four minutes to urge me to hurry back to Milwaukee. I hated her.

Back on Cedar Street in Wauwatosa what we would now call the jet set had been limited to two *Life* photographers, Frank and Joe Schershel, who lived there when they weren't off on exotic assignments. I found Frank in New York and he took me to *Time* and *Life* job seeking, but things were so discouraging that he gently suggested that Washington might be a better spot. I knew no one there, but Frank did. He called a friend and she said that I could stay with her.

It was dusk as I reached the capital. Waiting for me at the depot was the girl I'd never met, Frank's friend who worked at the CIA. As she drove me home, we stopped at the Lincoln Memorial. Since that night I've come to regard it as a sacred shrine, so I hate to admit that I experienced no profound impression when I first saw it. I've read memoirs of men and women who came to Washington and apparently had a mystic feeling about it as they gazed reverently at some meaningful historic site. Not me. I was anxious to get on with the business of changing the world and I had no time for old monuments. I'm not proud of that introduction because it reveals my lack of sensitivity at that time to what Washington is all about. At Harvard, Professor Bruce Hopper kept saying we had to have "history in your bones." That night my bones were empty. I do recall the sign on the front of the National Archives: "What is Past is Prologue." I made a mental note, but I was in a hurry to do something about the present.

Then my new friend drove me to the biggest brick mansion I'd ever seen, the home of Mr. Edward Burling, the founder of Washington's largest law firm and one of its most prestigious. She was staying there while he was away on vacation. When he returned and I met him, we became fast friends and he asked me to stay until I found a job. Although Mr. Burling was over eighty, he was one of the most exciting men I've ever met. To keep his mind alert, he memorized a verse of poetry each night. He was very rich and powerful, knew everyone, and in a short time he furthered my practical education considerably. For example, I learned that unless I read all the newspapers before going in to dinner, I'd be out of the conversation entirely.

One of Mr. Burling's former law partners was Secretary of State Dean Acheson, who was under great strain during that summer of 1950. The Alger Hiss case was just over, President Truman's popularity was low, and he was being less than friendly to his Secretary of State. One day Mr. Acheson came to lunch, and though I was not invited, I did pick the flowers for the luncheon table. For me, that was heady stuff.

I remember peeking out the window as Mr. Acheson climbed the stairs. He looked bone-tired, and it seemed to be an effort to lift each foot to the next step. I saw him many times after that, and he always exuded vitality; in fact, he embodied physical energy. But that day he was a weary man, and Mr. Burling advised him to tell Truman either to show a little more public affection and respect for his Secretary of State, or to let him go. That's what Acheson did, and the President began behaving better toward him.

When Mr. Acheson testified on the Hill, he had the arrogance of an emperor and the testiness of a spoiled child. Once he got into a semantic debate with old Senator H. Alexander Smith of New Jersey. They hassled for half an hour, at the end of which Smith said, "But, Mr. Secretary, you and I have no area of disagreement." Acheson's only reply was to sniff as if he smelled something bad.

Since there were no mustaches in Wauwatosa, I thought Mr. Acheson's made him look evil and sinister, though he carried it off much better than the half-dozen State Department underlings who tried to emulate him. To meet the Secretary of State was to see walking power. I was dying to tell him how to keep peace in the world, but I never had the chance. I wanted him to know how important student exchange was, and that he would have to work harder for freer and greater communication among peoples. I'm not sure how I wanted this accomplished, and in retrospect it sounds as if I was advocating a massive round-the-world love-in, but I was certain of one thing: he had to fight more vigorously for total commitment to the United Nations, a concept that was highly suspect at the time.

Every day for the rest of that hot and muggy summer I would leave the luxury of the Burling mansion to spend my time in the employment offices of government bureaus. It was a tedious exercise. I got to know the Pentagon by heart, and found that the colonels in charge of personnel were more interested in conversation during their coffee

8

break than in employment possibilities. I went to Capitol Hill and left a copy of my curriculum vitae at every senator's office, but it was clear that no one wanted to hire a Milwaukee schoolteacher with minimum typing skills who didn't know anybody.

The place where I most wanted to work was the Senate Foreign Relations Committee, but it was surfeited with applications from girl graduates, especially girls who had gone to school in the East and whose families knew senators. However, the committee clerk was one of God's princes, a dear, dear man named C. C. O'Day, who smiled, which very few people do during job hunts. I didn't know until many years later that Cy O'Day had written across the top of my application, "This girl has everything." That did it. After I'd spent a few months working as a registrar at Georgetown University, Cy phoned to say that I had a job with the committee.

To get that job I had said that I could take dictation. Since I couldn't, I had to learn it quickly. I bought a speed-writing manual, and every night for four weeks my beaus had to sit for an hour and dictate as I tried to teach myself some form of shorthand. Despite the effort, it was a disaster. I showed up at the committee with a brave smile and a façade of authority, but to this day I cannot see anyone taking dictation without suffering for them.

However, I knew how to type, so Carl Marcy, who later became the distinguished chief of staff of the committee, let me write the letters myself, while another staffman, a sadist, dictated speeches, hour after hour—a first draft, second draft, and *ad infinitum*. What I returned to him had little resemblance to what he had dictated, but he didn't seem to realize it. I never thought he knew what he was talking about, anyway; when he wrote speeches for committee members, they always had more rhetoric than reason. This characterizes much of what is said in Congress, so it didn't make much difference. My shorthand soon became an open joke and a stenographer was hired who first had to take a stiff shorthand test. By then Dr. Francis O. Wilcox, the scholarly staff chief, who thought more about writing than typing, had assigned me to edit hearings and to help write speeches.

One classic speech was a collaboration with Carl Marcy in support of foreign aid for Senator Theodore Francis Green of Rhode Island. Carl took the substantive parts of the bill as it had been marked up, section by section, and explained the meaning and intent. Armed with *Bartlett's Quotations*, I wrote the beginning of each paragraph, which was then meshed with Carl's part. As each section came off his or my typewriter, a Senate pageboy standing by would grab it and rush it upstairs to the Senate floor to the aged senator. Later we were astonished to find that Green had that speech reproduced to send to every library in his state. Rich though he was, I don't think it was worth his money, but it was nice to think it was going to be kept forever in Rhode Island.

My job at the Foreign Relations Committee had started in the spring of 1951, shortly before Truman fired General Douglas MacArthur. On the chilly day in April when he gave his farewell speech to Congress, saying, "Old soldiers never die, they just fade away," I felt as if I was really in the center of things, right where I wanted to be. At the time there was a lot of talk about a groundswell movement to run MacArthur for President, but after listening to the speech I agreed with the old pros around the Hill who knowingly told me he'd never make it.

After watching MacArthur in the crowded House chamber, I went back to the other side of the Hill, to the Senate gallery, which was empty except for Foreign Relations Committee staff members. As the drums rolled outside and sirens wailed the departure of the fading MacArthur, our little group listened to his colleagues' eulogies for the late Senator Arthur H. Vandenberg, the beloved former committee chairman who had done so much to create bipartisan foreign policy after World War II. It's often said that a Senate speech never changes a single vote, but Vandenberg was an exception; his integrity and personal charm gave him unique power and standing in the Senate. Indeed, whenever it became known that Vandenberg was preparing a speech, his democratic counterpart, Senator Tom Connally of Texas, would hole up in his office to write one too, as he tried to outshine Vandenberg and get a piggyback ride on his publicity.

Vandenberg's most important Senate speech was on January 10, 1945, when he endorsed the concept of the United Nations and thereby helped swing the country away from isolation toward internationalism. Two years later, in Cleveland, when he said that "politics ends at the water's edge," he created a tradition in U.S. foreign policy for years to come. He imbued committee members with the thought that partisanship had no place in foreign affairs—that while dissent was permissible and welcomed at home, when we presented ourselves to other nations we should appear as a unified whole. This attitude permeated the staff as well; we worked equally for senators of both parties, unlike other committee staffs which were often divided into Republican and Democratic staff members. As a result, purely partisan politics rarely entered Foreign Relations Committee deliberations. To be sure, there were strong philosophical differences, especially on foreign aid, but the senators and staff worked mightily toward a compromise so that as much as possible the committee could speak with one voice to the Senate and the world on all major issues.

When the Democrats regained control of the Senate in 1948, Tom Connally had succeeded Vandenberg as committee chairman. With his long white mane curling over his collar top, he not only looked like a lion, but roared like one too, and he intimidated me and a lot of other people. Whenever he spoke in the Senate, the word went around the Hill, and staffmen and senators would hurry over to see the fun. One bout which became famous was with his *bête noire*, Senator Robert A. Taft, who vigorously opposed such a "giveaway" as foreign aid. Since Taft was not on the Foreign Relations Committee, Connally accused him of meddling in affairs not of his concern, and chastised him for "supererogation." Taft jumped up and demanded to know what "supererogation" was. Old Connally slowly turned his massive bulk around, leered at Taft over his half glasses and said, "I haven't time to educate the Senator from Ohio; I refer him to *Webster.*"

Connally could be gracious, and prided himself on looking like a senator, but mostly he was grumpy and cunning. He considered Senator Brien McMahon of Connecticut something of an impostor, and was jealous that his colleague was being touted as a presidential possibility. In Senate protocol, one senator never calls another by name, but refers to him by his title, or as "the Senator from ____," but at every opportunity Connally would call McMahon by name and purposefully mispronounce it, playing to the press gallery to make sure they got his little joke.

Once Connally gave a hot story to the AP and UP men who covered the Hill in tandem, but swore them to secrecy, saying that he was talking off the record. Minutes later he gave the same story with no strings attached to his favorite reporter, Bill White of the *New York Times.* The next day when the story appeared in headlines

11

in the *Times,* the UP and AP men who had been roundly scooped protested bitterly to the senator; how had White got the story? Without breaking stride, Connally said, "One of you two fellows must have leaked it to him."

Later when Senator Green, a sweet old bachelor in his eighties, became chairman of the Foreign Relations Committee, he told me that people didn't take him very seriously because he walked around with a stoop, the result of a wrestling accident at an early age. He said, "People think I'm stupid, but I'm not." He was considered the richest man in the Senate, and also the stingiest. He tipped a nickel at lunch, and he used to take out Ms. Daisy Harriman, but was too cheap to hire a cab. Instead he'd take Ms. Harriman, a grand old lady, by streetcar to the movies, and then home again the same way. She didn't object until the snows came; then, being over seventy years old, she refused to trudge two blocks through the slush to the car stop.

There are a lot of funny stories about Senator Green, most of them true. Once at a cocktail party I saw him take out a small index card on which his appointments for the day were written. When someone asked him if he was trying to find out where he was due next, he replied, "No, indeed; I'm trying to find out where I am now."

Green's departure as chairman of the committee in 1959 epitomized the difference between Democratic political savvy and that of the Republicans. The Republicans in the House had decided that their leader, Joe Martin, was too old and should be replaced, so after a public power struggle they kicked him out, rather in the way the Eskimos let their old people go out to sea on a floe. Not so the Democrats. Green was sleeping through most of the committee hearings, and finally it became obvious even to him that he should step down. He said he would, but the Democratic majority would hear none of it. They passed a resolution insisting that Green stay on. When the senator protested, they asked him to leave the committee room and reconsider. And when he returned to his waiting colleagues still insisting that he should step down, again he met loud protests. Finally the ritual came to a glorious teary-eyed conclusion, accompanied by much handshaking, and Green was voted the first and only chairman emeritus, a position which enabled him to continue to sleep through meetings while Senator J. William Fulbright took over. No one was sent out on a floe, but the mission was accomplished.

*　　　　*　　　　*

12

The Foreign Relations Committee had its own tradition and history, and all of the staff connected with it vicariously enjoyed its prestige. We liked to talk about the strategic phone calls from the White House, and the distinguished foreign guests who came to pay homage—and sometimes to ask for more foreign aid. There was a wonderfully comfortable chair that Winston Churchill had sat in when he visited the committee during World War II; it had become known as "the Churchill chair" and was always given to any guest of honor.

Undoubtedly it was the most prestigious committee on Capitol Hill, and a seat close to the head of the big oval table was coveted. For decades some of America's greatest men had charted our country's history there, and their places were designated by bronze name plates. Senator Henry Cabot Lodge of Massachusetts was more concerned about the placement of his seat than anyone else, for his grandfather and namesake had been committee chairman and leader of the famous "seven willful men" who had thwarted Wilson's plan to join the League of Nations. As chairman, the grandfather had sat at the head of the table, but the grandson, a relative newcomer to the committee, lacked seniority, so protocol dictated that he be at the bottom of the table, a placement that greatly irritated him. Therefore, on days when the committee was the center of public interest and reporters and photographers were there, we all watched to see how he would act. Invariably he would cup his hand to his ear as if he were hard of hearing, and then would move his own chair up just behind the chairman's, saying he didn't want to miss anything. This ploy helped to get his picture in the papers. Despite his arrogance, Lodge was a sexy, handsome man who looked very grand in his white suits from Boston, but he could be a problem. Once he complained bitterly to Cy O'Day about the draft at his seat and asked that it be fixed, or else that his place be changed, a ploy which would let him edge up closer to the chairman. Cy called in the air-conditioning engineers, who found no draft; this was explained to Lodge, who accepted the explanation for a meeting or two, and then complained again. Cy went through the same charade, and once again Lodge said that he couldn't sit in the draft and would refuse to attend all future meetings until it was eliminated or his seat changed. The engineers were called back once more, with the same result, but by then Cy was wiser. He dutifully reported to Senator Lodge that the engineers had indeed found a draft, had located the source and deflected it, and that they all hoped Lodge would be comfortable henceforth. The senator started going to meetings again.

At one point the committee conducted a study to determine the most effective way of telling the American story abroad. They wanted to know if they got more for their money by spending it on the Voice of America, on pamphlets, on magazines or fliers, on the student-exchange program, or on other programs of the U.S. Information Agency. Questionnaires were sent to all our ambassadors, and when their evaluations came in I collated them and wrote a report. Naturally, I was delighted that the ambassadors had unanimously endorsed student exchange and other people-to-people programs as the most effective way to tell the United States' story. This survey gave substantive support to my own convictions that people exchange was the best way to prevent future war. The ambassadors' conclusions were exactly what I had been imbued with in that postwar trip through Europe as a UN student delegate. Of course it's naïve and simplistic to think that such exchange can solve *all* the world's problems, but it can ameliorate many of them, and I still believe that as world travel increases, understanding among nations will rise proportionately. In my report I strongly emphasized the value of people exchange, and this dovetailed nicely with the predispositions of the senator from Arkansas, whose Fulbright Act of 1946 had authorized surplus war funds to be used by U.S. students abroad. The committee chairman had the report published as a staff study, introduced it in the Senate and gave it the widest circulation possible.

Nothing I've ever done has given me more satisfaction than that report. I've never believed anything so passionately before or since, and I was delighted that it would be seen by the people in power who could do something about it.

CHAPTER 2 ⌁

For me, the Foreign Relations Committee was a graduate course in government. The lab was the whole United States Senate and sometimes the House. I hadn't been there six months when I was assigned as a staff assistant on the Jessup subcommittee, the group holding hearings on the nomination of Philip C. Jessup as U.S. Representative to the United Nations, an appointment challenged by Senator McCarthy.

It is a measure of the initial lack of concern about McCarthy that the subcommittee didn't think him sufficiently significant to assign more experienced staffmen in the beginning. It was said that his charges were too preposterous to be taken seriously by reasonable men, but only a few months later there wasn't a senator who could ignore McCarthy without peril, and in the elections a year later, in 1952, he was credited with the defeat of eight of them.

McCarthy had been questioning Jessup's loyalty for more than a year, charging that Jessup was soft on Communism and had favored recognition of Red China over Chiang Kai-shek, which in those days was tantamount to being a card-carrying Communist. When the hearings opened, the senator shuffled in to testify. He was surprisingly short, especially from the waist down; his top half was barrel-shaped, and he had a big gut, which hung over and covered his belt, and a gorillalike smile which was bestowed indiscriminately on everyone. At first I thought he had a tic, but it turned out that he was winking at me.

The hearing focused on whether Red China ever was in fact even *considered* for recognition by Jessup and the State Department. Jessup contended that such recognition had been discussed, but never "considered" in the sense that they actually contemplated doing so.

McCarthy had selected certain facets of Jessup's career and association with certain organizations to demonstrate that he was trying to "sell out" to the Communists. When he lacked specific information under questioning, he would plead that he had no staff and shouldn't be held responsible for all data; his research would be more precise, he said, if he could have the help of the Senate Foreign Relations Committee staff. That was me. He'd give me a big wink, and Senator John Sparkman, who was then the subcommittee chairman, would say graciously in his Alabama accent, "Our staff will be very glad to cooperate in any way they can." Here I was trying to change the world, and the chairman had offered me on a platter to McCarthy! Fortunately, he never followed up the offer. He just kept on winking.

The hearings became so heated and contentious, and the pace and publicity grew so quickly that the cunning and venality of the creature we were dealing with soon became apparent. It was then decided that a senior staffman would have to be in constant attendance, and Dr. Thorsten Kalijarvi was chosen. He was my *bête noire*, the man who'd dictated all those drafts, and when he arranged to have me assigned elsewhere I was furious and crestfallen. He didn't want to spend his Saturdays in the files of the House Un-American Activities Committee, but I did. I wanted to prove that McCarthy's facts were wrong, and I did so in minor ways. For instance, he was forever getting page numbers mixed up, and his research was extremely sloppy. When it became clear that Kalijarvi hadn't done his homework and didn't know what was going on and that I did, I was called back to the assignment. It was a major victory for me, and when I returned I suggested, with as straight a face as I could manage, that if McCarthy wanted help from our staff, perhaps Kalijarvi could be appointed to the job.

During the Jessup hearings Senator Fulbright was incredulous at McCarthy's charges and their lack of substance. "I thought the fellow had something, but he's got nothing," he said. One charge concerned some ideas expressed by Mrs. Jessup. At this, Fulbright could take no more. Trying to point up the speciousness of the senator's logic, Fulbright noted that McCarthy was not a married man and therefore might not fully understand some things. He reminded the committee that McCarthy had just publicly attacked General George C. Marshall, who was then the head of the American Red Cross. Since Mrs. Fulbright was also a member of the Red Cross, did this make him, Fulbright, also guilty? It took years for others to catch on, but to his credit Fulbright quickly recognized the perniciousness and plain silliness of McCarthy's guilt-by-association technique.

There was a dramatic moment at the end of those hearings when Fulbright leaned back, balancing on the two hind legs of his chair, with his Benjamin Franklin glasses perched on his nose, looked McCarthy straight in the eye and said, "Senator, I want to say for the record that in my entire career in the House and Senate, never have I seen a more arrogant or rude witness before any committee." In those frightening days that took guts to say. For his pains, McCarthy forever after called him "Halfbright" or worse.

It was a time without courage, and few others were willing to challenge McCarthy. When the committee started an investigation of the United States Information Agency, which was within its purview, the chairman was the other Wisconsin senator, Alexander Wiley. But when McCarthy said his special committee would also investigate the USIA, Wiley put up no objection and acquiesced without a whimper; he simply didn't want to tangle with his colleague, even though jurisdictionally he was in the right.

Then as now, the FBI was ubiquitous, investigating everyone, and it suddenly occurred to the Foreign Relations Committee's chief of staff that none of us had ever undergone FBI checks. A crash program was started, and we were all quickly investigated. It was then I learned what a farce some FBI checks were. The agents would take us out of the office, one at a time, to the Senate snack bar and ask us questions about our colleagues. It was a joke and certainly superficial, but there was the terrible fear that McCarthy would find out that we'd had no FBI checks and that one of us might be pro-Communist; even if we weren't, he could blast the whole committee for lack of caution.

There's no question that an FBI clearance is essential for anyone exposed to national-security secrets, but it was pathetic to see one staff member who quaked at the thought of the investigation. Once, in line of duty as a State Department employee, he had attended a celebration of the October 17 Revolution at the Russian embassy, and he was terrified that he would now be fired and his family disgraced. Worst of all, there was no one he could go to for help.

That was early McCarthyism; what happened later is well known. The preposterousness of what the man did and his ability to get away with it remains mind-boggling, and I still wonder why more people didn't speak out against him. But they were scared, and it was frightening to see such terror warp the Senate and its decisions. It was extremely discouraging to have to sit by and watch grown men cringe, shrink, compromise and rationalize. There were very few heroes in the McCarthy era.

I remember a day in Jack Kennedy's senatorial office. He was sitting in his rocking chair and I was asking him to go on a program, and the name of McCarthy, who had just done something particularly outrageous, came up. Jack was never comfortable talking about the man; McCarthy had been entertained at Hyannisport a couple of times, and Bobby worked for the McCarthy committee. Jack shook his head and said, "Even Bobby is getting fed up." Then he dismissed the subject by saying, "He must be a madman."

In point of fact, Kennedy was baffled by the Wisconsin senator; he felt the whole concept of McCarthyism was ludicrous and couldn't treat it seriously. Also, he represented a vast Catholic constituency in Massachusetts composed of loyal McCarthyites, and to have taken on the senator would have been political folly. There were many on Capitol Hill who thought that Kennedy scheduled the date of his back operation in 1954 in order to avoid voting on McCarthy's censure. In any event, his lack of action disgusted liberals who hooted when he called his book *Profiles in Courage;* they wondered where his own had been during the McCarthy era.

During this period I was going out with Senator Henry "Scoop" Jackson, a belabored man, not exciting, but thoroughly honest and decent. He is also a man with an infinite capacity for hard work; no one ever knows his subject better, whether military preparedness or oil reserves. He is deliberate and cautious, but once he makes up his mind, he's a tenacious and well-informed advocate. As a member of the McCarthy committee, he slowly—oh, so slowly—came to a boil, and from that time on, he never wavered. When he walked off the committee with the two other Democratic senators, I cheered.

It would have been more valiant if he had done something earlier, but even at that late date it was not yet safe to take on McCarthy, and it took courage to oppose him in any way. Even Eisenhower, the great hero, victorious in war and in peacetime elections, was afraid to tangle with him. When Edward R. Murrow televised his famous exposé of McCarthy, he became an overnight hero. A few weeks later he was invited to a White House party, and when Ike congratulated him on the show, Murrow, who never gave quarter, said, "I've done my part, Mr. President. Now you do yours." But Eisenhower never did.

In retrospect it's difficult to convey how scared people were of McCarthy. They were not only scared; they were cowardly. I remember one staff member on the Senate Foreign Relations Committee telling Mrs. Jessup how one senator had struggled with his conscience before he spoke out against her husband, who was then under McCarthy's attack. "Yes," Mrs. Jessup replied, "he struggled with his conscience and won."

* * *

There wasn't a single minute at the Foreign Relations Committee that I didn't enjoy. I was at the center of things and adored it. Congress had not yet abdicated its powers and was stronger than now. But I had gone as far as I could on the committee; being a woman, I could not travel with its members, and since I was young and female, I was told that there was no chance for me to make investigative staff trips on my own, as male staff members did. Also, since I did not have my doctorate and was a woman, there was no chance that I could ever become chief of staff. In addition, I was getting tired of writing other people's speeches and wanted to say a few things of my own. I still was impatient about not being able to change the world faster, and I decided that a quicker way to do it was to be a reporter.

In the addictive jungle of Capitol Hill, some of the most exciting people were the reporters. I was in awe of them, and I was not alone —it was a point of view I learned from my mighty employers. Senators powerful in their own kingdoms, lionized by constituents who would travel miles to see them and pay homage, were in their turn awed, sometimes terrified and often sycophantically deferential to reporters. I heard committee discussions about various junkets and knew of at least one trip that was canceled because of fear that Drew Pearson might criticize it, which could result in a loss of votes back home. In no other capital of the world is the press so influential as it is in Washington, and when it was time for me to leave the committee, I saw no other option.

Moreover, I thought my background was good training for journalism. For example, I thought that reporters at press conferences could ask much better questions than they were apt to—at least in those days. I'd had some experience with questions; a part of my job on the committee had been to prepare them for members and other senators to ask witnesses when they came to testify. Jack Kennedy was one of few who didn't want questions prepared for him. He did his own. Other senators would ask questions I'd written for them, and then, after getting an answer, would fail to ask the proper follow-up question. Infuriatingly, many reporters did the same thing on the air.

Jack Kennedy wanted me to work for him, but when he found out how much I was earning he decided he couldn't afford me. As he said to a staff assistant, "Can you believe that they would pay a girl that much?" When he heard that I couldn't get in to see Lawrence

Spivak, producer of NBC's *Meet the Press,* he arranged for an immediate interview. But for Spivak seeing was not hiring, and I had similar non-success at the newspapers. The old Washington *Daily News* offered me a job as women's editor, but it seemed foolish to try to change the world writing about politics and international affairs via the shopping and food columns.

I had been going out with a UP reporter covering Congress, and he told me that CBS was looking for a man who knew Capitol Hill. My only reporting had been as editor of the *Hawthorne Junior High School Echo,* but I did know Capitol Hill, and despite the fact that I wasn't a man, I got the job. In April 1954 I was put in charge of two CBS radio network programs, *The Leading Question* and *Capitol Cloakroom,* both of which were radio versions of *Meet the Press.* My title was "Producer, Public Affairs," and we had a corny laugh at the committee about my leaving foreign relations for public affairs.

As producer of *The Leading Question,* I had to know not only the issues but who was the best-informed about them, and then ask two senators or representatives to go on the air and debate. I also had to produce a "body" for *Capitol Cloakroom* each week. This meant that I had to corral three politicians a week, a formidable task. Most people think that all politicians jump at the opportunity to go on radio and television. Not so. They especially do not jump at the opportunity to debate an adversary, thus risking making a fool of themselves and showing up second-best.

Also, at the time that I was recruiting guests for these programs, radio was beginning to lose its impact and politicians preferred to go on television. They were becoming more sophisticated about the media and would check the areas where *Capitol Cloakroom* and *The Leading Question* were heard. Both programs were more popular in rural sections, those which were the last to be blanketed by television, so I put on many farm debates, especially after I had exhausted every possible subject on foreign affairs.

In the process of getting these two shows on the air, I got to know most of the senators and congressmen in Washington. Since I was asking them for something, I also learned which ones were decent and which were not. It was hard work because I didn't know the ropes, and no one told them to me. In fact, no one could; it was a specialized field in which only Spivak was an expert. It took a while to realize which senators were often drunk and would promise to appear, then forget and never show up. And I soon learned about the ones who would agree to go on and then inevitably cancel at the last moment. There was no way I could get revenge; I needed them more than they needed me. Radio debates simply weren't that popular because they weren't that beneficial to the politician. The producer of *Capitol Cloakroom* right now probably dies a dozen deaths each week trying to talk someone into showing up.

In the beginning, *Meet the Press* was a free-for-all, with reporters asking questions by shouting the loudest and thereby demanding the attention of the guest, but now such programs are far more tame, akin to a carefully measured minuet with each reporter taking his turn. A side effect has been the unhappy disappearance of tough reporters not worried about their image. Today many reporters are consumed by concern for how they appear to the public, and as more and more people get their news from television instead of newspapers, it has been interesting to watch a schism develop among journalists. At first newspaper and magazine reporters denigrated television reporters; they considered them a lower form of the species. All this has changed drastically; with few exceptions, reporters now crave television exposure because they know that after one appearance "on the tube," as they self-consciously call it, they are more widely recognized than they were for a lifetime of writing. Most reporters try to do both, not only for the exposure, but because television pays more. In the early days all the reporters on television came from newspapers, but then the medium came into its own and began to be taught in journalism schools, and today it is filled with journalists who have never worked for a newspaper. In the meantime, the inferiority complex has switched. Recently, a *New York Times* reporter was telling me about the lack of impact a piece of his had had, and he said, "But of course on television you never have that trouble."

Also, there is nothing to exacerbate an inferiority complex like inequity in money. Television salaries, particularly for anchormen, are astonishingly higher than those paid to the writing press. Yet former prejudices persist; in the competition between Sally Quinn when she was on CBS and Barbara Walters, then of NBC, on the two networks' morning programs, many journalists believed that Sally would be better than Barbara simply because she had been a *writing* reporter. That's idiotic. Reporting skills and the techniques of getting and understanding the news are the same, as is the basic intelligence.

21

Only the form in which the news is presented is different—and that of course is as great as the difference between lawyers and engineers. Some of the best writing reporters are the least articulate on the air.

In any case, those public affairs programs are more enlightening now, and by that criterion an improvement; but they are also far less fun, no longer have the excitement of a live news conference, and more often than not are simply dull.

In 1954 *Meet the Press* was the uncontested newsmaker of the day. It pre-empted the Monday-morning headlines and was such an influential maker and shaper of opinions that CBS was forced to compete with a program of its own. I was made an associate producer of *Face the Nation,* and naturally we wanted a blockbuster for our opening show. This meant inviting McCarthy, for the next week the Senate had scheduled a special session to consider his censure. He and his new wife, Jean, arrived at the studio in a big black Cadillac of which they were both very proud; McCarthy said that it was a wedding gift from a rich Texas supporter. Of course he never thought about the impropriety of such a gift; he had no convictions about anything, and didn't think anyone else did either.

Just before air time McCarthy tried to con one of the panelists, Bill Lawrence of the *New York Times,* and later of ABC. He told Bill that he had a tip, "a sure thing," he said, on some Texas oil stock. He told Bill to buy it right away, and he'd let him know when to sell it. Bill never bought it, of course, but we both watched the stock soar within the next few days.

That first program of *Face the Nation* was historic in Senate and American history, for it was then, on November 7, 1954, that McCarthy called the Senate a "lynch bee," thereby providing his colleagues with an easy excuse to censure him. Heretofore, despite his outrages, senators had not been anxious to condemn one of their own; after all, the Senate is called the "most exclusive club in the world" for good reason. Besides, their previous remarkable lack of courage still lingered because of hard-core McCarthy support throughout the country. But when the senator labeled the whole Senate a "lynch bee," it made it easier for the timid and wavering to vote against him with impunity. While it would have taken courage to censure him earlier for character assassination, it was easy to condemn him for denigrating the sacred name of the United States Senate. Hence,

22

based on the transcript of *Face the Nation,* McCarthy's immediate influence was ended.

But the true evil of McCarthyism lingers even today, especially for those of us who had to deal with that nightmare. So discredited were his accusations and charges, and so often did he cry wolf that we now are hardened to cries of danger from any quarter and tend to underplay them. I know that this period increased my own cynicism, and at the same time it dulled my perception of wrongdoing because I grew to dismiss charges and accusations as "just politics." Many of us baptized by McCarthyism developed our own special form of myopia. For example, when Watergate first began to unfold I was incredulous and kept comparing it to McCarthyism. Just as McCarthy's allegations were phony, I thought that the charges against Nixon were so idiotic that they too would turn out to be phony. But as we soon learned to our horror, they were not.

CHAPTER 3 ⌒

After a speech at a college seminar a young girl once asked me, "But how do you meet people and get to go everywhere and do everything in Washington?" To begin with, the first two young men I met were Congressman Jack Kennedy and Congressman Scoop Jackson, and I went out with them both. That was my introduction to dating in Washington. While I was on the Foreign Relations Committee, I also went out with a lot of other young men on Capitol Hill, many of them young bachelors who had come to Washington either to change the world or to make their fortune. I had a wonderful time with them all.

There is always a young group in the capital—lawyers, researchers, aides and assistants—waiting in the wings, and eventually they take over and run the place. They are the "contacts" that older reporters advise younger ones to develop and learn from, the men and women who start at the bottom of the bureaucratic ladder and eventually work their way up to become heads of departments. As a committee staff assistant I was a part of that group—the same group that has been so helpful to me ever since as we've all grown older and they have become more influential.

After I left the committee and went to CBS, I met even more people. I was young and female and in a man's job, which set me apart; moreover, it was a job that put me in daily contact with the most powerful men in the world. When I asked them to go on network radio and television programs, I was dealing with them as an equal, not as a subordinate.

For Washington officials and those who have business with them, it is hard to keep one's social life separate from one's professional life. As Mary Ellen Monroney, wife of the former Oklahoma senator, once said to me, "A dinner party at night is just an extension of the committee meeting during the day." In the higher echelons of social and political life, this is certainly true.

My job was a natural bridge between the two. I called on senators, Cabinet officers and congressmen during the day, and at night I would often see them at press parties or political gatherings I was assigned to. For example, on opening day of Congress in 1960, *Life* had a two-page spread of President Eisenhower, Nixon, LBJ, Hubert Humphrey and the other congressional leaders, all laughing, at various parties. On the same page there was a picture of me laughing too, wearing a new green silk dress from Dior. As I got to know people, I was often invited to the much-touted candlelit dinner parties when an extra woman was needed. And it was during this period that I became acquainted with the Lyndon Johnsons. As Majority Leader, his decisions affected my programs, and I often saw Lady Bird on the Hill because she was an involved wife and handled many of the Texas visitors to his office.

The first person I asked to go on the air was Congressman Kenneth Keating, a New York Republican, later a senator and New York judge, and finally our ambassador to Israel. I couldn't have made a better choice. I asked him because he was the first Republican of any prominence to have the courage to speak out publicly against McCarthy. He was one of the finest and most decent of men, and one of the few politicians with a sense of humor. After the broadcast he took me and my roommate to dinner, and soon he became my dearest friend. He was a member of the Chowder and Marching Society, the Wednesday-afternoon group that originally consisted of GOP congressmen first elected in 1948. It was here that I met

Richard Nixon, Gerald Ford, Melvin Laird and their wives—the group that later became the power structure of the GOP. As freshmen, they started meeting on Wednesday afternoons to discuss legislation. Later they held parties at night which included their wives, and Ken Keating used to take me and my roommate.

I remember one party the Nixons gave in the early fifties at their big suburban home. He was an uncomfortable host, disappearing from time to time, only to return and urge guests to have another drink, with a vigorous show at being friendly. Being a host did not come easy for him. We ate outdoors in the pretty backyard, and afterward Nixon played the piano and we sang. But what I remember best about the evening was seeing Checkers, the famous cocker spaniel who lives in history. Ken Keating teased me about being more impressed with my host's dog than with my host. Actually, I wasn't impressed with either of them, but Checkers did confirm to me that I was right in the center of things. After all, lots of people know Nixon, but how many knew Checkers?

Mr. Keating also introduced me to many other men whom I then had on my programs. He had lived apart from his wife for many years, but since I was a Catholic I could never have married him even if he had been divorced. Paul Niven, the late CBS news correspondent, incorrigible, curious and certainly one of the best interviewers on the air, once asked me if I was having an affair with Mr. Keating, and when I told him to save his questions for television, he dismissed the subject saying it was irrelevant, since so many people were whispering that we were, anyway. According to Paul, we were well received in social circles, the only such couple who were, he said, which was unlike other world capitals where there were many such relationships, but not so openly accepted.

Although Congressman Keating was as old as my mother, we went everywhere together. All this was in 1955 when life styles were quite different, and what might have appeared scandalous then would be commonplace today. The interest in our relationship was particularly strong around my office. The CBS vice president in charge of lobbying once warned me to stop going out with Mr. Keating—on the theory, I suppose, that my alleged immorality might harm the company's corporate image. "Just wait until Dr. Stanton [the president of CBS] finds out," he said.

Dr. Stanton was highly regarded, for good reason, in the profession and treated like an Oriental potentate by everyone at CBS. He lived and worked in rarefied circumstances. His employees were in awe of him, partly out of respect, partly out of fear for their jobs, and he was just as puffed up as certain senators from one-party areas who grow complacent because they don't have to face a questioning electorate. Still, no one at CBS threatened me again, and in all fairness, Dr. Stanton may never have known about his underling's threats. Years later I was delighted to learn that he secretly sent big red roses to a pretty young girl in California.

In 1958, when Keating ran for the Senate, I became his secret, unofficial campaign manager. We talked constantly, devising policy and strategy, and when he won, he gave me his official certificate of election, signed by the New York State authorities. After his victory I never went out with him again. It was a sad farewell, but he had the Senate and I had to get on with a life of my own.

While I was writing this book, Ambassador Keating died. Two weeks before his fatal heart attack he was in Washington and we had lunch and laughed a lot. He was joyously happy with his new wife, and we made plans for my husband and me to visit them in Tel Aviv. A few days later, when I heard he was in the hospital, I phoned and he blamed our luncheon for his heart attack. We both laughed, which is the only way to end a lifetime's conversation with a man who kept his sense of humor at the same time that he had the courage to denounce Joe McCarthy and to challenge Henry Kissinger before either of those acts became the popular thing to do.

Through Mr. Keating I met two women who couldn't have been nicer and who incidentally gave me a special kind of entré in Washington. The first was Laura Gross, the chatelaine of the 1925 F Street Club, which she had started when she was broke. She was an indomitable old dame, big and feisty, with a voice like a cement mixer and a heart equally large. Her godfather was Mark Hanna, and as a child she had played at the White House with the Roosevelt children. She loved life, and her zest for it was communicated to the diverse group of politicians she chose to have around her. When she lost her money in the Crash, she asked four hundred people to join the club she started—and every single one of them did.

Mrs. Gross prided herself on being a party-line Republican, though many of her dearest friends were Democrats. The club flourished and was considered "the hardest door to crack" in Washington. There was a long waiting list, but if she liked you, you got in immediately. The club became a second home to me, but I could never enter it without recalling that I had gone to night school right next door when I first came to the city. I was taking Diplomatic Relations 1-A at American University, and during the break we'd go out on the fire escape for a cigarette. Once, as we stood looking down at the mansion next door, at the big tent stretched across the garden with colored lights bobbing from the trees, and at the orchestra playing and guests dancing, our professor told us that the F Street Club was *the* place in Washington, and that only the rich belonged to it. That didn't interest me, but when he said that powerful people had gathered there ever since the days of FDR, and that Ike himself entertained there, I was fascinated.

Later Mr. Keating took my roommate and me to the club. With beautiful eighteenth-century American and English furniture and crazy Victorian curtains and draperies, it was decorated just as it had been when it was Mrs. Gross's home. The dining room had once been her children's playroom, and when she became a backer of Herbert Hoover, she sent the children's toys to storage, replaced them with rented desks and typewriters and started his nominating campaign right there. The Lodges had once lived in the house, and Ambassador John Cabot Lodge was born there. It was a very cozy place and Mrs. Gross ran it with the autocracy of a rich woman used to many servants from childhood. We became fast friends, and my social education began. It was she who taught me how to seat a dinner table for the most fun, the value of antique furniture, and how to decorate. The greatest politicians of the day warmed to the hospitality there and felt secure and protected, since Mrs. Gross wouldn't permit reporters to write what went on within the confines of the club.

Mrs. Gross was an intimidating and imposing woman, and at first I thought she was a pillar of moral rectitude, but I soon came to learn another side of "Aunt Laura," as she asked me to call her. As a young woman she had wanted a divorce, and since this was not socially acceptable at the time, she had gone to Paris to get one (apparently a Parisian divorce was somehow much less scandalous). Because of French law, she had to work in France for several months, so she packed up her maid, nurse and three children, got a job at Madame Vionnet's House of Couture, the finest of the day, and since her father's best friend was the ambassador, she became the hostess at the American embassy. Later she remarried her first husband and then divorced him *again;* in between she kept things humming in Washington.

Like any good Washington politician, Aunt Laura knew how to maneuver and to get her way. For example, she told me that once one of her friends was having an affair with the Deputy Attorney General and that the two would meet for lunch in her study, where their courtship flourished in secret bliss. At this same time Aunt Laura was having trouble getting "No Parking" signs placed in front of the club, so one day when the gentleman was coming to lunch she collected him in her car at the Justice Department, and while waiting, ordered her chauffeur to put the Justice Department "No Parking" signs in the front seat. When the Deputy Attorney General got into the car, he said nothing, and the signs were placed in front of the club, where they remain to this day.

The F Street Club was the scene of many famous meetings and dinners, but perhaps the most publicized took place a few months before the Republicans chose their presidential candidate in 1952. Both Ike and Senator Taft, who were potential candidates, were invited, and Aunt Laura seated herself between them. There was always a lot of wine at her dinners and that night was no exception. The conversation turned to income tax, and it grew lively and then overheated when Ike declared that in time of war there should be a 100 percent tax on war profits, a view totally opposed by Taft. Their argument turned into a shouting match, and for a moment it seemed that they might come to blows. Worst of all, someone leaked the story to the press.

I was something of a social Gigi to Aunt Laura, and she taught me well. We never discussed sex, which she seemed to think that ladies ought to pretend didn't exist, but she did instruct me in the art of entertaining. She gave big glamorous dinner parties that included members of the Cabinet and the Vice President, and always seated me in the most auspicious place. Her tastes were the best and most expensive, and under her tutelage I learned a lot of do's and don'ts that I never would have thought of on my own, since they were hardly of paramount importance in Wauwatosa, Wisconsin. But more important, she had that exciting zest for life and everything that was going on. Today we would say she wanted to be where the action is, where it's happening, to be involved. But as she put it, she always wanted to be *"Among Those Present."*

There are very few women I giggle with—I've never had the time for that delicious kind of female friendship because I've been too busy working—but I do like to giggle with Mrs. Alice Longworth. She has the fastest laugh in town. She also has the wit and indomitable spirit of her father, Teddy Roosevelt, and she enjoys recalling the time he was visited at the White House by an indignant senator who came to complain about her shenanigans. As a wise and resigned father, he listened and then observed, "My dear sir, I can either run this country or take care of my daughter, Alice, but I cannot do both."

Once Mrs. Longworth regaled me with stories of going to the boxing matches with her father, who liked nothing better than a good fight. Since I had never been to the fights, she promised to take me and her daughter, Paulina, who had never been either. A party was organized, including Congressman Keating; Walter Robertson, then Assistant Secretary of State; Joe Alsop, the columnist; and Mrs. Robert Low Bacon, another Washington grand dame; and after dinner at Mrs. Longworth's house, we went to the old Uline Arena. We were among the few white people in the audience, and I shall always remember Walter Robertson, a Virginian, scrutinizing the audience, realizing that it was almost totally black, and then observing to Joe Alsop, "I might say, sir, that this is a very strange audience." To which Joe replied, "I might say to you, sir, that it is no less strange for our being here."

Mrs. Longworth brooked no interruptions at the fights, so she placed her guests apart so that she didn't have to bother with us. Each time there was a particularly lethal blow, I could see my hostess raising her clenched fist in approval, shouting "Bully! Bully!"

The seating arrangements at the matches were as carefully planned as at a diplomatic dinner. In those days the fights were televised regularly, and we made something of a ceremonial entrance, sitting in the center of the first row so that the television cameras could focus on us, too. In between matches we were all given a piece of Kleenex by our hostess and told to hold it up for a couple minutes—a signal to Mrs. Longworth's sister, Ethel Darby, who watched the fights on television in Long Island, so that she could distinguish us from the rest of the crowd. The instructions on how to hold the Kleenex were very specific, and were a custom dating back to the Roosevelts' days at Sagamore Hill in Oyster Bay. At that time, when there were boating races, every family would be out at the water's edge waving their handkerchiefs and cheering the family's sailors on. But the handkerchiefs all looked alike, so TR devised his own signal: handkerchiefs were to be held up square by the corners, so that Roosevelts could be distinguished from others waving along the shore.

Sometime after one of these evenings, Senator Keating was interviewed about the difficulties the sport of boxing was suffering, and suggested that there be a boxing "czar." When asked who his candidate would be, he solemnly nominated Mrs. Longworth.

Years later, after I was married and had inherited Elizabeth, Ann and Jane, the children by my husband's first marriage, I took them and Michael Dickerson, then aged two, to tea at Mrs. Longworth's. Luckily, it was summertime and the rugs were up, so that when Michael crumbled the thin-sliced buttered bread which is a tradition of hers on the floor, no one minded. Tea at her house—no cocktails until later in the day—is always a gay time, and the conversation moves fast. She loves to go to a good party, and her presence makes it one. Men prefer to talk with her rather than to anyone else, and it is always worth the effort. She enjoys being wicked, or pretending to be, and though at this writing she is ninety-two, and as she says, an old lady, her mind is attuned, quick and sparkling.

CHAPTER 4 ⌒

As I struggled to make news with my two radio programs, CBS assigned me to other special projects on television. I didn't mind working late at night or on weekends. In the six years I was a producer —from 1954 to 1960—I worked every Thanksgiving and Christmas Eve, and when everyone else wanted a night off they assigned me such special tasks as producing the telecast of President Eisenhower's birthday message to the country. The men in our office felt such productions were beneath them and were glad to let me take over. They were jaded about the White House, but I wasn't then and I still am not. I was so young and so energetic and so eager that I was available for all tasks.

Soon I was put in charge of some specials on both radio and television, and in 1956 I was assigned to both political conventions and to headquarters on election night. At those big political spectacles, correspondents were often assigned an assistant or producer to bird-dog newsmakers, since the old-fashioned equipment prevented reporters themselves from leaving their mike stands. I became popular as a producer because through my experience on Capitol Hill I knew most of the politicians and could pry them away from their maneuvering to be interviewed. During Eisenhower's second inauguration, in January 1957, there was a delicate moment when it was decided to name me as assistant or producer for Edward R. Murrow, the chief star in the CBS News stable. But no one had the nerve to tell him that he even had a "producer," let alone a *girl* producer. There was unbelievable fretting over Murrow's sensitivities, and finally when the assignment sheets were mimeographed, my name was listed next to his as "Communications Assistant." When Murrow noticed this, he said, "What the hell is that?" I replied, "That's me." And that's how we met. We became fast friends. Later Murrow and Fred Friendly went over the heads of the Washington hierarchy to ask that I be the Washington producer of some segments of their programs. Friendly, later the president of CBS News, had the fastest mind in the business, and in our phone conversations he invariably began by saying, "Who knows the most and should talk first?"

From the moment I started at CBS in 1954 through the entire six years I was a producer, I wanted to be a correspondent, but this possibility was so far-fetched that I never even asked. Still, CBS didn't discourage me when I asked for time off to attend Catholic University to study speech. All week long I collected old wire copy, and then on Fridays drove across town and pretended to be a correspondent for Bill Graham, a top-notch drama coach. One bit of short-sightedness on the part of networks is that they often put reporters on the air without teaching them the basic techniques of speech, phrasing and communication. How often have you listened to a television news report and afterward couldn't remember what was said because the reporter was just mouthing words, not communicating? I remember Sevareid complaining about producers who made him walk across the set, point to maps, then return to his original position, sit on the edge of a desk, fold his hands and do various other bits of business. As he said, "It takes an actor a lifetime to learn to walk across the stage. Why do they want me to do it when I could give the same information in one place?" I didn't study walking but I did learn voice control.

Looking back, I see now that parts of my life fit together like a jigsaw puzzle, and one of the most important pieces fell into place when I met General C. V. Clifton, a dynamic Pentagon press officer who later became JFK's military aide. Together we concocted a plan for me to go to Europe in the summer of 1959 on a military transport, with the rank of general, provided that CBS News would carry my reports on women in the Army stationed abroad. The CBS brass in New York agreed, with the odd stipulation that I must not refer to the WACs as "a group of attractive women." (Networks always have been a strong bastion of male chauvinism.) I went to several Army camps, saw a great many WACs and then went to West Berlin, where General Clifton helped me set up lines to New York for my first broadcast. Earlier in the day I had gone to East Berlin, and after I did a report on the WACs I followed with a piece about the Communist sector. At the time, Khrushchev was in the United States, and I reported that in East Berlin there seemed to be preparations for a Khrushchev visit, which was a subject of lively speculation then. After Germany I flew to Vienna, interviewed our ambassador and described the city, which had become a listening post in the Cold War. CBS was delighted with this report too, and said they'd take any others. In Rome I joined a papal audience, and since His Holiness mentioned Khrushchev, I did another broadcast there. By this time I had created a new career out of reactions to Khrushchev's adventures in the United States, and by the end of my trip to Europe I considered myself a foreign correspondent. A prophet is without honor in his own country; while CBS would not think of my broadcasting from Washington, in Europe I had acquired new wisdom, previously unapparent to them.

Back in the capital I suggested every conceivable story idea that wouldn't infringe on the jurisdiction of a male CBS correspondent. Obviously no male correspondent would want to cover a luncheon for the First Lady, so I went. Luckily, it was one of the few times in Mamie Eisenhower's life that she actually made a speech, talking about Ike, so CBS again let me report it on radio. But resistance to my on-air activities grew, and not just because I was invading men's territories. It was also a matter of economics. In addition to our yearly salaries we were paid commercial fees for each broadcast. I was paid the same as a man, and if I was on the air, that broadcast time was unavailable to a male, with his income lowered as a result. It was even pointed out to me that since I was a woman and unmarried and didn't have a family to support, I should stop trying to broadcast.

I realized that the only way I could get on the air was to report news no one else had access to, so I went to House Speaker Sam Rayburn. He did not like television because the bright lights made his bald head look even balder; in fact, he once sat through an entire television interview with his hat on. But he had always been nice to me and he liked women; they adored him and flocked around him at parties. His attractiveness was undoubtedly similar to Henry Kissinger's, who explained it by saying that the greatest aphrodisiac of all is power. Speaker Rayburn was powerful and knew more about leadership than most Presidents ever learn. Out of deference to him, the House used to reopen every year on his birthday, January 6, and on that night Scooter and Dale Miller, Texas friends, always gave a big party in the Speaker's honor.

The day before his birthday in 1960, I asked Mr. Rayburn if I could have an exclusive interview, and he told me to come back the next day. By now CBS was grudgingly beginning to believe that if I said I would produce a certain body, I would do it; so far I always had. But though they didn't know it, this was the one time I thought I might fail. However, since no one else could get the Speaker on television, they let me have a camera crew in great secrecy so the other networks wouldn't learn about it and try to horn in, or complain about exclusivity and abort the whole interview. We went to the Speaker's office, set up the equipment and waited for him. When he arrived, he roared—literally roared—when he saw the cameras and lights. Then he tripped over a cable and I wished I were someplace else—anywhere else. I said I was sorry. Then there was a dreadful long silence. I reminded him that he had agreed to an interview—or at least I thought he had agreed to an interview. In steely tones through clenched teeth he admitted that he had, but not with those unholy cameras. It was a royal scene, with half the Rayburn staff looking on. Then I began to see the humor. (Fortunately, I can usually detect the ridiculousness in situations where I play an inadvertently comical role.) And we did look pretty silly: he at his desk, pouting and grunting, sitting there with his hat still on; me, knee-deep in cables. Apparently the Speaker admired my guts. I was the youngest press person around the Hill and the only one courageous or foolish enough to ask him for a television exclusive. And he liked the drama, too, as I kept insisting that I couldn't interview him without cameras and lights.

I asked him what was ahead in the legislative year, and he made a lot of news with his answers. I ended by asking him what he most hoped for in the coming year and he said, "To be back here." To which I said, and I couldn't have meant it more, "Well, I hope we're back with you, and now back to CBS News in New York."

The interview went off perfectly and we got rave reviews, but I never saw the program because I was celebrating the Speaker's birthday. It was a late party, and the next morning, when the producer of the CBS nightly news, Don Hewitt (now producer of 60 Minutes), phoned, I was still asleep and didn't quite realize the significance of his remark, "We want you on the air every night."

As producer of their major news program, Hewitt dictated much of what went on at CBS, and he was heard to say, "If she were a man, she'd have been a correspondent long ago." That did it. He also said that I should never cover "women's news" because he didn't want me to be typecast. This eliminated the fluff and I started right out at the top, doing major hard-news stories on the network. This would have been unusual even for a man, because they almost always start out either on a local station or a newspaper, covering minor developments.

For many years people asked two questions about my becoming the first woman CBS television-news correspondent: How did male correspondents treat me, and did I have to sleep with anyone to get the job? Those questions aren't asked so much now, but in 1960 there was no women's movement, no mass demand that women be hired. Since there were no other women on television news, it was automatically assumed that I must have slept with someone to get ahead. This simply was not true—which is not to deny that in the years that followed, reporters, producers and executives at both CBS and NBC asked me out, hinted at sex or even suggested it outright. But so did politicians and businessmen, and I don't think my career was affected because I refused to go to bed with them.

As for the reaction of male reporters, they treated me as one of them. If I was a threat to my colleagues, it was the same intimidation they felt from another male; they didn't feel menaced by me as the forerunner of a mass women's movement, which didn't begin until years later. The news sources themselves—congressmen, senators and other officials—were highly deferential—as they are to most network correspondents, for the simple reason that network reporters are powerful, and by one night's report can profoundly affect a political career.

Still, not everyone at CBS was delighted that a woman had been made a news correspondent. Ted Koop, the head of CBS's Washington bureau, was a friend, but he had once written a musical making fun of women reporters, and it was therefore ironic that he had the task of asking me if I would like the job. I couldn't have been happier if he had offered me a million dollars.

To honor the event, LBJ and Lady Bird gave a big party in the Majority Leader's quarters, and he invited the whole Senate. They all came. (No senator turns down an invitation of the leader.) The Johnsons also invited all the New York CBS brass, who also came, partly because he was Majority Leader and highly influential in broadcast legislation, but also because Lady Bird owned an important CBS affiliate in Austin, Texas.

In honor of the occasion I went to Bergdorf's and got a vicuna suit and a Dior coat of camel's hair which I called my foreign correspondent's coat. The Johnsons had a Texas-sized cake baked in the shape of Texas with a big CBS eye in the middle, and it was inscribed, "The Eyes of Texas are on Nancy." Eric Sevareid sent me a cable from London saying, THE QUALITY OF CBS NEWS IMPROVED PERCEPTIBLY TODAY . . . LOVE, SEVAREID.

What a day! It was February 22, 1960, the day the civil rights debate started, and my assignments were civil rights and LBJ, the first Southern senator to lead the fight for racial equality. At the time, LBJ was a presidential candidate, though he hadn't announced it officially, and when he started traveling around the country on an unofficial campaign, I went with him.

In the period just prior to a presidential campaign, networks always assign one reporter to each potential nominee to develop contacts and sources so that they'll be ahead of the game if the man is nominated. I was assigned LBJ and followed him so closely that in

35

some people's minds I became part of his entourage. As with every candidate, the reporter assigned to him wore his press badge; these are essential to get through Secret Service barriers, onto official buses and into places where the general public is barred. In true Johnson fashion, his press badge was far larger than any other candidate's, featuring a big picture of him, which made those of us wearing the badges look like enthusiastic Johnson supporters. While I was wearing one of these in a Texas shopping center one day, a woman came up to me in a rage, shouting incoherently, tried to pull my coat off me and in near-hysteria accused me of every black deed she felt LBJ had committed. Security guards rescued me, but it was indicative of the depth of the hatred a political campaign can evoke, especially a Johnson campaign in Texas, where passions were intense and divided.

During this period of barnstorming LBJ started his practice of coming up to my mike to drawl, "Hello, Nancy," and for this trademark I soon became famous.

But I also covered other candidates. With a camera crew I went to Baltimore to film JFK's announcement of his entry in the Maryland primary. In one of her rare campaign appearances, Jackie appeared with him. The camera crew went on ahead and I drove back with the Kennedys, Jackie lying down on the back seat of the convertible while Jack and I sat in front. He explained that she got carsick, and though I weakly pointed out that I did too, he drove over eighty miles an hour all the way. He tried to talk politics but I felt too ill, and when we reached the Senate, both Jackie and I were sea sick green.

When presidential candidates are trying for the nomination, they are easily available to the press and usually travel on the same plane with them, but once they get the nomination, everything changes. In 1960 Vice President Nixon was assured of the GOP nomination, and he conducted his travels accordingly. I went across the country with him once or twice, and at the end of each trip he and Mrs. Nixon boarded our press plane as if they were traveling royalty on an imperial state visit. Although Nixon's press relations were not yet as bad as they were to become later, even then he was uncomfortable with reporters. He had studied De Gaulle and was already trying to emulate him.

Health became an issue among the Democratic candidates in the

1960 campaign. Kennedy was accused of having Addison's disease, which he virtually denied, calling it a "mild adrenal deficiency." LBJ carried a laminated copy of his cardiogram which became dog-eared from use, since it was constantly flicked out of his pocket for display. Kennedy's supporters encouraged rumors that LBJ's heart attack had been so debilitating that it precluded his nomination, a point which riled him. To counter this he held a news conference in Pierre, South Dakota, early one Sunday morning, saying that he'd had only a few hours sleep, but adding with a sly wink that even so there had been a vigorous interruption. In case we hadn't yet caught on, he suggested that if we didn't believe him, we could just ask Lady Bird. To her credit, she sat in the room with her head raised as if she hadn't heard him.

CHAPTER 5 〜

When the Johnsons went to the convention in early July 1960, I flew with them. In retrospect it seems incredible that he arrived in Los Angeles thinking that he had a chance to get the presidential nomination. JFK already had it sewed up, but Johnson didn't know it. As Majority Leader he had played Senate politics, and for a national campaign it simply didn't work. While senators were powerful in Washington, where they ruled over their little fiefdoms, they rarely controlled the state party apparatus. Normally this was dominated by the governor and by other state officials, and it was these men who chose a presidential nominee, not the men in Washington.

Johnson never understood this. During the months before the convention Bobby Baker, his trusted aide, would whip a chart out of his pocket showing what delegates LBJ expected to get from each state. There was an elaborate plan based on second and third ballots, and detailed notes about when each delegate would switch over to Johnson from the other candidates. It was all nonsense. Kennedy had it locked up in the first ballot because he had gone the primary route and worked through state organizations, whereas LBJ, out of touch with the political fiber of his own party, was working through his trusted Senate friends, who simply did not have the power to deliver their state delegations.

But though JFK was certain he had the votes, there was momentary nervousness when Adlai Stevenson made his first visit to the convention hall. His supporters gave a wild demonstration, proving little more than that Stevenson had passionate and devoted followers ready to march on his behalf; there were few delegates among them. His appearance, championed by Eleanor Roosevelt, infuriated the Kennedy camp, who believed that Stevenson had violated the unwritten rule of not appearing in the hall until nominated. JFK had always disdained Stevenson; he didn't really respect him. During the campaign I once had dinner with half a dozen other reporters, all men, and they discussed Kennedy's well-known derision of Stevenson. Out of deference to the presence of a woman, one of them wrote on the tablecloth what Kennedy had said of Stevenson, rather than quoting it out loud. After dinner I sidled around to the other side of the table and read the penciled quote: "No balls."

Like the other candidates, LBJ made the rounds of the delegations at the convention. He was received cordially, in part because as Senate Majority Leader he had the power and ability to help state programs after the convention, but he often misinterpreted this cordiality as tacit endorsement. During the wooing of the delegations he got what he considered a brilliant idea: to invite Kennedy to visit the Texas delegation and debate with him in front of the pro-Johnson audience. To everyone's astonishment Kennedy accepted. Facing the Johnson loyalists, JFK stunned the crowd by announcing that he had come to endorse Lyndon Johnson; that he admired him, had great affection for him and strongly supported him . . . for Senate Majority Leader. Even the Texas loyalists laughed, and Kennedy fared extremely well.

My notes from the 1960 convention are sketchy, but I remember how hot it was in Los Angeles, and how the brass at CBS developed a crush for the wife of the Tennessee governor, the keynote speaker. She acquired instant notoriety, and I had to chase after her all over Los Angeles trying to get her on the air or simply to find out her whereabouts so that they could film her in her flowered hat and mink stole (in all that heat!). I never caught up with her and was exhausted from the effort.

I also remember talking with Jackie and Ethel Kennedy sitting together at a little table in a makeshift refreshment area, both of them heavily pregnant, watching the proceedings on a portable television set they had commandeered. Jackie looked especially beautiful and a little scared. They were not as sanguine about the results as the males in the family, and anxiously asked for the latest news. Shortly afterward, Jackie flew back to Hyannisport to await the outcome.

One thing that amazed me was the eloquence of the Johnson daughters. Luci had just turned thirteen the week before and Lynda was only sixteen, yet without any warning their father would call upon them to speak at a meeting of the Texas delegation or some other group, and each time they would say something meaningful and appropriate.

Just as LBJ arrived at the convention not knowing the political realities, I arrived ignorant of broadcasting realities. I had been a correspondent for four months and had done several radio spots at campaign stops and some television, but I was a virtual neophyte. To me the candidates and other politicians were inconsequential compared to the awe in which I held my colleagues—all older men—and I was both intimidated and thrilled to attend the first convention staff meeting of correspondents and network brass. Already there was Edward R. Murrow, the guru of CBS and its sometime conscience —when they permitted him to be. When I walked in, he stood up and with great formality, in front of everyone, complimented me on my broadcasts. It was not only a kind thing to do; it put the imprimatur on my reporting and made an exceedingly helpful impact on the network bosses, because at CBS praise from Murrow was the zenith. Later he took me aside and gave me a critique of my radio reports: "Don't tell everything you know," he said. "Just tell them the one thing you want them to know and tell it straight so that they understand. It's not necessary to establish your wide knowledge." This was the best advice any aspiring broadcast reporter could receive, and it focuses on a major distinction between writing for listeners and writing for readers. Good broadcasting prose should be Aristotelean in its simplicity so that the ear can catch the complete meaning easily; writing for readers can be more intricate in structure because the reader has the opportunity to go back over a complicated thought, an option denied to listeners. One of the first news directors in the early days of CBS radio put it another way: he said, "Tell them what you're going to tell them; tell them; and then tell them what you told them." Simplicity of style is even more pertinent to news broadcasting than to writing other words to be spoken, such as stage dialogue, because trained actors can make prosaic lines meaningful, whereas many news broadcasters are untrained and have poor delivery; when deficient delivery is added to imprecise prose, the chance for communication is hopeless.

Murrow and Sevareid took me under their wing and between them taught me everything I was to learn about the techniques of broadcasting. Murrow also told me that while the most important thing is to have something to say, substance amounts to only 51 percent of a broadcast; the other 49 percent—how you say it—is almost equally important. He had other tips: he said I looked like a "sexy madonna," and as such, should wear simple clothes on television. He also recommended that I try to find some shoes that made my feet look smaller. On decorum at receptions and cocktail parties: go to them only when mandatory, and when there, do not dash about talking first to one person and then to another like a butterfly; stay in one place and people will come to you. I came to learn that such behavior was more applicable to Murrow than most. Sevareid was always more introspective, and confined himself to advice about broadcasting. To him, "The cardinal sin is to bore." And he had once done a brilliant telecast contending that Washington was in less danger from a Communist takeover than from a takeover by stuffed shirts.

I was an oddity in Los Angeles because there had never been a woman reporter on the convention floor before. In addition, the camera equipment was primitive, bearing little resemblance to the sophisticated mini-cameras of today, so floor reporters had to lug around a heavy pack and two long antennas. Realizing how tough this was going to be, one of the engineers had asked his wife to fix a headgear for me to wear, a sort of Brownie cap with the antennas sticking out, which, when worn, made me resemble a space-age Minnie Mouse. The gesture was appreciated but rejected. Like a packhorse, I lugged the equipment around on my shoulders like everyone else.

For maximum convention coverage, the CBS engineers had devised a technical setup which rivaled Rube Goldberg's finest efforts.

As a floor reporter I was told to find the most newsworthy person there, ask for an interview, and once he agreed, to convey this information through my walkie-talkie to Central Control. At the same time I was supposed to wave a special red flashlight vigorously toward one of the distant corners of the ceiling where the CBS cameras were perched. In the pulsating mob below them, the cameramen were miraculously supposed to find me and my flashlight, and when initial contact had been made, strong floodlights were to be switched on to pick me and the interviewee out of the seething thousands below. If by this time the great man hadn't given up and departed in search of a more profitable way to spend his time, the interview was supposed to begin through high-powered zoom lenses. It was a mess. The men being interviewed couldn't see the distant cameras in that cavernous amphitheater, so they were never sure when they were on the air. Neither was I. Once I interviewed Teddy Kennedy, with both of us staring into blinding spotlights at the faraway corners, and I remember thinking that it was like communicating over a mountain. Of course, Speaker Rayburn never conceded that the cameras could reach us from that distance, so my interview with him showed only the backs of our heads.

In all, it was a classic example of technical difficulties when television was learning how to cope with conventions. It was impossible to make much sense, and as a result reporters often appeared as idiots. Under these circumstances, it was devastating to learn that some of my superiors were saying that I wasn't quite projecting the CBS News image. Neither was anyone else on the floor and NBC won all the kudos for convention coverage—as well they should have with the emergence of the Huntley-Brinkley combination in their anchor booth.

When Kennedy won the nomination I was where I had spent much of the convention: outside the Johnson suite at the Biltmore Hotel. A dozen other reporters were also waiting for LBJ to appear and make the statement we had been told to expect, but the minutes went by and LBJ remained secluded. CBS Central Control switched to me, but there was no story and no Johnson, so they switched back and Walter Cronkite kept filling in. Finally, as Kennedy was en route to the hall to accept the plaudits of the crowd, a Johnson aide appeared with a sheaf of mimeographed copies of LBJ's statement. I grabbed my copy and raced down the long hotel corridor to our

41

cameras as Cronkite, the greatest ad-libber of them all, vamped in the anchor booth, saying, "We had expected Senator Johnson to come out and make a statement . . . We had been told he would join us . . . We understand now that there has been a change of plans . . . We understand that the Senator has issued a statement instead —that he has . . . uh . . . put on his pajamas, gone to bed . . . and we switch now to Nancy Hanschman, who is covering him." Whereupon I burst on camera and breathlessly read the Johnson statement conceding defeat and congratulating Kennedy, never dreaming of the remarkable introduction I had just received. I was greatly embarrassed when someone teased me about it, and became even more so when I heard that LBJ was amusing his friends in Texas with the story of that introduction.

After Kennedy thanked the crowd and we went off the air, I had a nightcap with the Johnsons and their entourage and heard a postmortem of what went wrong. The general consensus was that LBJ could either run the Senate or run for the nomination, but not both —which was just malarky, since for months LBJ had been actively using the Senate as a springboard for the Presidency.

The next day came the vice-presidential choice. What actually happened in the eighteen hours between John Kennedy's nomination on Wednesday, July 13, and the announcement of Lyndon Johnson as his running mate will always be debated. The confusion involved is endemic to a political convention, a confusion magnified by the natural jealousies that go hand in hand with power, and by the physical impossibility of anyone being in several different places at once. And in this case, the confusion was magnified by Kennedy and Johnson themselves: JFK told different versions to different people, and Johnson swore that the Kennedy offer was without reservations, even though he knew Kennedy tried to withdraw it.

Leading up to the convention, these were the facts: as far back as the West Virginia and Wisconsin primaries, Ambassador Joseph Kennedy had broached the vice-presidential nomination with Thomas Corcoran, the famous Washington lawyer who had been a close confidant and adviser of FDR's. The senior Kennedy was concerned with nothing but victory, and he thought the combination most likely to win was a Kennedy-Johnson ticket. Any opinion of

Joseph Kennedy's was highly significant; his influence on his sons was tremendous.

As the convention drew nearer, JFK had three secret meetings with Clark Clifford, who was handling the campaign of Senator Stuart Symington. The first was a luncheon at Kennedy's Washington house, where, through Clifford, he offered the Vice Presidency to Symington, provided Symington's Missouri delegation votes went to Kennedy. Symington turned down the deal. The second conversation, which took place in Los Angeles, was a repeat of the first, and again it was refused. The third conversation was in Kennedy's hideaway in Los Angeles, during which he told Clifford that he was fairly certain of a first-ballot victory and asked if Symington would be his running mate. As Clifford later told me, "There were no strings attached. It was a straight offer." The Symington and Clifford families conferred, Symington agreed to run, and Clifford relayed the news to Kennedy.

Clifford was playing a unique role: he was not only Symington's campaign adviser but JFK's personal lawyer as well. He is one of the world's most sophisticated men, and he does not make mistakes about matters like this. As he told me, "We had a deal signed, sealed and delivered."

On the day before Kennedy was nominated, Bobby Kennedy told a news conference that he favored Scoop Jackson as a running mate. Privately he'd told Scoop, "You're my choice; you're the guy. I don't know what's going to happen, but I want you to have it." Also on the day before the nomination, Kennedy visited the Minnesota delegation, put his arm around Minnesota Governor Orville Freeman and said that this was the kind of man he'd like to run with. No promises were made, but Freeman thought he had a pretty good chance.

After Kennedy was nominated, beating LBJ out by a vote of 806 to 409, phone calls started coming in to the Johnson suite. One of the first was from Speaker Sam Rayburn, who said there were whispers at the convention hall that Kennedy was going to offer the Vice Presidency to LBJ. Rayburn strongly advised against it. John Connally brought news of the same rumors. When others phoned, LBJ asked them if they'd heard the rumors. As the night wore on, various groups of Southerners and others got together and reasoned, with logic, that if the Democrats were to win, they would have to carry the South, and the best way to accomplish this was to have a Southerner like LBJ on the ticket. None of these meetings were triggered by LBJ. During the night the Southerners relayed their conclusions to Kennedy, and they made sense. Confirming this viewpoint was Philip L. Graham, publisher of the Washington *Post*, a man who also had a tremendous influence on JFK. However, the most influential of all was Joe Kennedy, and he too was for Johnson.

As Kennedy's brother-in-law Sargent Shriver described the mood in the Kennedy camp, there was much talk about Johnson being the second most popular Democrat, because his presence on the ticket could determine the difference between victory and defeat. They all were saying, "Who will do the most good?" Besides, said Shriver, "They had to consider Johnson's enormous ego." As Majority Leader, LBJ was accustomed to hearing himself called "the most powerful man in Washington, next to Ike." JFK worried that the hostility engendered by the rough nominating campaign might linger and imperil victory in the election; even if he won, it could endanger future relations with Congress. Some believed that Johnson would be too proud to take second place, but that he would be flattered. They told JFK, "Offer it to him; he'll turn it down, and you can have your own man by noon."

Early the next morning, Thursday, July 14, John Kennedy walked down the flight of stairs from his suite to call on Senator and Mrs. Johnson. There was a new sense of seriousness about him, a reserved inner calm that was perceptible not only in the way he walked, but in the way reporters and onlookers gave him a new deference, standing aside to let him through. I never dreamed that he was there to offer the Vice Presidency to LBJ—and if any of those among the more than fifty other reporters outside the door were thinking about it, they didn't say so. It never crossed my mind because Johnson had sworn to me a dozen times, both on the air and off, that he would never take the Vice Presidency.

For his part, Johnson had been expecting the offer; he took it at face value and said he'd think it over. A politician to his bones, he could see the merits of a Kennedy-Johnson combination. All the Johnson aides believed that it was a serious offer, and LBJ went to his grave saying he thought so, but there were many in the Kennedy camp who believed that it was only a courtesy.

Once the rumor of a Kennedy-Johnson ticket started, it spread like wildfire, igniting violent opposition in both the Kennedy and Johnson suites at the Biltmore. LBJ's friends, particularly Sam Rayburn, thought it heresy for him to accept. To run with Kennedy was to run with the devil.

In the Kennedy suite, Bobby Kennedy was upset; he thought LBJ was a crude wheeler-dealer. The campaign had been nasty, and Bobby did not forget Johnson's remarks about his father's alleged Nazi sympathies, nor what he considered to be unfair suggestions that his brother's poor health made him an unacceptable candidate. Liberals, labor and big-city politicians said they could not and would not stomach Johnson. This triggered more doubts in the Kennedy camp. Impassioned appeals were made to JFK to change his mind, and he started negotiations.

According to newspaper columnist Charles Bartlett, it was to get himself off the hook that JFK sent Bobby down to the Johnson suite around one o'clock to warn LBJ of the possibility that he might not be accepted by the Kennedy delegates. Bobby told LBJ's advisers that there was going to be trouble, that there were threats about throwing the vice-presidential choice open to the convention, and that if Johnson wanted the nomination, "He'll have to fight for it." Rayburn swore and said, "Never." He told Bobby to go back and tell his people that John Kennedy was going to have to speak out and tell everyone that he wanted LBJ. A crusty, tough old man, Rayburn considered Robert Kennedy a "kid" and a "punk."

Bobby was only thirty-five then and looked younger, and his voice was naturally strident, foreign-sounding and extremely irritating to Texas ears. The Johnson people simply did not understand the close relationship between the two Kennedys; besides, it was more convenient to believe that Bobby was there on his own rather than as an emissary of his brother. It was an angry, hostile meeting. Bobby left, grim-faced.

Years later at Hyannisport I asked Bobby about his attempt to keep LBJ off the ticket, and he replied that while he often disagreed with his brother, he would never have gone against his wishes and prevented him from choosing the man he wanted. There's no doubt that Bobby was acting at Jack's behest.

Opposition to Johnson continued to swell all over Los Angeles, especially from those liberals who had worked so hard for Kennedy's victory, and once again Bobby went downstairs to see if he could keep

Johnson out. At this point LBJ knew that JFK was trying to back out, because as a sop he was offered the chairmanship of the Democratic National Committee. When the offer was made, Rayburn exploded. Glaring at Bobby, he said, "Shit, sonny," and stomped out of the room. When he erupted from the Johnson suite, I walked down the hotel corridor with him to his room while he muttered about "the goddamn Kennedys" and how "We'll teach them how we do things . . ."

At some point during all this frenetic maneuvering, I interviewed Johnson and once again asked him if he would accept the post of Vice President. "No, no," he said. I repeated, "No, no, never?" And he emphatically said, "No, no, never."

Meanwhile, private planeloads of Texans left for home, saddened that their man had lost and never dreaming that he would accept second place. As the Johnsons were planning a big party for their supporters who had remained in Los Angeles, word continued to spread that the Vice Presidency had been offered to LBJ, but no one was certain what would happen.

Consultations continued during the afternoon. Johnson's feelings, bruised from the meeting with Bobby, were soothed by Phil Graham, who urged LBJ to take the offer. Johnson speculated that if he turned it down, Kennedy would be angry, and then, in victory, might try to reorganize the Senate and dump Johnson as Majority Leader. Further, even if the Democrats lost, Kennedy would be the titular head of the party and still might try to dump LBJ.

Rayburn was changing his mind, a highly significant factor, for Johnson, who used to say "He's like a Daddy to me," never would have gone on the ticket without Rayburn's approval.

In his suite directly overhead, Kennedy was breaking the news to Clark Clifford that practical politics demanded that he choose LBJ. Later Clifford said that JFK was considerably embarrassed because he'd promised the post to Symington and now was reneging. But Clifford saw the merits of a Kennedy-Johnson ticket, said he and Symington understood, and that it probably was for the best.

Kennedy also met with Scoop Jackson and gave him a different version. As Jackson quoted JFK, "Rayburn has intervened and insists that LBJ be on the ticket if the party is going to carry the South." Kennedy then offered Jackson the chairmanship of the Democratic National Committee, which Scoop turned down.

Still later Kennedy told his close friend and adviser, the highly regarded Pulitzer Prize-winning columnist Charles Bartlett, that he had "discussed" the Vice Presidency with Johnson on the supposition that LBJ would turn it down. Bartlett represented a solidity and adherence to principle that Kennedy greatly admired, and he probably didn't want Bartlett to think that he had given up ideals for political expediency. In any event, in explaining his choice Kennedy told Bartlett, "I never offered it to him. I just sort of held it out here," and he made a funny little gesture of a man pulling something part way out of his pocket but still hanging on to it. According to Bartlett, Kennedy said he had already picked Symington, and that Symington aides had started drafting an acceptance speech.

LBJ made up his mind alone, in his bedroom. It was a logical decision, but Lady Bird did not expect it, had hoped that her husband would not take the job and argued strongly against it. She changed her mind, but only much later. Back upstairs the Kennedy brothers locked themselves in a room and JFK told his brother that Johnson had to be the choice. Bobby was dreadfully disappointed. Eventually Phil Graham, the gentle and much respected friend of both Kennedy and Johnson, got the two men on the phone together and the deal was clinched.

Next, frantic maneuverings began to line up sympathetic liberals to place Johnson's name in nomination. Simultaneously, wheels were greased with the parliamentarian to thwart the liberals' potential demand for a roll-call vote, a vote that LBJ might have lost. Instead there was a voice vote and the chairman gaveled the noes away to announce the Johnson nomination.

Again JFK called Jackson to ask him a second time to be the Democratic party chairman. This time Jackson accepted, and he also agreed to join in the public orchestration of support for Johnson.

More frantic calls were made as each side tried to placate its purists who opposed the choice. As the afternoon wore on, Kennedy asked Orville Freeman to come to his suite. Thus summoned, Freeman was fairly confident that he had been chosen as running mate. He and his wife entered the little Kennedy hideaway which had one small unmade bed, dirty glasses, and ashtrays filled with cigars and cigarette butts. When JFK told them his choice, the Freemans were shocked; they couldn't conceive of the post being offered to Johnson or of his accepting. Just as Kennedy was starting to explain, Bobby, having heard that Johnson was already telling everyone the news, stuck his head in the door and said to Jack, "Hurry up! Announce it right now or the son-of-a-bitch will beat you to it." Kennedy ran out of the room. No further explanation to the Freemans.

When the Johnson loyalists arrived at the party he and Lady Bird were giving, thinking to drown their sorrows at the loss of the nomination, they were stunned to hear he was the vice-presidential nominee. They stood around in bewilderment watching the news being broadcast on television. When Lady Bird saw Scoop Jackson come on the screen to confirm the selection, she burst out crying—unheard of for this disciplined and controlled woman. Many thought that Mrs. Johnson did not know about the decision until she heard it on television, but that's not true, for she said wistfully to Bill Moyers beforehand, "But I was so happy being the wife of the senator from Texas." That's all she wanted.

Breaking the news to some Johnson loyalists was not easy. Bobby Baker took Senator Robert Kerr into a men's room to tell him, and for his pains got slapped in the face. As Baker said, "He thought I was a traitor." Perle Mesta left the party in disgust; like many others she felt she had been betrayed, and she switched her support to Nixon.

So unanticipated was the choice of Johnson and his acceptance that even one of his daughters didn't know about it. Lynda Bird had been told she could skip the party and go to Disneyland, and an inordinate amount of time was spent that afternoon trying to locate her so that the four Johnsons could appear together, projecting the image of a united family—an aura that was thought particularly desirable since Jackie, because of her pregnancy, was unable to stand at Jack's side.

After the decision LBJ refused to be interviewed by anyone but me, and of course I had some recouping to do. After all, I had been confidently predicting for months that he wouldn't take the spot even if it was offered, and pointing out that the position of Majority Leader of the Senate was a more powerful job. When we got on the air I reminded LBJ that only hours before, he had specifically told me that he would never accept the office, and he blandly replied, "That's right. I wouldn't run *for* it, but I'm indeed honored to run *as* the vice-presidential nominee." I wanted to throttle him. The nuances of grammar had never before been one of his major concerns,

48

but it was symptomatic of what was later to create havoc in LBJ's press relations.

At the convention that night with Lady Bird and Luci—Lynda Bird was still missing, which irritated her father greatly; he kept saying, "After all, if you can't count on your family, who can you count on?"—LBJ again refused all interviews except mine. Everywhere they went I leapfrogged in front of them to a camera position, and as they passed by, Johnson would stop to smile, say, "Hello, Nancy," and answer all questions. Since he was the man of the hour, this annoyed the other networks considerably, and it coincidentally skyrocketed me to a certain prominence. After a final interview, when I could think of nothing more to ask any member of the family, director Don Hewitt summoned me to the anchor booth to join Cronkite and Murrow in a convention wrap-up. As I walked into this inner sanctum filled with network executives, writers, technicians and onlookers, Murrow stood up, bowed low off camera and said, "Goddamn good news reporting, ma'am." I beamed.

After it was all over, both the Johnson and Kennedy camps were downhearted and in some instances disgusted. At the Kennedy hideaway it was gloomy until Joe Kennedy said, "Don't worry, Jack. Two weeks from now, everyone will say it's the smartest thing you ever did." On the Johnson plane flying back to Texas, it was also like a wake. Mrs. Johnson was glum, and LBJ consoled at least one supporter by saying, "Don't worry; we're not going to win, anyway."

The day after the convention I flew to Texas to cover the Johnsons, and they invited me to stay at the LBJ Ranch. At breakfast an assessment was made of the Democrats' chances for victory. The problem of JFK's Catholicism, particularly sticky in the Protestant South, was analyzed, and was followed by an oblique reference to his reputed love affairs. I'll always remember Lady Bird's crestfallen face as she said, "Oh, no! Not that too!"

As a postscript to the whole business, Orville Freeman told me many years later of a conversation he'd once had with President Johnson at Camp David. They were alone by the pool, sunning themselves, when LBJ broke the silence. "You know what?" he said. "When JFK offered me the Vice Presidency, I asked him who he'd take if I didn't accept, and you know what he said? He said, 'Orville Freeman.' "

CHAPTER 6 ⌇⌒

After the two 1960 conventions, there was a special session of Congress to cope with. LBJ had engineered it as part of his own campaign to get the presidential nomination, and now he and Kennedy were stuck with it when they had no time to spare. JFK needed to make himself as well known as Nixon, who had benefited from the prominence of the Vice Presidency for the past eight years and was ahead in the polls. Moreover, Kennedy had never been comfortable in the Senate. He was not a member of the inner group that ran the place, the so-called club, and the Senate's politics were of little use to him in a national campaign.

On the other hand, for Johnson the Senate was home. Although its politics had failed to win him the nomination, he was back in the Capitol, where his personal contacts and consummate power-balancing held sway. He ruled there with the autocracy of an emperor permitting certain older men to counsel him, or as he put it, "to reason together." Though those senators had not been able to deliver the nomination to him, he still thought they could help in the coming campaign. Even at this point he did not fully comprehend that the real power throughout the country was generally held by state leaders, who ruled from home with little concern for their representatives in Washington.

For their part, the Senate elders considered Kennedy a mere boy, were somewhat astonished that he actually had the nomination and were not at all sanguine about his prospects. Because of the gap between "the old men" of the club and "the boy" who was potentially their leader, LBJ thought the best way to prove himself to Kennedy was to get him into the club—no easy feat. To this end he persuaded old Senator Allen J. Ellender of Louisiana to give one of his little luncheons in his hideaway.

There are only a handful of these hideaways in the Capitol corridors; no name or door number is posted outside, and their very existence is known only to a few. They are a perquisite of seniority, so Ellender had one of the best, with a window that overlooked the Mall. He had installed a small oven and a bar, with a big table, deep Victorian sofas and low-slung chairs. Ellender's lunches were always the same—shrimp gumbo, made by the senator himself with shrimp flown up from his native Louisiana—and everyone was importuned to have second and third helpings before the traditional dessert of pralines. In this cozy setting a cast consisting of such Senate powers as Richard Russell, Harry Byrd and John Stennis, and two men who had thought they might be Kennedy's running mate, Stuart Symington and Scoop Jackson, had gathered. Inexplicably, Perle Mesta was also there.

Once the stage was set, LBJ and the rest of us waited for the candidate—who was late, so the occasion was virtually doomed from the start. Finally he bustled in, thin and wiry, papers under his arm, moving fast and giving the impression that he had many more important things to do, whereas the waiting group looked as if they would be more comfortable on the veranda of a plantation. He shook hands with each of them, all of them older, addressing each of them formally with "Hello, Senator," to which they all replied, "Hello, Jack." He was plainly uncomfortable being chaperoned by LBJ and making his debut before older men who were all too aware that if elected, he would have much more to say about the country's affairs than they would. Only Senator Symington, with his grace and innate gentlemanliness, seemed at ease.

The atmosphere was stiff from the start and got stiffer. Though we talked a great deal about the food, JFK ingested only a little of his lunch, which didn't please his host. The conversation never got rolling; it just lurched forward occasionally, responding to an energetic poke or two. Kennedy kept calling them all "Senator," and they kept calling him "Jack." To top it all off, he left before anyone else, which gave them a preview of the role he had in mind for them in his forthcoming campaign—that is, no role at all.

As the luncheon broke up, the indefatigable LBJ sidled up to a couple of his old friends and said, "See, I told you he really was a nice boy," but by any criterion, the luncheon was a failure.

Just as soon as they could, Kennedy and Johnson left the congressional session to go out on the campaign trail full time, and I spent most of the subsequent weeks assigned to LBJ.

Traveling with a vice-presidential candidate is much more relaxed than with a presidential nominee because he is not as important or as much in demand, and the pressures aren't as severe for him or for those assigned to him. As a result, the LBJ entourage had a certain amount of fun. While the reporters assigned to the presidential candidate were expected to produce a story each day, those of us following LBJ had to plead to get our stories on the air—a fact of life that galled LBJ, who thought his activities had great news value.

I learned something important about Johnson early in the campaign: never to disagree with him unless I had lots of spare time and energy equal to his own. If anyone differed with him he would literally spend hours trying to convince the person of the wisdom of his position and the folly of any other view, and it made no difference whether the argument was on politics or on beagles. I learned not to take him on unless I had finished writing my radio and television pieces and had plenty of time before the next campaign stop. One night when we arrived at our destination after a vigorous argument of several hours, one of Johnson's aides conveyed to me the grateful appreciation of the staff: when he was occupied with a reporter they all had a breather from his constant demands.

But though they found him exhausting, the members of Johnson's staff were exceedingly loyal and were seldom irreverent about their employer. Bill Moyers, however, who had been trained as a preacher and therefore perhaps enjoyed a closeness to the Lord which enabled him to see Johnson as a mere man, sometimes saw his bigger-than-life boss in perspective. Once when there had been a reference to the Bible in a debate which I couldn't recall verbatim, I asked Bill if he had one I could borrow. Bill shook his head, and with a nod in the direction of Johnson, said, "Why should we, when we've got Himself?"

LBJ was proud of "going first class," and he insisted that all who accompanied him go the same way. He had an Electra with a specially fitted interior, and because in the past these planes had occasionally crashed because of insufficiently strong struts under the wings, he made a point of calling to assure me that his plane had been reconditioned and was safe. American Airlines made sure that the best-trained and prettiest stewardesses were on board, and there was a steward who soon learned our special likes and dislikes. As soon as we got back on the plane after each frenetic stop, the crew would have each reporter's favorite drink ready and waiting, along with a delicious snack—there was seldom enough time for a whole meal—to eat en route to the next spot in the tour.

This was the routine when we got to Helena, Montana. It was a quick stop, and afterward LBJ was anxious to get under way again. His ever-efficient staff had everything programed for minute-by-minute perfection, and takeoffs were always on time so that we wouldn't be late at the next city. (At the time Kennedy was being criticized for his late arrivals, and LBJ thought it was outrageous to keep welcoming crowds waiting.) But this time we didn't take off right away, and the delay greatly irritated the candidate. At first he fussed and fumed, and finally we were treated to a minor temper tantrum. At last, when he was about to burst with frustration, we took off, and only when we were in the air did we get an explanation. Evidently there was only one adequate caterer in Helena, and the last time that he had serviced a vice-presidential campaign plane—when Estes Kefauver had passed through four years earlier—the bill had never been paid. The man was determined that this wasn't going to happen again, and he refused to hand over any food without getting cash in return!

The quixotic Johnson campaign was always full of surprises. There is a certain sense of power that comes with having a large chartered airplane at your disposal, and LBJ relished it. It was nothing to him to fly anywhere at the drop of a vote, and it never occurred to him that such midair changes were either a surprise or an inconvenience for anyone else. As a result, my expense account listed such unusual items as pants, shirts and boots bought in Kansas City because of an unscheduled trip to the ranch, for which I had no appropriate clothes.

It was amazing the way Lady Bird adapted to these changes involving large numbers of guests. Once when we were in Austin, LBJ phoned the ranch to tell Lady Bird that he would be there in an hour —and incidentally was bringing nine reporters with him for the weekend. Accustomed to such calls and being organized, flexible and efficient, she simply kept the beds made and the freezers full of steak and venison. I never once saw her appear grumpy. Having my own house now, I know all too well what a chore nine extra people can be. While I wouldn't mind it once in a while, it was something of a habit with LBJ, who really meant it when he said, "You-all come."

Catholicism was a major issue in the campaign, and both sides used it to their advantage. Kennedy had made a brilliant appearance to answer questions about his religion before a group of Protestant clergymen in Houston, and a tape of this was shown wherever it was advantageous to thwart anti-Catholicism. However, Republicans complained, with some validity, that the film was also shown in some regions where there was no prejudice, as well as in heavily Catholic areas to drum up sympathy.

LBJ was not anti-Catholic, though he was mildly suspicious of the religion; it was a foreign, unknown force to him. But in his barnstorming speeches he took every opportunity to tell "the Wiley story," a true story strung out with many embellishments about a Protestant pilot who was killed in the war. After a dramatic pause he would roar at the crowd, "Did they ask Wiley's religion when he gave his life for his country?" And the crowd would shout back, "No!" And then, after another pause, he would follow with a story about Joseph P. Kennedy, Jr., JFK's older brother, "a young Catholic boy," as he put it, who had lost his life in the war. Poking his finger in the air, Johnson would demand in a stage whisper, "Did anyone ask *his* religion when he gave *his* life for our country?" Of course the crowd would roar back an even louder "No!" This made an impact, especially in the Protestant South.

LBJ's campaign style was as different from JFK's as it could be. A product of the Texas hill country and of the rugged individualism that such geography molds, he could stand up in front of a crowd and say how he loved his country, "this great country of ours," so sincerely that it wasn't even corny. Had someone else used the same words, it would have sounded false, but for LBJ, raised in the rural South, where oratory, debate and the art of talk is a way of life, where patriotism is a specific rather than amorphous concept, it was utterly natural. He regarded political speeches as a form of folk entertainment. As he once explained to me, "We didn't have things to do the way the people in the city did, and talking was the way we spent our time." His full-blown oratory was an extension of what he'd seen and been all his life.

In time there was considerable criticism of this "style," especially from the sometimes arrogant aides who were handling Kennedy, and LBJ became so self-conscious and sensitive to any hint that he was "corny" that he tried to change his way of speaking. I think that he conjured up the image of himself as a preacher; in any case, his

54

speeches took on a singsong cadence full of tremolos as he rolled out what he thought a proper Sunday-morning sermon should sound like. And just as a half-hour sermon is considered long enough in many places, a full-hour sermon is considered more appropriate in parts of the rural South, so he applied the same logic to a campaign speech; a brief appearance was not considered to be a voter's money's worth in certain areas, particularly if one had traveled a great distance to hear the candidate. He felt very strongly about this, and often mentioned the occasion when, as a young boy, he had traveled for hours on horseback to see a vice-presidential candidate ride by in a train. The candidate had never stopped—the train only slowed down at the crossroads—and LBJ vowed that he'd never do this to anyone. If it had been possible to shake hands with everyone in sight, he would have done it. Certainly he never passed up a crowd if he could help it, and while Eastern liberals often criticized him for his vanity and for the ego-massaging he got from crowds, part of it was an effort not to disappoint a small boy.

On the other hand, LBJ's attempts to present himself as a rural preacher were less successful because he was pretending to be something he was not. Once Lady Bird nodded in agreement as I tried to convince him to let people take him for what he was, but this was extremely difficult for him, just as it is for many other Texans who seem to have an inferiority complex about their origins. It didn't work. His campaign floundered in certain Northern states, and as a result, the Kennedy people tried to keep him out of some strategic areas where they thought he might actually lose votes. In addition, there simply was not a great demand for the presence of the vice-presidential candidate. The organizers of any political meeting much preferred the nominee for the Presidency, and though this has also been true of every other campaign, it still rankled. So his friends spent some time cooking up places for him to go while he was trying to convince everyone that he was as popular in the North as in the South —which simply wasn't so.

The Kennedys always were an irritant because he felt that they didn't accept him—and they didn't. At one point in the campaign he pleaded, "Nancy, you know the Kennedys; will you tell them what a good job I'm doing?" Then, as an afterthought: "Or at least will you tell them how hard I'm trying?" In spite of opposition by some Kennedy aides, he continued to go where his senator friends invited him to appear, and naturally this led to friction between the two nominees. At one point the relationship became so strained that peacemakers arranged for the Johnsons to visit Hyannisport for a weekend, where the exacerbations were smoothed over temporarily —not in any substantive way, but at least soothing LBJ's ego.

Not only had LBJ a terrible time adjusting to Kennedy's nomination, he also had a low opinion of JFK's ability to run the campaign. On the night of the first Nixon-Kennedy debate he was at his ranch, and several of us were also there, enjoying the unparalleled Johnson hospitality. Lady Bird had arranged a superb dinner to be eaten during the debate, just as millions of other Americans were doing all across the country. With the time difference in Texas, television stations delayed the debate for an hour, but we all gathered in the living room to listen on the radio. We all thought Nixon had won, for we could not see how dreadful he looked. Throughout, LBJ kept score, saying "One for Nixon" or "One for the boy"—but the boy always seemed to come out behind. To Johnson, JFK clearly had lost. Later, on television, the debate seemed more even, but Kennedy's running mate still felt Nixon was the winner.

Although the two men were never natural allies, the rawness between them was in part created, nourished and encouraged by eager and jealous staffs. This abrasion laid the groundwork for an enmity which still lasts, long after both are dead, an undercurrent that forever poisons loyalists in both camps.

Toward the end of the campaign there were worries, as there always are, about whether the ticket could win, and specifically whether the Democrats could hold the South, which was essential to victory. When there were signs that Nixon was gaining fast, LBJ cashed in every Southern IOU he had. His good friend Richard Russell, the Democratic senator from Georgia, had never liked Kennedy—he didn't trust him—so LBJ prevailed upon him to join the campaign. Russell was immensely popular throughout the South because he personified the classic prototype of Southern virtue and deep-seated convictions about segregation and patriotism. He always received a tremendous ovation and reception anywhere we went, and though he only spoke for a minute or two, endorsing Johnson lavishly but never mentioning Kennedy's name, his efforts paid off handsomely.

In the final week Johnson virtually commuted between New York and Texas. On Election Day the entourage was back in Austin, uncertain about the outcome. As usual the pollsters were ambivalent, but LBJ was sanguine because of his own particular poll: he drove around Austin counting campaign stickers on cars. In a country where a man's car is often his castle, LBJ believed that a sticker on a car represented total commitment, and he predicted the results accordingly. He called the Texas vote precisely, projected it nationally and was right on the button.

The representatives of the three networks had called a production meeting on election-night coverage from Johnson headquarters, part of which was devoted to a plan to thwart Johnson should he come over to my microphone to the exclusion of the others. We all agreed to pool our access and thus preclude exclusives on the part of any single network. But it was a waste of time; during the evening LBJ came out from time to time, talked to me and that was that.

Immediately after the victory the Johnsons got one more taste of the low state in which Vice Presidents are held. Speeches were planned by the Kennedys from Boston, but no one asked for LBJ's; in fact, neither NBC nor ABC even *wanted* his statement. The CBS television lines to Austin were down when I finally persuaded the network to agree to carry an interview. I felt sorry for LBJ: the victory was as much his as Kennedy's, but precious little credit came from Boston to the big sensitive man in Austin.

History says that vice-presidential candidates have not mattered much in a campaign, but this was not true in 1960. It may well have been the first time that a vice-presidential nominee *did* make a difference: without the South, Kennedy would have lost, and of all the other potential running mates he might have chosen, none could have delivered, with certainty, more than his own state—and perhaps not even that. Johnson delivered not only Texas but several other Southern states as well. This gave LBJ a certain leverage: he was there by sufferance because Kennedy had chosen him, but it worked both ways; without Johnson on the ticket, JFK wouldn't have made it to the White House. It was never a marriage of love, only of mutual dependence.

57

CHAPTER 7 〜⌒〜

After the election Kennedy flew to Texas to pay a courtesy call on Johnson. CBS sent me down to cover the event, and I interviewed JFK when he arrived. It was comical; the Texans had bought an especially big cowboy hat for him, and we all placed bets about whether he'd wear it. He didn't. He would only pose holding it.

Victory was sweet, and JFK didn't seem to be able to do anything wrong in the weeks that followed. When the Kennedy baby was born, it was a boy, which was especially pleasing to his father's male-chauvinist heart. The Kennedy verve displayed itself early; a news conference in Palm Beach was punctuated by the appearance of little Caroline clomping across the terrace in her mother's high-heeled shoes. With no inhibition she stopped at my chair, and every camera in the place recorded her enchanting antics.

The Cabinet was selected with all the flair of a Sol Hurok production. The major question was what job Bobby would have. The President-elect didn't want him to be Attorney General, Bobby didn't want to be Attorney General, but his father wanted him to be Attorney General; he thought it would give him stature. Several advisers argued that it would be foolish to have a Kennedy in charge of the civil rights fights looming ahead. They thought Bobby's presence would link JFK unnecessarily to the tough and often unpopular decisions to be made. But the father prevailed. It was one more example of the extraordinary influence the old man had on all of them. (Joe senior had once said that the Presidency wasn't so important as two other jobs in Washington: those of the Attorney General and the head of the IRS. He saw to it that a Kennedy was one and that a professor who had taught a Kennedy, Mortimer Kaplan, was the other.)

For those who covered the inauguration, it is remembered as much for the snow as for the era it ushered in. The Washington snowplows, which are so seldom used that they get rusty, were hopeless, the weather bureau was asleep and there was no warning. Before the streets were finally cleared, most of us had spent hours in traffic jams and had stayed up half the night. I remember that Garfinckel's could not deliver my new dress to be worn to the Inaugural Ball, so I lugged it all over town, along with matching shoes and a typewriter, looking more like a moonlighting secretary than a reporter.

On Inauguration Day the plows had not reached my Georgetown house and no car could get through, so I tramped down O Street early in the morning wearing snow boots, past Holy Trinity Church, where Jack had attended services earlier, past the Kennedy house on N Street, which looked no different from its snow-covered neighbors— though I did note that the snowplows had been there—and eventually to my assigned spot at the Capitol Rotunda where I had to be in position four hours before the ceremony.

I had plenty of time to think back to the first inauguration I'd attended, which was for Ike. I was still working at the Senate Foreign Relations Committee then, and watched it from our office window. There was an aura of patriotic pride in our war-hero President, and much talk about how George Washington had also been first a general and then a President.

It's a miracle that we can switch power from one party to another with so little rancor; it proves how well our system works. But even so, such a switch inevitably produces irritations, and these were exacerbated by Ike and Truman, who didn't like each other and showed it. This was reflected all the way down the staff, which was inexcusably insensitive to the changeover. Also, the new gang at any inauguration is always so anxious to take over that the amenities of life are often forgotten. While Ike and Truman rode together to Capitol Hill, with undisguised animosity toward each other, Beth Short, Truman's press secretary, closed down the press office at the White House and then was driven in a White House limousine to the inauguration ceremony. When it was over, her car and driver were gone—the new crowd had it—and Beth took the streetcar home. That's democracy's version of "The King is dead. Long live the King." I no longer react so violently, but at the time I was appalled by the way power affects people. I was beginning to see not only how power enables you to change the world, but how it can turn human beings into ogres.

I also remembered Ike's inauguration because Jack Kennedy had just been elected to the Senate. With his large family, he needed all the tickets he could get, and since I had some extras, I offered them to him. Outside the Senate entrance to the Capitol the security guard would not let anyone in, and Mrs. Rose Kennedy called out loudly from the center of a pushing mob, "I am Senator Kennedy's mother. Please let me in." It worked, and several of JFK's sisters trooped in after her. Now, eight years later, they wouldn't have to ask anyone; they *were* in.

Waiting in the bitter cold was agony, and the wives of dignitaries seated in the grandstand near the podium, along with various freezing officials, began to drift into the warm Rotunda, where our cameras were while they waited for the President-elect. This large crowd had to be cleared out before Kennedy could go out onto the platform and take the oath. Jackie had already arrived, and as she came up the steps I heard her say, "There's Nancy." After I started appearing on television she always treated me as a celebrity, which I found thoroughly unnerving. Part of her charm is her way of treating others as if they are more important than she is or they are.

Finally the President-elect, wearing no overcoat, appeared. Since he wore thermal underwear, he didn't need one—and he did look grand, as the Irish lady would say. But he was a little anxious and nervous, like a groom waiting to claim his bride who is late for the wedding, and in the interval he came over and talked to me. I asked, "When did you think this would finally come to pass?" and was surprised to learn that he'd thought it would happen ever since his youth. He added that he wasn't half as surprised to be President as a lot of people were to see him there.

He was pleased with his new morning dress, and equally impatient with the delay. He wondered "when the hell" they'd get the place cleared out; he was irritated that it took so long to herd the dignitaries out of the warm Rotunda and back into the cold. At this point I saw Herb Klein, then press secretary to the defeated Vice President Nixon. I introduced them to each other; though they had been adversaries in the long campaign, it was the first time they met.

The minutes dragged on. JFK said he wasn't cold; I said I was. He asked me who various people were and I identified them. He whistled and rocked back and forth on his feet, hands behind his back. During all this my CBS colleague, Howard K. Smith, was doing the running commentary, vamping while they cleared the Rotunda, and he told the world that while everyone waited, JFK was talking to me.

While the new President was telling Americans to ask not what their country would do for them, the three networks were jockeying in the Rotunda. There was an elaborate ploy to position me right next to the door so that when the President moved by, I could talk with him again. With the same idea, NBC put Sandy Vanocur in the same spot, banking on the fact that he had spent the past two years following Kennedy and knew him well. This kind of one-upmanship has since become the subject of policy decisions, but at the time the networks were still fencing. We were rather like horses in a race, with the additional chore of choosing our own stall at the gate. Our task was further complicated by the writing press, who liked to have their families back home see them on television. Eventually this got to be such a problem that NBC had to send along extra crewmen to block other reporters when I did live interviews.

As Sandy and I bumped around in the bitter cold, I tried to keep my wits about me and remember not to call the new President "Jack." (Once a President is inaugurated it is improper to call him by his first name in public, and I never did.) Obviously Sandy was thinking along the same lines because when JFK finally reappeared we both flubbed it and said "Congratulations, Senator." President Kennedy thanked me first, so that next day the *Times* could record that the last person before and first person after his inauguration that President Kennedy had talked to was CBS correspondent Nancy Hanschman.

Though it's trivial, this kind of thing is helpful to one's standing at a network, and I wrote the President to thank him. By return mail he sent me a handwritten letter on the special light-green White House stationery:

Dear Nancy:

Thank you for your note. I am glad our exchange was useful. You may be sure that I shall be glad to give testimony for you coast to coast on any occasion when it might be helpful. You can do the same for me.

Best,

Jack

Others at the White House use engraved white stationery; only Presidents use the light-green paper—a custom started by FDR. There are relatively few of these handwritten Kennedy notes; most of his letters were either dictated or written and signed by others.

President Kennedy's Inaugural Ball may have been a hassle, but I loved it. I had my own car and driver and enough credentials to get through the traffic and the snow. In addition, the news department relaxes a little when it comes to covering a dance and therefore it's easier. I even had an assistant to round up guests for interviews. Our cameras were about twenty feet from the presidential box, and I never considered the evening as work; I simply had a marvelous time dressed up in a lot of chiffon and sequins that cost more than I was being paid for the evening's job. When Mrs. Rose Kennedy arrived, wearing the spectacular gown she'd worn twenty years earlier to be presented at the Court of St. James's, she told me that I looked as if I was having a better time than anyone, and maybe I was.

Vice President and Mrs. Johnson, who arrived before the Kennedys, had agreed to let me interview them in the presidential box. This was an exclusive, and it took massive preparation and planning with the security guards because live cameras are bulky and the cables are unsafe in crowds. Unless you've been involved with live coverage of major events, it's difficult to realize how complicated the arrangements are, especially if the Secret Service is there. People are crowded everywhere and want to get closer, so that it's difficult to move. A mike won't stretch where it's supposed to, because people are standing on the cable; aides don't want you to have access and become even more officious, and when a Secret Service agent refuses to let you through, there is no argument.

I stayed in the box interviewing the Johnsons until I was beginning to run out of anything more to ask, and then a guard whispered that I'd better get out of there, that the President and Mrs. Kennedy were waiting to enter. When they did appear, I asked them, "What took you so long?"

CHAPTER 8 ⌒

When I first went out with Jack Kennedy I was working on the Foreign Relations Committee, and he wanted to know everything about the foreign-aid debates. He never deprecated an opinion because it was a woman's, and once when someone cut me off in midsentence, he made everyone keep quiet until I'd made my point. He didn't denigrate women, but he didn't idealize them either, or treat them in the courtly way of a Southerner. On the contrary; one night when he came to take me out, he didn't bother to get out of the car and simply honked the horn. I didn't like it, and he never did it again.

Kennedy had great sex appeal. I know one prominent woman who adored him and when her future husband proposed, she said she'd let him know; she wanted time to sound out Jack to see whether there was any chance for her. And she was one among many. The Capitol Hill secretaries were the forerunners of the squealers who became famous during his later campaigns. This appeal extended even to old Republican ladies who would never have voted for him. Thinking back on it, I realize that part of his charm was the fun; you never knew what would bubble out at the next moment. To Jack the cardinal sin was boredom; it was his biggest enemy, and he didn't know how to handle it. When he was bored, a hood would come down over his eyes and his nervous system would start churning. You could do anything to him—steal his wallet, insult him, argue with him—but to bore was unpardonable.

That's something he himself never did. His mind went like a saber through fuzziness, right to the crux, and it annoyed him to spend time with people whose minds were slow or flabby. He used to worry about who I should marry; he was afraid that I'd get bored. But though he recognized that women could be bored just running a household, the idea of putting one in charge of something important and giving her the same pay as a man was quite another matter. It may surprise some feminists who revere him to learn that Jack Kennedy was the complete male chauvinist. He saw women primarily as sex objects, and though he loved to be around them and often asked for and paid attention to their opinions, he thought it ridiculous to pay them the same as men.

Once when the Kennedys and I were on the same plane to New York, en route to a convention of women in radio and television, where I was to be a delegate and he was to speak, he gave me a copy of his address and asked for suggestions. It was amorphous—something about the need for general improvement in the quality of life via the media—and I told him he'd do much better with his audience

63

if he said, "Let's get women off the weather beat and let them be newscasters." He looked at me as if I were certifiable, but he did change his speech to include a call for women to broaden their scope within the broadcasting world.

The early glimmerings of the women's movement began to surface during JFK's Administration, and Eleanor Roosevelt stated publicly that he should appoint more women to high office than he had. She was right, but he didn't change his ways. In the meanwhile Jackie had become the darling of the world, setting fashion in everything she did. JFK was fascinated by his wife, partly because, as he once said, "I never know what she's going to do." He liked her because she was different and because of her feyness.

In her youth Jackie was quite different from her later image. She had a lighter step, laughter came more easily and there were practical jokes. Essentially she was motivated by a desire for money. Though she grew up in the midst of luxury, extravagant amounts were not spent on her, and early on she had vowed to marry someone "richer than Uncle Hugh D.," her stepfather. She was often unhappy growing up at Merrywood, the family estate in Virginia. She was not particularly close to her mother, and there was a sadness to her adoration of her father, whose life she saw sinking away. She had few strong friendships, and with the possible exception of her father, few loyalties. As one of her oldest friends said to me, "Even when she was married to JFK, she would mimic him behind his back and make fun of him. It was immensely amusing, but also discomforting."

Jackie enjoyed printed publicity that was favorable, but she didn't like the reporters assigned to her or those she thought inferior. Early in 1961 she gave a White House luncheon for women of the press, and everyone was dazzled by her. Just ahead of me in the reception line was Doris Fleeson, the highly respected political columnist; on seeing her, Jackie said, "Oh, Doris, what in the world would you be doing here with these others?"—a dig at everyone else within hearing distance. As we walked away, Doris whispered, "That young woman has a lot to learn!"

She didn't like the crowds that surged around her in campaigns, and I understood why the first time I was assigned to cover them both. It was a large meeting of Democratic women who were so excited to see the Kennedys that they almost trampled them just to touch her, or to get over her to touch him. It was terrifying.

Jackie's appeal was that she had a mystery about her. She kept her privacy, which only whetted the public's appetite for more. JFK was quick to capitalize on this, and in the 1964 campaign he planned to use her and the children in many more photographic stories. He liked what he called Jackie's "class," and perhaps was even intimidated by it, despite the fact that he considered himself an aristocrat and never suffered the anti-Irish frost his parents had.

Jackie could also be extremely endearing. When I was on *Face the Nation* and her husband was the guest one week, she came to watch, and before the show slipped little notes on the desks of the reporters she knew; each said, "Don't ask Jack mean questions."

When they first moved into the White House, the Kennedys went to a few private parties, but this soon ceased. JFK thought the practice lacked dignity; he didn't want to be just another swinger in town. Another pattern that changed was a conscious drawing away from the press, except for old friends such as Charlie Bartlett, who had first introduced JFK to Jackie, and Ben Bradlee, then of *Newsweek*. Though Kennedy liked the business of journalism and had excellent press relations—after all, as he used to say, he had once been a reporter himself—he soon decided that the overt courtship of the press that was necessary during a campaign was absurd for a President. He invited a few "super journalists" to lunch, but he was under no illusions that it made much difference. By becoming more remote from most reporters, JFK was paying them a supreme compliment; he was admitting that they couldn't be conned. In any case, he had no taste for it. But though he continued to be curious about individual reporters' lives and how they wrote, when he didn't like the way *Newsweek* treated one story, he banned it from the White House. At a dinner party immediately afterward I heard Bobby Kennedy say jokingly to Phil Graham, the publisher of *Newsweek*, "Don't worry, Phil. When a book is banned in Boston, it sells better everywhere else."

One of JFK's most attractive qualities was his lack of pomposity, and he enjoyed immensely telling stories on himself, such as an incident that occurred in May of 1962. At the time, his relations with Congress were in poor shape; there was a slump in the economy, and unemployment was at a high level. To combat this, friends helped him draw up a guest list of the fifteen or twenty top businessmen in the country to be invited to the Oval Room for a pep talk. On the theory that confidence is half the battle, JFK tried to explain and convince these men of the wisdom of his policies. As a clincher to wind up his argument, he said, "Why, gentlemen, the economy of this country is in such good shape that if I weren't President today, I'd go into the stock market heavily." To which one of those gathered there replied, "Sir, if you weren't President, so would I."

The Kennedys had a compartmentalized relationship with their friends. JFK loved his political pals, but they weren't invited upstairs to the White House. Lemoyne Billings, his roommate at Choate who had been a close intimate for years, was a delight, and JFK loved to laugh and relax with him, but he would never have appointed him to federal office. His relationships were like the spokes of a wheel, with himself as the hub. He expected his friends to be amusing and his associates to be right, but he never demanded that the two be interchangeable.

The Kennedy family didn't quite know how to cope with Jackie, and were seldom at ease with her because she was so different. Family gatherings at the White House were much more relaxed when she was not there. But she was tough and learned how to live with the clan, which was not easy because of their tremendous competitiveness. She started out playing touch football with them, but when she broke her ankle she gave this up and let them have their own games while she had hers. However, they always respected her—if for no other reason than her own considerable public following, which in some cases surpassed his. Her zenith came on their visit to France. A year or so earlier I had been at a party at the French embassy in Washington when Jackie first met De Gaulle. It was easy to see that she captivated him, and when she arrived in Paris she did the same with millions of other Frenchmen—so much so that President Kennedy opened his news conference by identifying himself "as the man who accompanied Jacqueline Kennedy to France." When they got back home his mother-in-law, Mrs. Auchincloss, asked in amazement if he *really* had said that. She was never a big Kennedy fan until he attained the White House, a residence which can convert the most critical.

Throughout our history, the sex lives of Presidents have been a subject of intense interest, and when the President is as young and dashing as Kennedy was, the topic was irresistible. If he saw as many women as it was rumored he did, he couldn't have had time for anything else. Still, it is true that Jackie was away from the White House frequently, and sometimes for long periods. At times she simply needed a rest; JFK was taxing intellectually, and it was a strain for her to be with him constantly. While she was away he did entertain other women, sometimes in a group and sometimes alone. He was fascinated with other people's sex lives and talked about them. When one bachelor ambassador went through a White House receiving line, he told me later that he was astonished when the President asked him, "Are you getting any lately?" When he first moved into the White House, JFK told a friend that he intended "to keep the White House white," and though he changed his mind, he was extremely discreet about it. But some of those who took women to the White House, for him or for themselves, were not so discreet. One, a former senator, said after a night at the White House, "I felt sacrilegious screwing in the Lincoln Bedroom."

Women charmed and delighted JFK, particularly if they were attractive. I'm sure he'd have laughed out loud if he could have heard a remark made at a memorial service ten years after his death. When a plain woman of generous proportions rose to read the lesson, Charlie Bartlett leaned over and whispered, "Jack would have preferred a better-looking broad!"

The Kennedys had pizzazz. As Dickens might have said of those thousand days, it was "the best of times." In fact, it was called Camelot, and its intrinsic characteristics were surprise, change, style and zest. Of JFK's inaugural address, Robert Frost said that it was Irish because it sang and had a lilt. So did the Kennedy White House. It was Irish, which made it fun, and blended with the spirit of Harvard and the patina of Jackie's finishing schools, the mixture was intoxicating.

When asked why he wanted the Presidency during the campaign, Kennedy said, "That's where the power is." Once in the White House, the Kennedy style was to use that power and the office in every way. What his Administration did captured the imagination of the country and the world. Everybody was swept up in the dazzling ambiance of beautiful women coming down from New York for parties, state dinners of unprecedented elegance—and a nursery school for small children on the third floor. It was a time of involve-

67

ment; people felt guilty if they weren't doing something. Even more important, they felt that what they did would make a difference. It was an era of optimism, when everything was possible, when the word "no" didn't exist.

There was also the flattery of imitation. When Jackie started to redecorate the White House, furniture classes sprung up all over town as young women studied the difference between Sheraton and Queen Anne, and between Lowestoft china and Chinese export. State dinners, formerly held at long formal tables in the L or U shape, were changed to small round tables. Immediately hostesses all around town bought or rented round dinner tables to seat eight or ten. Eisenhower parties had often been white tie; the Kennedys switched to black tie. The Eisenhower preferences for canasta, Lawrence Welk and Guy Lombardo were replaced with a pony named Macaroni, Pablo Casals, French dresses and a New York interior decorator named Sister Parish. There were other obvious differences: the Army discipline of the Eisenhower White House, contrasted with the openness of its new occupants. For example, the reporters in the press room on the first Sunday morning after the inauguration were surprised to run into the President and the First Lady on a tour of their new home. The Eisenhowers had rarely appeared anywhere without forerunners, and I remember once being escorted past the Oval Office on tiptoe; Ike was there, and people outside were speaking only in whispers. Just after the Kennedys moved in, however, I was talking to his secretary, Evelyn Lincoln, and when JFK saw us through the open door of the same Oval Office, he waved me in and a photographer who was doing a story on me took a dozen pictures.

Every Kennedy had an unabashed delight at being at the summit; they loved the White House and savored every minute. At one luncheon the President gave for the Queen of the Netherlands I was seated next to Bobby, the Attorney General. He took out his pen, handed me the menu card delicately scripted with the date and occasion and said, "Sign it." (Bobby always spoke in commands.) After I signed his and he mine, we passed them around the table for the other guests to sign. I've done the same thing at every White House dinner since, which has provided a collection of unique souvenirs.

There were gay parties elsewhere too—at Bobby and Ethel's Hickory Hill, and at Eunice and Sargent Shriver's place, Timberlawn. The first time I ever met Teddy Kennedy was at Hickory Hill, at a dinner to celebrate Bobby and Ethel's wedding anniversary. He burst inside, shouted loudly, and then stood in the hallway, arms outstretched like a huge tree, and all of Bobby's children came tumbling down the stairs and climbed all over him, hanging on to their uncle like so many monkeys on a branch. I thought of what his mother had told me: that when she was pregnant with Teddy someone said to her, "Oh, you poor thing—a ninth child." She vowed then and there that no one would ever feel sorry for her or for that child again. You can have any number of emotions about Senator Kennedy—distrust, anger, love or compassion—but not pity.

After JFK became President the pace of the Hickory Hill gatherings increased. There were children's parties on Sunday afternoons, seated dinner parties in the garden by night, and smaller dinner parties where congressmen were wooed on issues important to the Administration. The zest for life was everywhere, and competition was king. The Kennedys liked to be with people who excelled: the best football player, the best reporter, the best novelist, the best singer, and such superstars as John Glenn. But the competition was greatest among themselves—for example, who gave the best parties? Once, at Eunice's house, there were some Hollywood people, Carol Channing among them, and Ethel, surveying the crowd, asked me, "Does Eunice really *know* all these people?" I said that I thought she must or she wouldn't have invited them, but Ethel didn't seem to hear: she just kept ogling the stars.

The entertainment competition occasionally took absurd twists. Once Ethel phoned me to say that her father-in-law had offered a thousand-dollar prize to the sister-in-law who gave the most scintillating dinner for ten and provided him with the best dinner partner. I was her candidate and she wanted to book me "before Eunice gets you."

Ethel's secret of entertaining was to make you feel as if you were the favorite guest she had been waiting for. She would ask single women to "mix it up" because she didn't want anyone to get stuck.

Early in the Administration, the ranking guest at one of Ethel's parties was LBJ. Since Lady Bird was out of town, he had come alone, and though he was obviously pleased to be there he was clearly uncomfortable. He and Bobby and I were talking about the convention the year before, and Bobby remarked that when people talk about working sixteen-hour days, they are usually exaggerating. When I replied that at the conventions we'd worked almost twenty-four-hour days, Bobby, always ready with a thrust, retorted, "All I remember seeing on television at the convention was you sitting on a bed with the Vice President here." It was true. Fire laws had prohibited our using the halls, the only place we could put the camera was in the bedroom, and that's where I frequently interviewed LBJ.

Bobby Kennedy, who could be brutally ruthless, could also be equally compassionate. In any spare time he had, he'd dig up a charity or something to be done for somebody. His particular concerns were the orphans in Washington, D.C., and their facilities at Junior Village, as well as the less advantaged children in the Washington high schools. He was constantly inviting hundreds of them to the Justice Department, giving them parties, or taking them to Hickory Hill to run around in the fresh air. Since there were no votes among these orphans, no political motives could be ascribed to these substantial efforts.

After he decided to run for the senate in 1964, Bobby went to the playing field of an inner-city high school where students from all over town had gathered to say goodbye. The outpouring of affection for him was overwhelming. There wasn't a vote in the place, but had he been running there, no one could have competed against him.

I had started doing a little entertaining of my own, using the F Street Club, which had become just like home, and one night I gave a formal dinner party for fifty to introduce the new CBS bureau chief to Washington. Since I was not married, I asked Vice President Johnson and the Secretaries of Labor and Welfare to be hosts at three tables; at the fourth, where I sat, I put the French ambassador, Hervé Alphand, on my right and Defense Secretary Robert McNamara on my left. When the French ambassador and his wife, Nicole, arrived —she looking splendid in a Dior gown—they checked the seating chart, had a hurried, whispered conversation and then entered, looking puzzled. At the time I had no idea what was wrong, but it turned out that I had accidentally made a mistake in protocol in the seating arrangement. Since I had confirmed this with the State Department, I was perplexed, but in transferring names to a diagram, my secretary and I had gotten right and left mixed up, and put Madame Alphand on the Vice President's left instead of his right. I phoned her the next morning to apologize for inadvertently breaking the rules and hurting her feelings. Nicole, always gracious, said she'd had such a good time that she hadn't even thought about it.

For those whose lives don't involve entertaining public officials or foreign dignitaries, protocol may seem ridiculous. But it is essential, especially at large multination functions. Protocol is like preventive medicine: it precludes difficulties. It makes life easy because if everything is handled according to prearranged, agreed-upon rules, no one will feel slighted. As Monsieur Alphand once explained to me, protocol demands that he be seated in his rightful place; if not, it is a slight to France, not to the French ambassador or his wife. Some diplomats feel very strongly about this. A few weeks before, I actually had seen an ambassador check the seating arrangement at a dinner, find it not to his liking, throw his place card across the table and demand a change.

Obviously this rigidity does not extend to informal gatherings at home, but though entertaining in Washington, like life styles everywhere else, has become more relaxed, there remain many people in the capital who feel slighted if they are seated too far from the ranking guest or from the head of the table. Such people, however, are generally bores.

By bringing the best and the brightest in the country to the White House, the Kennedys established different criteria in Washington guest lists. Jackie had her jet-set, socialite friends down, but there was also a marked emphasis on ability, as manifested by the celebrations for the Nobel and Medal of Honor winners. Bobby and Ethel were probably as responsible as the President and Jackie for promoting a nationwide social change already in progress; country clubs, ancestors and money were no longer the principal qualifications for social status. As JFK said, "Happiness is the fullest use of one's powers along the lines of excellence." This was the Holy Grail of Camelot, and it was respected far more than one's bank account or pedigree.

CHAPTER 9 ⁓◯

In the pervasive euphoria of the Kennedy takeover there was a lot of talk about a new openness in government, and of how the structured ways of the General-President, holdovers from Army life, would be thrown out. The rigidity of Ike's staff operation was to be exchanged for "free-flowing ideas from the best brains in the country," and a lot of other fine-sounding phrases. In the new *modus operandi* the routine of the National Security Council meetings and other such structured meetings were dispensed with, and the new look was heralded as fresh, open and honest.

But when the old apparatus was thrown out, it wasn't replaced with anything, which produced a vacuum of consultation that was directly responsible for the ill-conceived and ill-fated Bay of Pigs invasion in April.

In assessing this fiasco later, Kennedy told Charles Bartlett that he had asked his National Security Affairs adviser, McGeorge Bundy, "Mac, does this thing check out?," and that Bundy had replied, "Boss, it checks out one hundred percent." Essentially, that was it, and the operation was given a green light. Had there been a little more consultation and staff work, let alone a clear idea of what was involved, the mistake might have been avoided.

Afterward Bundy was so frank in admitting his mistake that it didn't damage his standing with Kennedy. The two men understood each other and this travail only solidified their working relationship. The invasion did hurt Dean Rusk's position, however; JFK felt that he should have been more forthcoming about the potential hazards. In any case, Rusk's style did not appeal to the President. The Secretary of State preferred to give a private presentation of his views, and was not good at sitting around a table working out all the facets of a situation. Rusk had the wrong chemistry for Kennedy—another example of the simple but profound truth that our lives and destinies are controlled by and at the mercy of the personal relationships of men in high office.

After the invasion there was a post-mortem at the White House which LBJ told me about. He said that he had asked each person around the table whether the man had advised against the invasion beforehand. In relating the story, LBJ, who was a marvelous mimic, impersonated everyone, and one after the other admitted that they had not foreseen the results.

JFK was visibly irritated at what he considered to be his Vice President's awkward attempts to take over, and afterward he called LBJ into the Oval Office and demanded, "What in hell did you do that for?" According to LBJ, he replied that he wanted everyone there to be on record, thereby preventing a rush of leaks as various staff members tried to place the blame on others. It had already been leaked to the press that Chester Bowles, Undersecretary of State, had had the foresight to oppose the invasion from its very conception, and though this was true, LBJ thought that the comparison made Kennedy look foolish. Johnson was unfailing in that kind of protective loyalty to Kennedy, and in time the President came to appreciate it.

My personal life and professional assignments continued to intermingle. Jim Aubrey, the president of CBS, wanted to impress a New York convention of television advertisers by producing Vice President Johnson as its main banquet speaker in May 1961. It took CBS weeks to get through to LBJ, and when he turned down the invitation, Aubrey called me for help.

Then as now, vice-presidential speeches are rarely televised, so I asked Aubrey if he would put Johnson on the network. When he agreed, I asked LBJ if he'd speak, and he accepted on condition that I introduce him. Aubrey was delighted with the deal, but I told him that I didn't think it would work because of complications in my schedule; how could I be in New York on Friday night to introduce the Vice President and still keep my long-standing date with Congressman Keating at the Kentucky Derby in Louisville? Aubrey gave me a quick lesson in corporate power and decision making by loaning me the CBS plane. It was fascinating to see the alacrity with which business got its way, in contrast to the impediments of governmental red tape, and it was amusing to observe the different values of the two worlds. For example, when Johnson returned Aubrey's phone call, LBJ's secretary said, "The Vice President is calling"—to which

Aubrey's secretary replied, "Which vice president?"

Derby weekend is always the first Saturday in May and always a delight, and this was especially true since my hosts were Senator and Mrs. Thruston Morton. We were swept up in the graciousness of the city and the encompassing hospitality and happy atmosphere, and just as I was beginning to unwind from the pace of the last few days, and even thinking that I might like to stay in Louisville forever, CBS tracked me down to ask if I could hurry back. It had just been announced that LBJ was leaving in twenty-four hours to go around the world, and the network wanted me to go with him.

"Around the World in Eighty Days" was a popular hit when the Johnson trip was announced and the obvious comparison was made: "Around the World in Fourteen Days—Texas Style." The trip was both hilarious and historic, the forerunner in style and impact of many later whirlwind presidential and vice-presidential journeys.

Our arrival in Saigon, our first stop, was more befitting a folk festival than a fact-finding mission. The airport ceremony was memorable, at least in LBJ's eyes, because the celebrated Madam Nhu, President Diem's powerful sister-in-law, was there wearing the traditional *ao di* in a very untraditional manner. Instead of the usual turtleneck, hers was cut revealingly low, and underneath the slit skirt she had replaced the customary white pants with light-blue "bloomers," as LBJ called them. Large crowds lined the streets into town. The Vietnamese are little people, and since both men and women wear knee-length pants and kimono tops, and since we landed at dusk, they looked like a nation of children in pajamas having a last fling before bedtime.

LBJ was pleased at his welcome; he had expected far less. Warming to it, he set about lecturing everyone on American democracy for the rest of our stay. To him this meant going "among the people," to the astonishment of dozens of passers-by who were half his size and had no idea who this giant creature was that so vigorously pumped the hand of everyone in sight. He was trying to impress President Diem with the necessity of circulating among the populace, and he kept saying pointedly that everyone—meaning Diem—had to "get off his ass" and make himself visible so that people would know he was one of them. As he put it time and time again, "These people out here have to stop wearing white Bermuda shorts and sipping gins, and get to the people."

74

For his pains, the *New York Times* criticized LBJ, and papers back home wrote editorials suggesting that he was behaving as if he were campaigning for sheriff in Texas. When this reaction was radioed back to Saigon, it infuriated Johnson and propelled him to even more roadside handshaking, much to the consternation of those who had to protect him. One day we went fifty miles out of Saigon to see some war games. Our route was highly guarded; every twenty feet a soldier was stationed, his back to the motorcade, gun at the ready should any guerrilla sneak through the underbrush out to the highway.

During this expedition LBJ saw a little village, stopped the motorcade and walked through it, shaking hands with everyone, smiling as they smiled back. It was a bizarre sight: the tall American gabbing away vigorously, giving lessons in democracy, and the Vietnamese, totally bewildered, nodding back. Afterward we learned that LBJ had chosen an enemy stronghold to invade, and that his security guards had been near apoplexy.

Next, at a textile plant that had recently been attacked by guerrillas, Johnson climbed through barbed wire to reach some natives. At several street corners he engaged in lively conversation, his hands flailing the air, admonishing one and all to "fight the Communists," and pleading, "We'll stand behind you. If you fight the Communists, we'll stand to your right; if you fight, we'll stand to your left; we'll be with you. You can count on us." It was an exhausting process, and no one worked harder than he. Apparently his goal was to impart stern resolve in every person in South Vietnam. For their part, the Vietnamese were amused and a little embarrassed.

Next came the Philippines, where we darted around Manila trying to follow the Vice President, who by now was so hoarse that he had trouble making himself heard when he addressed the Philippine Congress. With no time to catch our breath, we then flew to Taiwan, where Chiang Kai-shek had arranged a tumultuous welcome. I don't think I've ever seen so many people in one place before. Traveling with us were JFK's sister and brother-in-law, Jean and Steve Smith, and when he saw the size of the crowd at the Taipei airport, Smith said admiringly, "Not even Mayor Daley could top this." And not even LBJ could touch all those people.

In front of the motorcade there were dancing dragons who gyrated to the delight of the crowd, halting the cars from time to time. For their part, the Chinese were fascinated by him because whenever

Chiang Kai-shek went out, which was rare, he drove in a black car which sped through town with the shades down.

For the sake of the American press accompanying LBJ, Chiang held a rare press conference. The first question was asked, Madame Chiang answered it, and with that the news conference ended. This charade aside, we were invited to the Chiang house, which was a great treat: ornate with massive pieces of teak furniture and spectacular pottery filled with brilliant flowers. We were told that reporters never before had been allowed inside, but though I was fascinated by this opulent and imposing house, there was no news story in it.

By the time we left Taiwan we had settled into a pattern of no rest, but if you worked at top speed and were lucky enough to avoid technical difficulties, you could occasionally get a television spot filmed and onto a plane for the States. In Hong Kong we were supposed to "rest" for a night; however, since communications for the press were better here than in any other city so far, we worked most of the time. But LBJ didn't rest either. While all of us were in touch with our home offices, he heard about a great place for silk shirts and personally picked out a present for every person on the entourage.

In Hong Kong the State Department staff was obsessed with fear that when the Vice President reached Thailand, he might cause an incident: the Thais are offended by bodily contact and his habit of shaking every hand in sight would be a disaster. Since they didn't know how to handle this, they tried to get the press to warn him. En route to Bangkok one diplomat tried to teach him the way Thais greet each other, which is by putting their hands together as if in prayer and simultaneously bowing their heads. I saw the Vice President do it only once; he went right on handshaking, to the horror of his State Department keepers. Although the escort officers were beside themselves, the Thais seemed to enjoy it. Afterward, through an interpreter, I asked several of them whether they knew who he was. Of course they didn't.

In India we visited the Taj Mahal in what must have been one of the most extraordinary pilgrimages to that noble structure. We took the hot dusty train to Agra and then walked in excruciating heat to the entrance. The approach to the Taj is designed so that you cannot see the temple as you near it; you must go through the entrance, and then, after passing through a thick Palladian arch, the magnificent structure looms before you. When the Johnson entourage, a bedraggled perspiring crowd of nearly a hundred, reached the arch, LBJ stopped us for an important announcement. He explained that the Taj was a temple of love, built by a husband out of love for his wife; that all the world loves a lover; that it was the wedding anniversary of President Kennedy's sister and Steve Smith; that Steve Smith was a great lover; and that all the world loved Steve Smith. Armed with this introduction, we proceeded to the Taj. It is as breath-taking as advertised, its foreground dotted with languid pools of water spanned by beautiful, delicate crosswalks. Never one to miss a good photographic opportunity, LBJ grabbed Lady Bird, led her to the middle of one footbridge, put his arm around her, and leaning down in true Valentino fashion, gave her a passionate kiss. With the Taj as a backdrop, cameras snapped.

Inside the building, which the Indians consider to be sacred, two religious guides called out a Moslem prayer that echoed and reverberated startlingly up the towers. Not to be outdone, LBJ roared a Texas "Yahoo!" Raised Indian eyebrows. Outside, I tried to explain the LBJ brand of exuberance to my Indian escort, and he smiled wanly. "Not to worry," he said, and added that when Eisenhower visited the Taj, he'd mistaken the four love towers for gun turrets. Meanwhile, to the horror of the State Department escorts, Jean Smith had removed her shoes and was cooling her hot, tired feet in one of the reflecting pools.

Back in Delhi, there were snickers about the prospective meeting between two such diverse personalities as Johnson, the robust activist, and Nehru, the ascetic intellectual who wore a rose. In point of fact, the two hit it off very well together, much to the surprise of the State Department officers, for whom the entire trip had been a hand-wringing experience. Later, as Johnson described their meeting, he compared it to seducing a woman, and with great relish he told about winning one point in the conversation; according to him, it was "just like putting your hand up her leg."

On to Pakistan, a more comfortable atmosphere for LBJ, for President Ayub Khan was a practical politician schooled in the art of the possible who wasted no time on academic niceties. There, of course, we ran into Yashir, the camel cart driver, who was promptly invited to visit America. It was classic LBJ. Once again he was out talking with people and found an immediate friend in the affable Yashir, whose darting dark eyes and quick smile were infectious. In the usual Johnson manner, he asked Yashir to come to the United States, and as everyone remembers, he came. At the time, however, sophisticates hooted at the invitation, and LBJ was the target for more criticism.

After Pakistan we flew to Athens for one day, drinking champagne at midnight on the Acropolis, and then to Bermuda, where there was a farewell party at which everyone lost their inhibitions. Observing the gaiety from the sidelines, the Vice President was seated between Jean Smith and me. In the tradition of the Kennedys, Jean asks blunt questions, and demanded that the Vice President tell her which one of us he thought the most glamorous or sexy, to which he replied that he never did like "to fool around with any of you Catholic girls."

We had been around the world in two weeks on a trip remarkable for its juxtapositions: an incorrigible LBJ, who was at once a formidable and uncaged Texan let loose on an unsuspecting Southeast Asia. Originally slated as a fact-finding mission, it ended much more significantly by setting policy. What we didn't know then was that our journey was the beginning of a sad and crucial decade of American life; it was the first of dozens of such missions that gave the wrong answers, leading to wrong policies which eventually immersed the United States in the first war we ever lost.

The trip had originally been proposed because President Kennedy was concerned about the political and military stability of the non-Communist countries in the Far East. In 1954 President Eisenhower had begun our commitment to South Vietnam, writing President Diem that we would support him in developing a strong state capable of resisting military aggression. In exchange for reforms, Ike pledged that we would help Diem "discourage any who might wish to impose a foreign ideology on your free people." In hindsight, the people were not free by our standards, and "foreign ideology" has become a defunct concept of the role of one side in a civil war. By 1961, American military aid was estimated to cover about 80 percent of the South Vietnamese defense budget, and we had already sent Diem about $1.5 billion. He had nearly been toppled by a coup in 1960, and in order to secure his position, he was vigorously repressing all opposition. Nevertheless, his regime was in some jeopardy, and Kennedy wanted to know what was going on out there.

JFK made it a practice of having his own man, either a personal friend or someone with acknowledged expertise, give him independent reports, rather than relying on the bureaucrats on the scene. The advantage of this is a fresh viewpoint unencumbered by loyalties to past policies which must, for reasons of face, be defended. The disadvantage is in trusting an instant expert who has acquired a little knowledge. Laos had tilted toward Communism, U.S. pledges were suspect, and Kennedy wanted to send someone of sufficient stature to ensure an accurate perception of our commitment to the people who lived in that part of the world. Therefore he chose LBJ, who was not particularly anxious to go and said so. "Don't worry," JFK joked. "If anything happens to you, Lyndon, we'll give you the biggest funeral they've ever seen in Austin, Texas."

While everyone on the trip knew there was serious business at hand, we had no idea just how serious it would later become. Almost certainly the trip would result in increased aid to Southeast Asia, but there was no way of foreseeing that it would be the first of a series of missions by U.S. officials for the next dozen years which would always conclude with the same theme: Send them a little more aid and perhaps a few more men and we'll be able to end it.

LBJ embarked on the mission inwardly unsure of himself; his uncanny feel for domestic issues did not carry over to foreign affairs. Though he was skeptical and asked hundreds of questions in a quest for more knowledge, he simply did not have the background, did not understand the area, and was gullible.

En route to Asia, Carroll Kilpatrick of the Washington *Post* and I had a long discussion with LBJ about Vietnam. In the spring of 1961 we were just emerging from the Cold War, but Communism was still perceived to be a monolithic threat. Remembering our experience in Korea, I asked Johnson if he thought that increased U.S. aid and advisers might not trigger involvement from the Chinese Communists as well as from North Vietnam. LBJ replied that he didn't see any difference between North Vietnamese and Chinese Communists; they were all alike, and if you were fighting one group, you were fighting them all. In retrospect, of course, this is an appallingly simplistic approach.

In Saigon, where I had a chance to talk with Vietnamese bureaucrats and reporters, I had dinner with a minor official. He said, "You Americans should either make it clear that you support Diem or that you don't. Being ambivalent about him only sows suspicion." Actually, we gave clear evidence over the years that we would support Diem or any successor to Diem, provided that he fought the war the way *we* wanted—namely, efficiently and obediently. But in a country where the military runs the government and the coup is a way of life, letting it be known that you will accept another leader may be enough to trigger assassination. This is what that Saigon official was trying to tell me.

After we made it clear that we'd support anybody who fought against "Communism," various Saigon factions began competing for U.S. aid instead of for the support of their people. Diem may not have been the greatest leader in South Vietnam, but he was an authentic nationalist. Unlike many of his successors, he would not always obey our wishes, and there is some evidence that at the time of his death he and his brother were trying to strike a deal with the North, thus preceding Henry Kissinger by ten years. The Diem brothers were not as foolish as painted by the U.S. government and press, and they were not prepared to let us tell them how to run their country. In the final stages of the war we got puppets like Thieu, who did let us run the country and the war our way—a fatal error for us both.

To his credit, LBJ did not call for U.S. troop intervention, but he returned from Vietnam unrealistically optimistic. He never understood what "finishing the job" involved. When our military-aid representatives requested more aid, he advocated an even greater increase than they did. He had foolishly called Diem the "Churchill of the East," and he reasoned that with this Churchill and further aid we could certainly "wind this thing up." One of LBJ's problems was his sparse vocabulary; he was imprecise and prone to overstatement, and his report to Kennedy on the Vietnam situation reflected it. One of the official U.S. advisers on the trip was Frank Valeo, who later became Secretary of the Senate, and as we flew back home he kept trying to tone down the tenor of the report. Lady Bird sat knitting while she listened, saying nothing as the debate heated up. But as Valeo continued to protest for mile after mile high above the Atlantic, she finally said, "Mr. Valeo, you keep protesting, all the time protesting." Later Valeo said that she reminded him of Madame Defarge, recording his name for future retribution.

If LBJ had no conception of what was involved, the next fact-finding mission had even less. By the fall of 1961, a few months after

Johnson returned, it was plain that Diem was losing the war, and Kennedy wanted to know whether the massive aid program recommended by Johnson made sense. This time he sent General Maxwell Taylor, whom all the Kennedys respected highly, and Walt Rostow, then on the White House staff for National Security Affairs. Though Taylor was known as "the civilian general" because of his knowledge of languages and literature, his findings were those of a military man. It was this report which initiated the disastrous policy of a U.S. military solution/victory in Vietnam, for Taylor and Rostow made LBJ's recommendation for more aid appear a timid, cautious half-measure. They encouraged U.S. military involvement, suggesting that U.S. troops become directly involved in airlifts and air reconnaissance. They recommended a U.S. armed task force of up to ten thousand men who would not only train the Vietnamese but also conduct combat operations in self-defense—in effect, providing a reserve force for emergencies. If LBJ had failed to understand the futility of American-imposed solutions, Taylor and Rostow understood even less.

Our Vietnam policy was always permeated by a strong flavor of *machismo*. Defeated at the Bay of Pigs, disturbed by the Laotian tilt to the left, and impotent in the shadow of the Berlin Wall, the Kennedy Administration simply did not feel it could afford politically another show of weakness. *Machismo* is a strong Kennedy trait instilled from birth, and it permeated not only the immediate members of the Kennedy family but key members of the Cabinet as well. (For instance, when McNamara spoke at Harvard and was booed by some of the students, he shouted above the uproar, "I'm just as tough as you are.") Always it was necessary to be tough and to have the trophies proving it.

During his own Administration, Johnson was the most blatant of all. As Commander in Chief, wearing a khaki uniform which he'd designed himself, he made an impassioned plea to our troops to "bring back the coonskin and hang it on the wall." Later, it was the same with Nixon. His perception of himself forced him to create the image of the tough guy, all alone, making the hard decisions. If there had been a few more tears at the death counts and less joy in the excitement of the game of war, Vietnam might have been a different chapter in our history.

When LBJ went to Vietnam in 1961, there were about six hundred and fifty Americans there. By the end we had lost over fifty thousand men, and in the interval there were dozens of trips by those considered to be our wisest men in government.

Being from Texas, LBJ felt, like Horatio Alger, that anything was possible if you worked hard enough, and in this he reflected the feelings of his country. But he was wrong, the country was wrong, and so were McNamara, Taylor, Rostow and all the rest.

CHAPTER 10

Doris Fleeson, the plain-talking columnist from Kansas, used to "tell it like it is" long before that phrase was popular. Contrary to the stereotype of female backbiting, Doris gave young women a boost whenever she could. After I became a correspondent for CBS, she gave a party for me—and more important, some good advice. She believed that a woman in our business had to work twice as hard and do twice as well as a man to survive. She also told me, "Go everywhere, learn everything, meet everybody, and it will make you a good journalist." I had a great time trying. Along the way I went out with scores of different men and was often the extra woman at dinner parties.

When Perle Mesta entertained Prince Juan Carlos, who later became the Spanish king, I was invited to the party. When the King of Jordan appeared on *Face the Nation*, his uncle later was dispatched to ask me to be with the king at his party that night. I refused, since my nephew was visiting and I had no baby-sitter. When I told Mrs. Longworth, she retorted that I was a fool and should have asked her to baby-sit; after all, how many more chances would I have to go out with a king, even a small one?

There were so many dates over the years that I can't remember them all, but I had a very good time. In his analysis of a proper husband for me, Jack Kennedy had finally decided that I should marry either a reporter or a politician because "You'll be bored by anyone else." Since I agreed, I was uninterested in available young men unless they were politicians or reporters.

As the years went on, I decided I'd better look for a husband in earnest, and promised myself that henceforth I would not date any-one unless he was "marriageable"—that is, a bachelor or widower; the Catholic Church has since changed a great deal, but at that time marrying a divorced man carried far more opprobrium than now and I would not have done it. My good friends Patty and Ed Cavin accused me of subconsciously not wanting to get married, and that this was why I only went out with "the impossibles"—meaning divorced or older men. They vowed they'd come up with someone, and they did: C. Wyatt Dickerson, a widower with three young daughters. We had dinner, and it was a fiasco; he talked only about Hollywood stars and California—two of my least favorite topics—and he was neither a politician nor reporter, but a *businessman.*

Still, I went out with Dick occasionally in the next few months to convince the Cavins and myself that I really was interested in seeing eligible men. Then I went to Europe on a press-club charter, along with my long-time friend and colleague Paul Niven. Dick, who knew London well, arranged to have us met by a chauffeur in a Rolls-Royce and taken to the Savoy, and Paul and I were duly impressed. Soon Dick himself came to Europe, and we roamed around London and Ireland before I flew down to meet Paul on the Riviera; he was squiring Mary McGrory there, and Dick joined us for a few days.

About a month later back in Washington, Paul, Bill Jordan, then of the *New York Times* and later our spokesman on Vietnam at the U.S. embassy in Paris, and I were celebrating Veterans Day over a raucous lunch in a Georgetown restaurant. By chance Dick and his eldest daughter, Liz, then age twelve, came in. Paul insisted that they join us and then regaled everyone with outrageous stories of our European escapades, most of which he embellished with creative ingenuity, all of which suggested improper behavior on my part. Every attempt to stop him only egged him on. Little Liz in her blue school uniform stared wide-eyed at the roguish Mr. Niven, and merci-fully, she and her father left rather quickly. An hour or so later, having happily celebrated peace and victory in all wars, Paul and I made our way back to my house for coffee. There and then he asked me to marry him. When I suggested that he first lose fifty pounds, without skipping a beat he asked, "What will you do for five?"—a line he loved to repeat later on.

As Paul left, Dick arrived, having sent Liz home to the country, and he too asked me to marry him. I said I'd have to think it over.

The next day he returned with his youngest daughter, Jane, then eight years old, an adorable little girl wearing a camel's-hair coat, white knee socks and black-patent Mary Janes. She said little as we drove her to a birthday party before we went on to the International Race at Laurel. Dick bet heavily on the horse TV Lark for the obvious reason and won—at which point we decided to get married.

Meanwhile Jane Dickerson, now back at Belgrove, Dick's house in Leesburg, Virginia, about forty-five minutes away, exercised her creative imagination and flair for drama. She declared, "Daddy is going to marry Nancy Hanschman!" at a moment when I hadn't even agreed. Naturally, her revelation riveted her two sisters and Louise, the wonderful housekeeper who ran Belgrove. The three of them hung on Janie's every word, and she was delighted to find herself the focus of interest. She sustained the story with proper embellishments long into the next day, and whenever the intense questioning died down, she would revive it by such additional bulletins as, "Not only is Daddy going to marry Nancy Hanschman, but you're going to have to be very nice to her or else she'll get sick and die, and then she'll go to heaven and meet Mom, and wow!" Hence, when Dick arrived at Belgrove the next afternoon, after we had agreed to tell no one about our decision for the time being, he was flabbergasted to be met by two leaping Great Danes, and by Louise and the three little girls all dying to know when the wedding would be.

After we announced our engagement a friend said to me, "I'll bet you looked over Dick's daughters long and hard before you took them on!" Actually, I'd seen Liz for fifteen minutes, Janie for ten and had yet to meet Ann. Years later Patty Cavin reminded me that I'd once said that we got engaged "in spite of the three girls," and that later I decided to get married "because of them."

On my first official visit to Belgrove, the girls and Dick and I took a long walk through the countryside. All the way Janie clutched my hand. She was a lovable little creature, with enormous blue eyes. It was a very windy day and I told her to hang on to me or the wind would blow her away. Ann Dickerson, who was ten, is much like me in mood and looks; to this day people who don't know our history say that we look and act alike, which I love to hear. Elizabeth had at an early age been burdened with the responsibility for her sisters over a long period when her mother was sick. She had tried to live up to the exhortations of various relatives and it seemed to be a relief to her when I promised that I would take over the worry.

The wedding date was set for late January or early February 1962, during the period CBS News had assigned me to cover John Glenn's wife during the first space flight. The launch was postponed eight times, and each time the wedding date had to be changed. Because I had been on the story for many weeks I had gotten to know Annie Glenn well, and there was no time to coach another reporter on the details of the story. One night Dick and I were at a pre-Christmas dinner at Eunice and Sarge Shriver's house, which we were planning to leave early because I had a pre-dawn assignment to be outside John Glenn's house in Arlington at the time of blast off. At that point two surprise guests arrived: President Kennedy and Vice President Johnson. Shortly thereafter the President got a phone call from space headquarters saying that the Glenn flight had been postponed once again, so I stayed on at the party, which was a smash, and made even more titillating by Kennedy's intense conversation with the beautiful wife of Italian car manufacturer Giovanni Agnelli. LBJ introduced Dick to the President that night and then invited everyone to our wedding. Finally, after the last postponement, CBS said I could go ahead and set a definite date even if the space shot had not taken place by then; they would get a replacement if necessary. But it wasn't; John Glenn went up and down on February 20, I covered the shot, and the wedding took place four days later.

It was a lovely wedding, only family—mostly children, the three girls and my niece and nephews—with a small reception later at the F Street Club, where little Janie stole the show by dancing the twist with the CBS bureau chief. Dick and I have lived happily ever since. Right from the beginning it was fun; the girls were delighted to have me around and would have welcomed me if I'd had two heads and a green nose, for their mother had been sick a long time. For me, the big difference was the switch from breakfast alone in Georgetown at 9 A.M. to breakfast in the country with four persons at 7 A.M.

CBS was generous in giving me time off for the wedding trip, but was touchy about my new name. One of the first memos I wrote on my return was to say that henceforth on the air I should be referred to as Nancy Dickerson—certainly a more euphonious name than Hanschman. I was astonished when the network balked and asked me to retain my maiden name. Its usual male chauvinism was surpassed by its financial concern; my superiors protested that they would have to change billings in newspapers and re-educate the public. We reached a compromise; it was agreed that I would be called Nancy Hanschman Dickerson for six months. Every time I signed off and mouthed that long name, I sounded like a latter-day Mary Margaret McBride, and it took Walter Cronkite so long to spit it all out that he said he was going to charge Dick time rates.

While CBS had let me cover politics and report from both Europe and Asia, my reports were often side-tracked to radio or minor television news shows, and in some cases my scoops, reported by me on radio, were later worked into an anchorman's script on television and announced as, "CBS News had learned that . . ." This infuriated me when I beat out the entire Washington press corps on the announcement of Kennedy's overhaul of the Joint Chiefs of Staff, a major story in the summer of 1962. I heard it at our dinner party the night before, but since I don't think it's fair to use information gained during the social hour, especially when drinks are served, I went the next morning to the Pentagon to confirm the tip. My source was in a meeting with JFK, however, and I couldn't reach him, so I went back to Capitol Hill and managed to see LBJ. He never gave me inside information and would not add to what I already knew, but he did say, "You know I wouldn't let you go on the air if you had your facts wrong."

We made the three o'clock afternoon news with the scoop, while the White House press corps was en route to Hyannisport with the President and his entourage. As was the custom, press secretary Pierre Salinger had planned to give the reporters the news of the Pentagon shake-up on Saturday, to be held for overnight release, for several reasons. First, it would ensure a major story emanating from Hyannisport on Sunday morning, giving the impression that Kennedy was working as well as relaxing—a routine ploy on most Presidents' vacations. The delay also gave the Administration publicists time to brief reporters, and by so doing, place the best possible light on the story. Lastly, the arrangement gave reporters enough lead time to file their dispatches and then go swimming while the lid was on, making it a nice vacation for all concerned.

The press releases from the White House and Pentagon had all been mimeographed and were ready for distribution, but when the presidential party landed on the Cape, its weekend plans were scratched; the releases were handed out with "Hold for Release" crossed out, and something else had to be cooked up for the Sunday morning papers. For all my pains, I wasn't allowed to present the story on the evening news. Instead, the anchorman handled it, once again saying, "CBS News has learned that . . ."

Assessing the situation, I realized that being a woman was sometimes helpful, but more often a hindrance. There were no effective antidiscrimination laws then, no groups to fight women's battles; television was having growing pains, and sexism was not of paramount concern in broadcasting. There were literally dozens of problems arising from being female in that world, and from the stereotype expected of women. To take a trivial example, if a male correspondent complained, he was merely analyzing his situation; if I were to do so, I was automatically "a bitch."

A typical instance had occurred during the Glenn space shot, when the live coverage was a pressurized jungle. Television reporters were not allowed inside the Glenn house, for *Life* had an exclusive contract with the astronauts and their families. But since I'd spent so much time in the Glenn neighborhood, I had gotten to know the neighbors; I had also talked to Annie Glenn about children and my forthcoming marriage, and had spent more time there than most other reporters. Hence, when Annie agreed to come out and speak to the television cameras after the shot, it was natural for her to approach me first. However, we three network correspondents on the scene had agreed among ourselves that we would question her in turn, and had drawn straws to choose who would ask the first question. I lost; Martin Agronsky of NBC was to be first. But when Annie came out, NBC was in the middle of a commercial; still, to honor our agreement, I kept nudging Agronsky instead of talking with Mrs. Glenn, but Martin had no intention of going ahead, since NBC wasn't even on the air. Simultaneously Don Hewitt, my producer-director, could hear on the network, as could the whole world, that Mrs. Glenn was talking to me but that I wasn't answering, so he started shouting into my earphones, "For Christ's sake, talk to her, open your mouth." In an attempt to explain the agreement we'd made, I said right on the air that we would take turns, and that I would begin as soon as my colleagues had preceded me. At the same time I was nudging Agronsky with my foot to try to get him going while Hewitt screamed in my earphones, "I don't give a shit who promised what to whom, she's talking to *you!* Take off your earphones and give them to her so that she can talk directly to Walter" —meaning Cronkite in the anchor booth. I tried to protest on the air, but Hewitt shouted again, "Take the goddamn phones off and give them to Annie Glenn."

By this maneuver Hewitt hooked up Annie Glenn and her children in Alexandria, Virginia, with television in New Concord, Ohio, where John Glenn's parents were. By the time Annie started talking to Walter, and the children were conversing with their grandparents, the other two network correspondents were back on the air, and they were furious. Their on-the-spot interviews made no sense because they were interrupted by Annie answering Walter's questions. In addition, NBC and ABC couldn't plug in their lines to pick up the children's and grandparents' exchange, so their audiences were, in effect, hearing only one side of a phone conversation. Since these viewers knew perfectly well who the "Walter" was that Annie was talking to, many of them undoubtedly switched channels.

When it was all over, I remember two comments: Agronsky said, "She kept kicking me all the time we were on the air," and Hewitt complained, "She's really not very responsive to directions."

After many frustrating experiences at CBS, I decided that I wanted to switch to NBC. But I didn't quite know how to let them know that I was available, especially since there was then a gentlemen's understanding among network news departments not to raid each other. Finally I went to see General Sarnoff, who had always been friendly to me. He said he would look into the matter, and a few days later he telephoned to say, "There is interest." In the meantime I had met Bill McAndrew, the NBC News vice president, who made it a joy and an honor to be in the news business. I did most of the bargaining myself until the very end; then Dick, who is the world's best negotiator on any subject, went with me. CBS was offering more money, but NBC presented more opportunity, I thought.

I told all this to LBJ, who, along with Walter Jenkins, entered the negotiations. Johnson was partial to CBS; their station in Austin was a CBS affiliate, and he'd always felt that Frank Stanton, the CBS president, was the outstanding man in broadcasting. In the crossfire LBJ and Jenkins became my negotiators with CBS, while Dick was chief negotiator with NBC. Johnson invited Dick and me to his house one night to talk over the two offers, and gave his guideline for such decisions: I should go with the company that had the best management at the top, and that was CBS. But he was concerned with financial statements and managerial practices, whereas I was more interested in the news operation. Also, by now I was a big fan of McAndrew, who felt that being a reporter was the highest calling, and that a network team had to operate like the Notre Dame football squad. While networks and the news business are highly competitive and often bring out the worst in people, McAndrew's leadership reduced this to a minimum. Moreover, his top assistant, Julian Goodman, who is now president of NBC, was another man I respected and liked.

For all these reasons, we eventually picked NBC. I asked Dick to attend the final bargaining session with me because I had a little problem that I hadn't yet mentioned: I was pregnant, and was too embarrassed to bring it up during the negotiations. Frankly, I thought that perhaps no one would want a pregnant news correspondent. But soon I could put it off no longer, so I told McAndrew. When he responded by asking, "When's labor day?" I was so flustered that I answered, "It's always the first Monday in September, isn't it?"

Luckily, McAndrew was a good family man who felt benignly about big families, so he hired me despite impending motherhood. Intellectually I knew I should switch networks, but I hated to leave CBS because my heart was there. The Washington news staff gave me a nice farewell party, and there was a cable from Sevareid, who was then stationed in London:

THE WHOLE THING IS NOTHING BUT A LOUSY NBC PLOT TO DE-
PRIVE ME OF MY CHIEF SOURCE OF NEWS GOSSIP WISDOM GOOD
COMPANIONSHIP AND THE COFFEE BREAK WHEN I GET TO WASH-
INGTON STOP I HAVE ASKED REASSIGNMENT . . . GOOD LUCK ANY-
WAY. DAMMIT. ERIC SEVAREID.

My first NBC assignment, in the spring of 1963, was a telecast from the White House lawn of a reception the Kennedys gave to honor all the winners of the Medal of Honor. I really didn't look pregnant, which irked me because when you're having your first baby you want everyone to know about it, and since the camera crews shot me from the chest up the audience never knew.

Jackie was equally pregnant at the same time, but our mutual obstetrician said that she was too fragile to attend the reception, so she sat up on the Truman balcony overlooking the White House lawn and watched. I remember feeling a little sorry for myself, but in retrospect I was far luckier, because unlike their baby, ours was born healthy.

On July 10 I left the office, went to a lovely dinner party for the Vice President and Lady Bird, got up early the next morning and produced Michael Wyatt Dickerson, who arrived with blond curls. By the time I came out of the anesthesia, Dr. Walsh was already en route to Hyannisport to care for his most famous patient. Even in birth the White House has precedence!

Since I had been so busy being a reporter, I had never really focused on the actual process of giving birth, so I was unprepared for the ordeal and did not enjoy it. The NBC press department issued a release headlined, "NBC News has its First Baby" and Paul Niven sent flowers with a card saying, "Let us hope that Michael takes after the network in which he was conceived rather than that into which he was born!" When the newspapers arrived to take his picture, Michael refused to wake up. I envied him; I was exhausted and realized that I had never been so tired in my life.

Michael is blessed to have Charlie Bartlett and his wife, Martha, for godparents, but between Charlie and me we had a tough time scheduling the baptism, which kept being pre-empted by various news events, one of them the civil rights march on Washington.

That was a glorious August day in the capital, hot but not muggy, and since there was fear beforehand that the occasion would trigger violence, NBC stationed me on top of a high platform, safe from the madding crowd. But there was no violence, only a vital spirit that took over the city. While the participants were trying to get themselves together, the march just took off, self-propelled and self-ignited. It started like spontaneous combustion, and the marchers thronged below our camera platform, which was none too stable in the joyous surge of humanity.

Infected by their marvelous spirit, I joined the demonstrators for a few blocks. A reporter is supposed to be detached, and I was while we were on the air, but once the action moved away from us I was with them. I still can hear the amplified voice of Martin Luther King, Jr., over the loudspeaker. Newspaper journalists are trained in words, but broadcast reporters deal in sound, and perhaps for that reason I have something akin to instant recall of voices, so I can still hear, as if it were being said this instant, the vibrant words and tones of King's "I had a dream."

Eventually the baby was baptized Michael Wyatt—to the vexation of LBJ, who thought a more proper name would be Lyndon. I explained that Lyndon was not a saint's name and therefore unacceptable, but after LBJ became President, Walter Jenkins returned from a papal visit with the news that the Vatican had newly discovered that Lyndon was indeed a saint's name—proving once again that the Church is always resourceful in matters of state. Still, I've never seen "Lyndon" in any known litany.

CHAPTER 11 ⌒

Everybody remembers where they were on the day President Kennedy was killed. I was in the NBC News room when someone saw the bulletin on the wire and shouted, "Kennedy's been shot!" We all rushed to the ticker room. The information was infuriatingly scarce; there we were manning a major news center, and we could find out nothing. I phoned the White House, and they didn't know anything either. Based on the early reports, it seemed certain that he had been shot, but whether he had been killed was unclear at that moment.

While we were still in the dark I was sent out to Andrews Air Force Base with instructions to try to get on the Kennedy family plane, which we understood was flying to Dallas with Robert Kennedy. The janitor was the only person available to take me to the base, and his car had no radio. The forty-five-minute drive was agony. There was no way of finding out anything. Arriving at Andrews, I still didn't know the outcome, and was afraid to ask. Then I saw Mike O'Neill, now editor of the New York *Daily News*. He didn't need to say anything. I could tell by his face.

It turned out that the family plane was not going to Dallas, so I was told to wait for *Air Force One* to return. The hours dragged by. In the interim Eunice Shriver, the eldest surviving Kennedy daughter, arrived sobbing. She had been especially close to the President, and she had been chosen to go to Hyannisport to break the news to her father.

There was a sense of panic at Andrews, and security was understandably tight. Already a feeling of guilt was spreading through the Secret Service, which felt responsible for Dallas. As the news spread, the airport was closed and no one could get out or in, including the network camera crews. I negotiated the entrance of some of them so that they could begin setting up equipment to televise the return. There were no wire machines at the base, and our information was limited to what we could glean from phone calls to our offices, where someone could read us the latest copy.

It grew cold and dark. NBC sent out Bob Abernethy to join me for the commentary when the plane arrived. There were hours of frenetic activity, confusion, agitation, misinformation, misdirected instructions and assignments. We couldn't get through to anyone who was running either the country or the network. The floodlights weren't working properly, and there was doubt that we could even get a picture on the air. Then suddenly, lights were on everywhere. With no warning, *Air Force One* screamed to a stop and the network switched to us.

In times of crisis a subconscious reflex takes over, and Bob and I automatically started talking. As we broadcast, I distinctly remember feeling confused and irritated. Dozens of times before I'd stood on the tarmac below a plane waiting for a candidate or President to alight. It's always the same: the front door opens, the Secret Service agents run down, there is a pause and then the President appears. This time I found myself thinking that the usual routine was all fouled up. Bobby Kennedy rushed up the steps at the front; then there was commotion at the back of the plane, and I wondered to myself why the operation was so confused. At that moment a hydraulic lift was slowly put in motion, moving upward at the back of the plane. Only then did the terrible reality engulf me. The lift was there to remove the coffin, and the President was coming off first, in a box. Thank God the television shots spoke for themselves; I had nothing to say.

When Jackie came down the steps, she ran toward a government station wagon, but the door was locked and she had to run around to the other side. I forgot we were on the air and put my mike down thinking that I could help. Everyone in the world would have liked to have been able to do something for her at that moment, yet no one could open the door. I saw the stains of the President's blood all over her dress, but didn't mention them on the air. Like everyone else, I was trying to find a way to protect her. I kept thinking of Shakespeare's phrase "Out, out, damned spot." In retrospect it's amazing that she was as composed as she was. Much later Nellie Connally, wife of John Connally, who was in the car with the Kennedys at the time of the assassination, told me that as they raced to the Dallas hospital, Jackie kept repeating all the way, "They've killed my husband and I have his brains in my hand. They've killed my husband and I have his brains in my hand."

With a blaze of sirens the President's body and his widow took off for Bethesda Naval Hospital, where there began the long process of funeral preparation. A messenger was sent to the White House for the President's clothes, and when they arrived, one of his friends there remembers thinking that his shoes weren't polished and how Jack would have hated that.

As his friends stood around the hospital, Defense Secretary Robert McNamara talked about the loss in terms of the bright promise for the future, of the hopes and goals they had set for the second Kennedy term. In his first term JFK's primary goal had been to get re-elected. A month or so before his death, on a glorious sunny Sunday afternoon he had phoned Charlie Bartlett, and together they had taken a long walk around the Washington monuments. At Arlington Cemetery they'd talked about where they wanted to be buried, and JFK said that he wanted his library to be in Boston, adding as an afterthought, "But if I'm here for only one term, nobody will give a damn, and I won't have a library."

Back at the airport the newly sworn President Johnson walked down the steps self-consciously, hat in hand, and with Lady Bird at his side, asked for our help and prayers. Then he was whisked off and we returned to the studio for hours of broadcasts. Later I was sent out to The Elms, the Johnson house, to report on his return. By then the neighborhood was swarming with security police, television floodlights were being installed, and the neighbors were out, quietly talking among themselves, just like everywhere else in the nation. People were anxious to be useful, to help in this time of sorrow, and everyone kept offering us coffee. Of course, other human emotions were also exaggerated by the focus of publicity, and several neighbors came up to say how well they knew Johnson, and to offer every conceivable bit of inside information about him and his family. Some were kind, others not, but all of them were trying to establish their own connection with the history of the hour.

When LBJ's car arrived, he was surrounded by Secret Service men whose guns stuck out of every window, something I'd never seen before. He had the inside light on to read the paper, which seemed silly because it made him a lighted target. He saw me and waved, and later said that when he drove up that night, as President of a few hours, and saw me standing in the street, microphone in hand, the enormity of it all struck him and he suddenly wished Speaker Rayburn were still alive. As he put it, "I could really use him now."

I spent Saturday standing in the rain across from the White House, trying to say something meaningful. JFK's famous rocking chair was carted across the street into storage, and I told a camera crew to get the picture. Friends and mourners started to arrive, and I spent much of the day identifying men and women who had known JFK all their lives, their faces riveted with pain. Members of the Senate and House came, both those who supported him and those who did not, united by the tragedy of death. Sarge Shriver, who made so many of the decisions in those dreary hours, talked to us briefly about the television coverage. He was yet another example of how resilient the Kennedys were—sad, yet stoic, courageously accepting what God had meted out.

By the day after the assassination, the networks had two objectives: first, to report on the family and funeral, and whatever could be gleaned about Oswald; second, to look ahead and try to inform the public about what kind of President Lyndon Johnson would be. Not many journalists of the national press knew him well; even though he had been Majority Leader for years, he wasn't friendly with many reporters, and genuinely liked even fewer. With a few exceptions he didn't know the White House press corps, and there was a dearth of information about him. In fact, up to then I had interviewed him at least as much as, if not more than, any other reporter. As a result, at one point during these grim days, I was speaking about him on NBC live television at the exact moment that my old network, CBS, was televising some old interviews I had done with him months earlier.

On Saturday night, November 23, NBC scheduled a panel discussion of reporters on "Lyndon Johnson: What Kind of President?" I said that LBJ had always thought of himself as being qualified, that whether you agreed with his policies or not, he had had as much government experience for the job as any man alive, and that he would take over with a firm hand. After thirty-five years in Washington, he knew the bureaucracy and how it functioned, and was both prepared and eager to lead.

Later in the program the subject switched to the controversy surrounding Kennedy's choice of Johnson as a running mate. Martin Agronsky said that it was particularly ironic because Johnson's closest adviser, the late Speaker Rayburn, had not wanted LBJ to accept the post. But I pointed out that while Martin Agronsky was right as far as he went—that Rayburn had indeed opposed the maneuver—I believed that he had later reversed himself and had endorsed the move.

As soon as I got off the air, there was a phone call waiting for me: The President was on the line, and there was no doubt that he was well into his role as Commander in Chief. Publicly during those days he was the silent, solemn leader of the nation's mourning. In private, he was very much in charge. He launched into a critique of all the details of our show, and said that its high moment had been my correcting Martin Agronsky "without making a fool of him." As he put it, "Agronsky was wrong; Rayburn changed. He did want me to take the nomination, and you set the record straight without making him eat crow in public. Only way to do it." Then he asked Dick and me to dinner, saying that he would send his car to pick us up.

When we arrived at The Elms, we had to wait a long time to get by the guards. Mindful of their failure in Dallas, every security officer in America was taking extra precautions. When we finally entered the house, the President had not yet arrived from the White House, Lady Bird was resting, and Luci was in the living room barefoot in a green Chinese robe. I asked her how she would like living in the White House, and she said that she thought it would be awful: "How would you like to be sixteen years old and have Secret Service men chaperon you every minute of the day?" Even now, she said, she couldn't talk to any boy late at night because the phone light would go on in her parents' bedroom, and her father, seeing it, would either monitor the call or interrupt to tell her that she ought to be asleep. What she really wanted most was a private phone, and we promised her one for Christmas.

Then Lady Bird came down in a dressing gown and had a drink and some popcorn. When LBJ finally showed up, he was still talking about my handling of that "other fellow" in public, and to make his point, launched into a long story of his early days in the House. He had wanted very much to have a public-works project approved, and he had finally maneuvered it into committee and then onto the House floor, only to be opposed by an older, stronger man. LBJ had finally won out and gotten his project through, but to do so he had to publicly put down the other congressman. Afterward Rayburn had taken him aside and said, "Lyndon, you feel pretty smart because you got what you wanted. But you also got yourself an enemy. A really clever fellow would have won without ridiculing another man on the way, ensuring himself an enemy for life."

It was the end of President Johnson's first full day in office, and he carried on a running monologue throughout the evening. Also, the television set was on, and he kept talking back to Huntley and Brinkley as they delivered the news. Right after the shots LBJ had thought that the assassination might well be a conspiracy to take over the government—that maybe "they were out to get us all"—and he had ordered that House Speaker John McCormack be protected. Even at this point he was concerned about possible collaborators and about a conspiracy. He was going to keep the armed services on alert for the moment because he still wasn't sure that the assassination was the work of one man and that there was no foreign involvement.

LBJ was also determined that there should be calm throughout the country, and whenever either Huntley or Brinkley said something that he thought might be inflammatory, he would talk back to the television set: "Keep talking like that and you'll bring on a revolution just as sure as I'm standing here." He was also worried about security; he wanted it improved, but not to the extent of hamstringing him; he wanted to have his own freedom and not be hemmed in.

The President kept skipping from subject to subject. He told us that the second letter he had written as President was to James Rowley, head of the Secret Service, saying what a fine job Rufus Youngblood had done. After the shots, Rufus had pushed LBJ to the floor of the car and for the eight miles to the hospital had covered "my body with his." He described Lady Bird "hunkered up" down on the floor of the car, and Senator Yarborough "hunkered up down there too."

LBJ was particularly concerned about the children involved. He said his first presidential letter had been to John and Caroline Kennedy, and he was terribly proud of Lynda Bird, then studying at the University of Texas. As soon as she'd heard the news, she had gone to the governor's house in Austin to be with the Connally children. He was also full of admiration for young John Connally, who had volunteered to represent his father at the funeral.

As always, LBJ was obsessed with the telephones. Now he picked up the receiver, pushed a button and said, "Is this the White House? Sorry . . ." Another button: "The White House? Oh, sorry." Then, helplessly, "Bird," while unsuccessfully trying once more, and finally switching to commands, shouting: "Bird! Come over here and get me the White House. That's going to have to be changed! The whole damn world could go up in smoke and I wouldn't even be able to get Dean Rusk! Take me ten minutes to reach the Secretary of State." Eventually he reached McGeorge Bundy, the Special Assistant for National Security Affairs, and reminded him "to get those wires out fast," meaning the cables he wanted sent to every other country recognized by the United States to assure them of the continuity of our government. As he put it, "I don't want any of them thinking that we don't know what we're going to do." Then he said that the most important thing he'd done that day was to phone Bob McNamara to insist that he stay on the job as Secretary of Defense. "I told McNamara that if he left town, I'd get a sheriff and posse to bring him back."

The President's mind was going a hundred miles an hour as he walked back and forth. There were only eight of us at that late supper, among them Judge Homer Thornberry, an old friend, who at one point phoned his daughter in Texas to offer her the same kind of reassurance millions of other citizens were giving each other that night. After a few minutes LBJ took the phone away from Homer and talked to the daughter himself. Then he asked whom she was with: "Is he your boy friend? . . . What's his name? . . . Buddy? Well, put Buddy on, I want to talk with him . . . Buddy? This is Lyndon Johnson, your new President . . . Just fine, thank you . . . Thank you very much . . . need all the help we can get . . . Well, Buddy, take good care of that little girl who's with you . . ." I still like to imagine the surprised look on the face of "Buddy," whose last name I never heard.

Later we all trooped to the Johnson bedroom, where newspapers from all over were spread out on the bed and on tables, with the overflow on the floor. LBJ was fascinated by the headlines and by the way newspapers were handling the story, and insisted on reading out loud and correcting the details of certain accounts. Finally Horace Busby, a long-time friend and aide, arrived, and they discussed the speech LBJ had decided to give to Congress. As they talked about it, LBJ suddenly seemed to wind down as he became preoccupied with the events of the next day.

Before Dick and I left the house, Lady Bird asked me what she should wear to the funeral, and I told her that she had no choice but to wear black. Since she didn't have anything in that color, I sent over some of my coats and dresses, then had Garfinckel's send her a couple of hats, and these were what she wore for most of the official mourning. Lady Bird, who is both rich and frugal, was astonished that anyone would have so many black clothes, and I was equally astonished that she didn't have any.

By the Sunday morning after the assassination, fatigue had set in, especially for those of us who had been broadcasting day and night. Sander Vanocur and I were assigned to the White House lawn to do the live commentary as the cortege left on its trip to Capitol Hill, where the slain President would lie in state. Before the procession started, a soldier led up Black Jack, the riderless horse, with his boots in reverse; positioned right next to us, he was full of beans that cold morning, defiantly rearing up on his hind legs so that the soldier had trouble controlling him. His futile flailings epitomized my feelings precisely and although I was a little scared of him, I couldn't move away because our cameras and mikes were assigned to this specific spot.

Sandy arrived; he was particularly saddened by the loss of Kennedy, whom he had long covered. At this point we were all beginning to crack, especially the technicians, who had been working even longer hours than we had. The human kindness initially following the assassination had been replaced by pettiness and stupidity. Many people displayed what Hemingway had called "grace under pressure," but some were second-raters and showed it.

Suddenly we were cut off the air entirely, and in a furious whisper I complained urgently to the control room. An equally pre-emptory voice at the other end of the walkie-talkie told me to start talking into the microphone as if I were on live, and that the spot would be taped for later use. I thought that the people in the control room had lost their reason, and said as much. "Just talk," was the reply, "and we'll explain later." Afterward, as I was being rushed up the back route to the Capitol, to leapfrog ahead so that I could offer commentary when the cortege arrived, I found out that it was at this moment that Jack Ruby had shot Oswald, and that Tom Pettit had done a brilliant piece of on-the-spot reporting.

Long before the cortege reached the Capitol it was preceded by the sound of horses' hoofs on the pavement. As I stood high up on the Capitol steps on a specially built platform waiting to go on the air, I kept thinking, Maybe it all didn't happen; maybe this is just a nightmare. But the walkie-talkie plugged in my ear brought me back to reality. It exaggerated the sound of the horses' hoofs approaching relentlessly, and for weeks afterward I woke up in the middle of the night hearing that cadence.

In the afternoon there was a State Department reception for foreign delegates attending the funeral, and Edwin Newman and I were told to identify them from the monitor in a studio. Prince Philip of Great Britain and De Gaulle were easy enough, but from there on it was a mystery. We had no official list, and for thirty-five embarrassing minutes we kept repeating, "Well, there are some more of the foreign dignitaries paying their official respects and condolences."

The funeral itself was the next day, Monday. We had to be in position by 8 A.M., and I've never been more cold than I was standing on a ramp across from St. Matthew's Cathedral, identifying the family and friends arriving: old Mrs. Longworth, who was much admired by the dead President; the politico who had been so helpful in the West Virginia primary; the old school friends; Cardinal Cushing, who had married the Kennedys and later had rambled through a long prayer at the inauguration; Caroline and John saluting the coffin just like the soldiers. Watching the Mass, it seemed like a regular Catholic Irish-family funeral. On this state occasion the Kennedys, through television, had allowed the entire world to share their sorrow, just as everyone had shared the family's joys and successes. The funeral was an expiation for the country. Through television, the nation was united in sorrow, and people's helplessness was made bearable by their chance to participate in the farewell.

All of us covering the event for television—technicians, executives and reporters—felt bound together on a mission, which seemed almost holy at times, to inform and help the country find itself again. In a sense, we reporters who worked day and night for those four days were fortunate, for we had work to keep us busy, and the sheer necessity of getting the job done postponed the sorrow. Our grief was mitigated by activity and the thought that our efforts might have meaning and make a contribution at a time when so much was meaningless. It was only after the interment at Arlington Cemetery that I went home and cried.

CHAPTER 12

The Johnson takeover was Johnson at his best. Those who hated him were impressed. Those who loved him were proud. He did it so well, and with such a firm hand and sure foot, that the transition seemed far more simple than it actually was. It was a dangerous time and one misstep could have led to chaos. But he walked with the right instincts, did most of what was right—or at least successful—and his honeymoon with the press and public lasted longer than expected because the country was anxious to be led away from the dreadful abyss of the assassination.

From the very beginning LBJ was inclined to think that the assassination was part of a conspiracy, and he went to his grave uncertain about it. He told columnist Marianne Means that he thought Castro was behind it, and he told me that we would never know the whole truth, especially after the death of Oswald. He kept saying that there were unanswered questions about Lincoln's death, and that he didn't want the same kind of mystery to surround the Kennedy assassination. This was why he appointed the Warren Commission. He felt that a blue-ribbon commission was also essential to promote unity in a country in a state of shock, and national unity was his first concern.

The make-up of the commission was typically Johnsonian. He

knew he needed well-known men of unassailable integrity, and his only choice for chairman was the Chief Justice. He was aware that because of constitutional separation of powers, Warren would not want to take the job, but he also knew that the Chief Justice would not be able to turn down an appeal to his patriotism. This arm-twisting, usually referred to as "the treatment," was typical of Johnson. The rest of the commission was a classic blend and balance of Republicans and Democrats, with representatives of both the House and Senate and a bow to the Kennedy family's wishes—meaning the suggestions of Attorney General Robert Kennedy.

When the report was finally issued, LBJ commended the panel, but he was not completely convinced that they had found out everything. Moreover, he was always influenced by John Connally, who never agreed with the commission's theory that the lethal bullet that had killed JFK was the same one that had seriously wounded him. (It is also a fact that Bobby Kennedy as well was uncertain whether there was a conspiracy connected with his brother's death. Though he always gave a standard reply supporting the Warren Commission when asked, he was not convinced that Oswald was the only one involved.)

LBJ was hit doubly hard by the assassination, not just because it had taken place in Texas, but also because of the anti-Texas and anti-Dallas feeling that was part of the emotional backlash. Still, despite the horrifying circumstances, he had long wanted to be President, and now he was. In his book he states that he never wanted to be, but this is simply not true. He wanted the job because he thought that he had the ability and could do it better than anyone else; because he passionately believed that the world could be a better place and that through the office he could give poor people a better break; and because in some subconscious way which he didn't articulate to himself he thought the Presidency would help him rid himself of all his nagging self-doubts. Like so many powerful, ambitious men, LBJ was an enigma: at once an egotistic braggart and an insecure, thin-skinned creature who loved Texas but was embarrassed by the real and imagined stigma of his origins. He was also sweet, loyal, generous, genuinely kind and considerate—yet obsessed with being big and tough (in Texas he ran against John Tower in a campaign that emphasized his size). But he could also cry.

After three years of inaction as Vice President, LBJ was itching to get power in his hands again, confident that he knew how to use it as well as any man. His first step was to get in touch with all the leaders of the country to rally them in a national effort to keep the country together. "Touching bases," he called it. He was on the phone constantly, calling everyone who had influence on a sector of our society, winning over long-time enemies by asking for their help in the difficult days ahead. He phoned black leaders and presidents of labor unions; he called industry tycoons and financial experts; he sought "counsel," as he called it, from every area.

Johnson also asked large numbers of people for suggestions and drafts of what he should say to the joint session of Congress, and dozens offered versions. Lynda Bird, then aged nineteen, made suggestions, and I was asked to go over a couple of drafts. Each of these ended with the last four lines of "America, the Beautiful," and I told him that I thought it would be awkward for him to stand up before a joint session of Congress and say words which are usually sung. Also, while I agreed with the sentiment, I thought it might be a bit corny. However, LBJ himself had inserted those lines, so they stayed in. And they were so much a part of him and his kind of uninhibited rhetoric that they were profoundly moving when he said them. I doubt that anyone else could have declaimed them without embarrassment.

That speech, the product of myriad drafts, was an unqualified success. LBJ always graded everything he did, whether it was a speech or a guest list, on a scale of A to F. That speech was an A+. Even given the universal good will of a nation and a world that at that moment desperately wanted him to perform brilliantly, he did not disappoint. He not only promised "to continue," he boldly demanded that as a memorial to JFK the civil rights bill be passed. If he had said nothing more than "We will continue," he would have been well received, but part of his genius was his ability to use any event, even an assassination, to get something done—a program started or legislation passed. Thus, he used this occasion to pull out all the stops for a bill which had been floundering. He was acutely aware of the irony of a Southern President pleading for the rights of blacks; it was high drama and he loved it. He also knew that it would be hard to turn him down, and it was.

The *New York Times* said that Johnson's speech convinced people of his strong and able leadership, and columnists and editorials all over the world heralded the remarkable new President. Writing in the *Times,* Arthur Krock said:

> The most "remarkable" aspect of President Johnson's speech to the joint session of Congress Wednesday is that his perfect matching of construction, content and delivery to the solemn occasion was so frequently described as remarkable. For, though he was addressing Congress, the nation and the world for the first time in the capacity of President of the United States, Mr. Johnson has displayed all these qualities—dignity, emotional fitness and eloquent prose—many, many times as majority leader of the Senate and as Vice President.

Krock's point was that no one should have been surprised at Johnson's ability. In all modesty, Johnson agreed; though he had many self-doubts and insecurities, he was on sure ground when it came to running Washington. Using all his years of capital experience and riding the crest of popular support, he called for a War on Poverty and rammed it through Congress in what must surely be a legislative record for speed. Most of his close friends came from Congress, and he played on these relationships to get through a remarkable amount of Great Society legislation. During that period there was no problem too big to be solved, convinced as he was that given determination, perseverance and a capable director for each program, everything could be solved.

In their book, *Lyndon,* Richard Harwood and Haynes Johnson wrote about these days:

> His manner of operating was not surprising to anyone who had followed his long career. Lyndon, in the old and accurate definition, was not a Southern politician nor a national politician, but a Washington politician. . . . He was a negotiator whose gifts of persuasion moved small collections of powerful men to adopt a common course of action . . . his political theory and his principle of government was that political power in America is closely held, that great decisions are not made by popular referendum but in the private interplay of what Wright Mills called "the power elite." The system, he believed, operated on *quid pro quos.* It was a principle that served him well in Congress and it was the central principle he took with him to the White House.

103

LBJ's assistant, Elizabeth Carpenter, put it more simply; she said, "He ran the White House the way he ran the Senate." Which in the long run didn't work. Once again Lyndon Johnson made the crucial mistake of thinking that congressional politics were national politics. Just as he had misjudged the country and its political system during the 1960 campaign and thus lost his quest for the nomination, his application of Capitol Hill politics to the White House was doomed. Still, during the takeover there was general acclaim, and the popularity polls showed that he was earning record high marks.

The LBJ social style was something of a shock to the capital. Starting right at the White House, the Johnson way was different. For example, Jackie had never invited the staff to parties upstairs, and had made a distinct separation between it and her social friends. The Johnsons were the exact opposite: some of their best friends were those who worked for them, and they were always included in the big parties. When Johnson moved into the White House, it was the first time that those presidential aides whose names are still linked primarily to JFK were ever asked upstairs.

It's difficult to comprehend the LBJ style because even by Texas standards he had large impulses. When the Johnsons said, "You-all come," they meant it. Their lack of inhibition was new in Washington, a Southern city in the East. LBJ was a cowboy, and though that mythic figure is in the best American tradition, the Washington establishment, the press and the country were unaccustomed to a cowboy in the White House. The city shook its collective head, not in the envy of the JFK era, but at the grandiosity of the LBJ style. Ann Lincoln, who had been the housekeeper for the Kennedys, pointed out one contrast between the two administrations for me. Once Mayor Richard Daley of Chicago had been in President Kennedy's office on business, and at noon, when he and an aide were ready to leave, JFK wanted to invite them to stay for lunch; first, however, he had checked with Ann to see if two more places could be added to the table. LBJ, on the other hand, thought nothing of inviting half the Congress for cocktails on three hours' notice. This was the way he had lived in Texas and in Washington before he was President, and he did not change.

As the assassination receded into history, the Johnsons began to put their own mark on Washington. If the Kennedy style had been to invite the best and the brightest, the Johnsons simply magnified it. At dinner one night there were so many celebrities that I couldn't count them. The President decided that it would be a thrill for every woman there to be able to say afterward, "I danced at the White House with the President," and he proceeded systematically through the distaff guests. In order to dance with every woman present, LBJ devised a plan of double-cutting. He would dance with me until he saw some woman he'd missed, then change partners, and I would find myself in the arms of John Steinbeck or Dr. Spock. In a few minutes Johnson would return, collect me for another twirl and then double-cut again. Observing this performance, the AP solemnly noted the next day that I had danced with the President eighteen times.

LBJ got things done on the dance floor. Whereas James Thurber once described dancing as a vertical excuse for something much better accomplished horizontally, LBJ always had other business in mind—that is, politics (in fact, he seldom thought of anything else). He never asked my political affiliation until one night on the dance floor, when he wanted to know why I had never told him that I was a lifelong Republican. When I replied that I was politically independent, he said that he had the information straight from Everett Dirksen, the Senate Republican leader; what's more, I was Dirksen's candidate for an appointment to the Federal Communications Commission, and did I want the job? I promptly turned down the offer, but afterward I got some pleasure out of imagining the expression on the faces of the network bosses if I'd accepted. They were obsequious to the FCC commissioners, and it would have been uproarious if they'd had to appear before me.

Although the open-door policy permeated the Johnson White House and the welcome mat was out, there was nothing corny about the state dinners, which were staged with style and grace. Monumental efforts were made to ensure that a Johnson entertainment was the best. The family and staff were hypersensitive to criticisms of the Texas style of hospitality, and they tried vigorously, and successfully, to compensate. The donation of a handsome stage for the East Room permitted more elaborate after-dinner entertainment, and headliners were invited to perform.

But the keynote to the Johnsons' hospitality was that it had a purpose. Just as LBJ capitalized on news events to get action on legislation and to achieve his goals, both of them used entertainment to further their pet projects. Lady Bird gave a series of luncheons to honor women "doers." These were greeted with bemused skepticism at NBC and elsewhere, but the critics were wrong. They brought to the White House women who had already made substantial achievements in their own fields, so that Lady Bird could seek their advice on how to settle other problems and initiate programs for the betterment of society.

One "Doers' Luncheon" was held to generate suggestions about what to do about the growing rate of crime in the streets. There had been a good deal of publicity about cases where cries for help went unanswered, and Mrs. Johnson thought that something could be done. She had invited women who worked in anticrime programs, and had opened a debate among us when President Johnson unexpectedly appeared. After he spoke briefly, Eartha Kitt rose and made an impassioned and intemperate speech about Vietnam. I was sitting next to Miss Kitt, who had been on a slow boil all during lunch. While I agreed with her sentiments, I disagreed with her tactics; also, she was extremely tense and was behaving erratically. I realize that if you're fighting for a cause you often feel obliged to take extreme steps, but I don't think that zeal precludes decency, and it seems to me questionable to accept an invitation and then deliberately thwart the host's attempt to push his cause by usurping the stage and promulgating your own.

One of the most exquisite luncheons I ever attended was in honor of Lady Bird's beautification program. The East Ballroom was breathtaking with spring flowers everywhere. Though much maligned at the time, "beautification" was a highly significant program with far-reaching impact. The word itself was a detriment, but no one could find a satisfactory synonym. Clumsy though the title was, "beautification" was the forerunner of many ecological programs which enhance our life today.

But probably the most dedicated efforts in entertaining were directed at Congress. For years LBJ's closest friends had been his colleagues on Capitol Hill, so it was only natural that they be invited to the White House frequently. In addition, there were regularly scheduled parties for the members of Congress whom LBJ knew less well. The wife of one Republican leader told me that during the Eisenhower Administration she had never once been invited to the

White House, and that she had virtually been ignored by the Kennedys, but that with LBJ in office she went there regularly. One big bash was even called "A Salute to Congress," and a musical history of U.S. politics, produced and directed by professionals from New York, was performed on a specially constructed stage on the South Lawn. One correspondent from each network was chosen to narrate: Walter Cronkite from CBS, Howard K. Smith from ABC, and I from NBC. The program itself was entertaining, historically interesting and with good dancing and songs, but the real significance of the occasion was that it dispelled the legendary antipathy between the White House and Capitol Hill. Traditionally, Presidents have never given much credit to "that other branch of government"; yet here was a Chief Executive giving the legislative branch a tribute on the White House lawn.

Since Johnson ran the White House as if he were the Majority Leader, it was difficult for him to realize that he no longer *was* the Majority Leader. On the Hill he had haggled, negotiated, trading away one vote for another, one committee seat in exchange for support when needed, but now he no longer had that kind of power. Congressmen jealously guard their domain and resent any intrusion, even if it comes from a son of Capitol Hill like LBJ. It was a tough lesson for him to learn that while he had increased his overall power, he had lost some of his leverage on the Hill. In fact, he needed his old friends and their votes more frequently than they needed him, so he grew irritated with Congress and frustrated by his inability to manipulate it as he once had. Consequently his relations with his successor, Mike Mansfield, soured. In a typical overstatement LBJ once told me that if he'd ever had a son, he wished he would be like Mansfield. Some Johnson loyalists believed that the relationship deteriorated because Mansfield was anxious to leave his own mark, which was tough to do following in the footsteps of the great Senate master.

Still, LBJ's old friends from the South were loyal and friendly as ever, and shortly after he became President, Senator Allen Ellender gave one of his luncheons so that LBJ could exert his legendary charm and pressure on some of his old friends. I was invited, and was seated between the President and Senator Harry Byrd, one of the few people besides Lady Bird who still called him "Lyndon." Those two understood each other and neither gave quarter in their badinage, but they were also "pokers." In fact, neither of them could carry on a conversation without poking, which was dangerous if you were sitting between them. They started out arguing about beagles. LBJ had picked up his beagle by the ears and claimed that the beagle didn't mind. Byrd, a country man who had many dogs, disagreed, and to emphasize, he reached across under my chin and poked LBJ in the shoulder. In reply, LBJ poked Byrd back. Then they argued about the tax bill, which was the real purpose of the lunch, because Byrd had life-and-death power over tax legislation, and the poking increased. Soon it became a matter of exquisite timing to get a mouthful of shrimp gumbo without colliding with one or another long arm snaking across to emphasize a point. Eventually LBJ arranged a compromise on the bill and I was able to eat.

Although LBJ ran into trouble trying to run the Congress from the White House, his constant massaging of its members did enable him to get through a great deal of his Great Society legislation. Eventually there were so many laws, commissions and committees that no more seemed to be needed; what *was* needed was implementation of the laws. This took far more time and irritated Johnson, who was frustrated by any delay.

One of my favorite White House parties was given by the President in honor of Courtenay Valenti, the daughter of Jack and Mary Margaret Valenti. Mary Margaret had once been the President's secretary, and he and Lady Bird were devoted to her and dependent on her husband. LBJ also adored Courtenay, a beautiful little girl, and one Christmas Eve, when the Valentis were at our traditional Christmas Eve party, he telephoned her to wish her Merry Christmas. It was an honor most people would have been impressed by, but Courtenay, who was anxious to get to the presents and festivities, considered the interruption a bit of an imposition, and kept trying to get off the line by saying, "Okay, Mr. Prez, see you later."

Besides Courtenay four other children were invited to the party: Billy Watson, son of the Postmaster General; Laing Rogers, daughter of Congressman Rogers; Angela Weisl, granddaughter of the New York committeeman who had long supported LBJ; and Michael Dickerson. They were each about four years old and were in their very best clothes. The invitation was for 5:30 P.M., and all of us were there in good time, waiting in the Fish Room, just down the hall from the

108

President's office. There was a large oak table in the room which the children kept running under and bumping their heads against. Little Billy Watson could bump his head the hardest and never cry. None of the mothers had thought to bring any toys, so there was nothing to entertain our rambunctious children with as the minutes dragged by. Moreover, it was dinnertime for that age group and there was nothing to eat, so someone went down to the White House basement to get a snack from the candy machines. By then the beautifully dressed boys and girls were thoroughly rumpled, and the chocolate candy they got all over their clothes made little difference.

More time elapsed, and the hungry children were becoming unmanageable, but LBJ kept sending out messages asking us to wait just a little while longer. I sent a message back suggesting that we return at a more convenient time, but the word came back that we were to wait. Finally, about two hours after we arrived, the children were ushered in—or I should say, rushed in—to the famous office, and when they entered, we met some added starters at the party: Vice President Hubert Humphrey, House Speaker John McCormack, Secretary of State Dean Rusk and Defense Secretary Robert McNamara. The group had finally finished an emergency meeting called because De Gaulle had just pulled out of the NATO military command. Typically, LBJ hadn't wanted to disappoint the children by canceling the party. He was always aware of history and the meaning that a White House visit had, and it pleased him to think that those children could grow up and say, "President Johnson gave a party for me at the White House."

It was dark by the time we were admitted, and Michael kept running over to the window, which has a magnificent view, to look at the Washington Monument, a landmark he could identify. But each time he got to the window, LBJ would command, "Michael, come here and give me a kiss." Michael would dutifully obey, and then sneak away to look out the window, at which point the President would again call him back. The Johnson presence, always formidable, was particularly awesome to children, and they naturally obeyed him, with no cajoling or loud tone necessary. I can still remember vividly standing there, watching Michael running around the Oval Office in his little red shoes, with a typical motherly thought running through my head: Would Michael ever be there in another capacity, perhaps even as President?

CHAPTER 13 〜◯

At the same time that my professional life kept me moving around the world, my personal life was equally peripatetic. When we were first married we lived at Dick's farm in Leesburg and used my little Georgetown house as a pied-à-terre. But the commuting was too much, so we moved to Wyoming Avenue, a half block from the French embassy. I loved the house—it was near a hotel and civilized stores, and a quick drive from the Capitol, the office or the White House—but Dick said we needed a place for exercise. I couldn't have disagreed more. I was working during the day, at night we often went out, and when I had any spare time I read the paper or a book. *I* didn't need any more room; I could stand in the middle of the house and shout up or down the four floors, and everyone could hear me well enough, but Dick said we needed more space for the girls and Michael to play.

During the early sixties the papers were full of the controversy over the Merrywood estate, which had belonged to Mr. and Mrs. Hugh D. Auchincloss, Jackie's mother and stepfather. A couple of years before, the Auchinclosses had moved to Georgetown and had sold Merrywood to developers who planned to build a massive high-rise apartment complex, thus ruining the skyline and destroying the natural setting, which was much the same as in the days of the Revolutionary War. (Even in early 1963, the area was virtually undeveloped, and wild deer often darted across the lawns at Merrywood.)

The citizens of McLean, Virginia, were outraged and protested, demanding that their bucolic neighborhood be saved. Coast-to-coast environmentalists joined the cause, urging that the land be preserved for its scenic and historic value. Irate neighbors picketed the house with signs saying, "Her daughter beautifies the White House and she desecrates our neighborhood." President Kennedy said privately that the one question he hoped never to be asked at his news conference was about Merrywood. Tempers flared, but the syndicators were adamant and pressed ahead; they knew they had a gold mine with their apartment zoning close to Washington on such a choice spot. Local politicians won and lost elections on the issue, and it evoked so much emotionalism that when two presidential friends, Robin and Angier Biddle Duke, were to be married, the President and Mrs. Kennedy didn't attend the ceremony when they learned that the wedding would be at the home of some of the neighbors who had picketed Merrywood.

At that time I was writing articles and appearing on CBS telecasts to protest the desecration of the land. Still, despite the protests, the bulldozers arrived to break ground—at which point the Attorney General, Robert Kennedy, also a Merrywood neighbor, took action. He discovered an old scenic easement, rarely if ever used, and slapped it on the gates of Merrywood. Construction stopped, and a legal battle ensued. Eventually Congress appropriated over $750,000 to buy the air rights to Merrywood in perpetuity. This means that nothing can ever be built there over forty feet high—the height of our house—and also that no trees over a certain diameter can be cut down. In effect, today all U.S. citizens own the air rights to Merrywood.

The Congress' purchase also meant that the syndicate of developers was left with a big mansion and nearly fifty acres of land zoned not for high-rise apartments but for one-acre houses. It was at this point that Dick began to think about buying it; we could live in the big house, and would develop the surrounding acreage. I wasn't interested. Nevertheless, one bright windy fall day Dick drove us out to McLean to look at the place. The trees were spectacular—the biggest oaks imaginable and the largest and grandest tulip poplar I've ever seen. All of them were in autumn shades of red and yellow, and the falling leaves floated down around us. The grounds and view were glorious, but the house was larger than I remembered, and looked bigger still since it was empty. In addition there was a four-car garage, above which were five bedrooms, two baths and a kitchen—all over a gigantic gym which was not quite big enough for indoor tennis. In the main house the bedrooms and bathrooms were mammoth, and the kitchen had a bigger stove than the one in the Mayflower Hotel. No thanks. But Dick promptly bought it and fifty adjoining acres.

The first time I ever saw Merrywood was with Jack Kennedy. Jackie was with Mr. and Mrs. Auchincloss in Newport while he was in Washington for the Senate summer session and staying at Merry-wood, where he took me for dinner. I never dreamed I'd own it one day, and it never occurred to me to want to. It seemed awfully big and stuffy; it needed a good airing and was dark inside. (Dick and I have since removed the mullions from the big windows and pulled back the shutters, so now it is much brighter.) Jack and I ate out on the terrace, above which there were, and still are, bug-repellent lights of a kind I'd never seen before. They had a wire cage around them which electrocutes insects when they fly into them, making a hissing sound. Those lights have been immortalized by Gore Vidal in his book *Washington, D.C.*, and I doubt whether that kind is made any more.

After dinner we went swimming in the pool a hundred yards away. It was Olympic-sized, with both high and low diving boards, and full of leaves and bugs, and Jack said that sometimes there were snakes. The bath house, modeled after a Swiss chalet, was placed in a clearing of the forest of gigantic oak trees. There were also a lot of mosquitoes because the pool was in a pocket above the river which didn't get a breeze. (We've since filled it in and built a new pool nearer the house.)

The best thing about Merrywood was the sound of the river below. There are some rocks down there in front of the house which give just enough ripple to the water, and now I cherish that sound every night.

It was a delightful place on a summer's night, and JFK obviously liked it. There's an intangible aura to Merrywood; it has a particular enchantment of its own, and those who have lived there seem to feel that here is where their roots remain. They like to revisit; it's that kind of house.

The Noyes family, who were among the original owners of the Washington *Evening Star*, were the first to live there, and the Noyes children, now all middle-aged, still like to reminisce about it. They sold the house to Hugh D. Auchincloss, whose succession of wives vied with each other in changing the place and adding rooms. The first was a Russian by whom he had a son, Yusha. Next Mr. Auchincloss married Mrs. Nina Vidal, who moved in with her son, Gore. She added the circular room at the end of the house which is called the card room, and whose décor was early *Queen Elizabeth*—meaning the ocean liner. The Auchinclosses had two children: a son, Thomas, and a daughter, Nina. When they were divorced, Auchincloss married Mrs. Janet Bouvier, mother of Jackie and Lee, and this marriage produced two more children, Janet and James.

After Merrywood was ours, Dick spent six months remodeling it. He changed everything about it except the wood paneling in the library, a glorious dark walnut that couldn't be reproduced today. Now it's beautiful here, and I feel lucky to be in this small stretch of riverbank. We are only fifteen minutes from the White House, yet live in a virtual wilderness with no other houses in sight. Our neighbors toward town are Charles and Lynda Bird Johnson Robb and Senator and Mrs. Edward Kennedy; upriver, about a block away, live Ann and Elliot Richardson, and a mile and a half farther out, away from the river, is Hickory Hill, Ethel Kennedy's house.

Though I love it at Merrywood now, I arrived there kicking and screaming. I really preferred the city. Reluctantly, I moved in with the help of a South American couple and their year-old baby and a maid—the couple on the verge of divorce, and the maid pregnant and unmarried. The three girls were wonderfully helpful, though they too were not enthusiastic about the change. However, for Michael it was a dream; two dozen workmen were employed there when we moved in and he had a great time with them.

Our family had the usual arguments over who was to get which bedroom. In the middle of all this Jaime Auchincloss, Jackie's whimsical half brother, stopped by one day. Like many others who have lived here, he has a special fondness for the place. It was here that Jackie played as a girl, reputedly "The Princess" in the games, and here that she became engaged to John Husted. It was while Jackie was engaged to Husted that she met JFK and started dating him. Since her mother frowned on Jackie's going out with Congressman Kennedy while simultaneously wearing Husted's ring, the fiancé was summoned from New York to Merrywood so that Jackie could break the engagement. But she wasn't home when he arrived; instead he was greeted by young Nina Auchincloss, sitting in the library in her little blue Potomac School uniform practicing her spelling. So she entertained Mr. Husted, who had a drink or two while waiting for his fiancée to arrive and anticipating why he was there. As Nina describes it, Jackie wafted in, completely untroubled, and took over the library while Nina quickly retreated upstairs to her bedroom.

113

Jackie must have been particularly enchanting that evening, because within a few minutes Mr. Husted, his ring returned, his engagement broken, was showing no signs of despondency, and along with Jackie, went upstairs to serenade the bewildered Nina.

It was at Merrywood that JFK courted Jackie, but there was a year's hiatus when they hardly saw each other because he was running for the Senate. This was typical Kennedy—politics before everything —and Jackie was pretty grumpy during that interval.

After they were married, the Kennedys stayed at Merrywood several summers while her parents were in Newport, and she gave her first dinner party here. Then, after JFK's serious back operation, he recuperated at Merrywood and wrote *Profiles in Courage* on the third floor. The children swear his ghost still roams the place, but I'm not so sure; I think that his taste for history would make him more comfortable with Lincoln's ghost, who, as is well known, regularly appears at the White House.

Gore Vidal liked that same third-floor room, which he occupied before Jackie took it over. Before I was married I had occasionally gone out with Gore; he was always fascinating, always a gossip and great fun to match wits with. He too took us on a tour of our house. When we reached the landing between the first and second floors, he talked about his first day there. At the age of ten he had been yanked out of school in New York, taken to a neighbor's house to witness the marriage of his mother to Mr. Auchincloss, and then whisked down to Merrywood, his new home—all in one day. He awakened at six o'clock the next morning and wandered around the big house, lost and alone, a forlorn little creature. He was sitting on the top step of the landing when his mother appeared and asked him, "Well, do you like it?" When he said he had not yet had time to decide, she said that she hoped he would, since she had done it all for him. To this day Gore resents his mother's imposing that burden on him. What he resents even more is that she also told him that it was to be a marriage of convenience—really *his* convenience. Obviously she changed her mind, since she and Auchincloss had two children.

Our children all wanted the "Jackie room," on the third floor, but we thought we could take better care of them if they were on the second floor, nearer to us. Gore liked that third-floor room because he loved the sound of the river from way up there. He wrote about it in *Washington, D.C.*, the third part of the trilogy that begins with *Burr* and *1876*. It is his only work, he told me, that is partially autobiographical. The story centers around Merrywood, renamed Laurel House in the book. He still loves to come back and reminisce about his early background, and breezes in as if he were the squire of Merrywood and has only loaned the house to us temporarily. In fact, when he gave me a copy of *Washington, D.C.*, he inscribed it "Welcome!" On his last pilgrimage here, he brought along a CBS camera crew that was doing a profile on him for *60 Minutes*.

When Gore's mother moved out, Mrs. Bouvier moved in with Jackie and Lee. Gore says he left his shirts behind, and that Jackie used to wear them. At any rate, he and Jackie were pals thereafter until one night at a White House dinner when Bobby Kennedy accosted Gore for being too friendly with the First Lady. Gore was incensed, and retaliated with a blistering article about the Kennedys which ensured his being *persona non grata* at the White House and created an irreparable breach with Jackie.

Raising children when both parents work takes patience and planning. I used to worry that they would suffer with our being away, but Dick, who is a superb father, convinced me that it was not a matter of how much time we gave them but how it was used. Whenever possible, we took the children with us. In 1964 the girls went to the Democratic National Convention in Atlantic City, and while I worked they went swimming by day and were exposed to the political process by night. However, little Michael was left at home, and when he was told his mommy wanted to talk to him, he ran to the television set instead of going to the phone. This upset me. Clearly I suffered more from the separation than he did.

I also learned about raising children from someone who had great experience and success at it: Mrs. Rose Kennedy. After dining with us one night she wrote a charming thank-you letter from the White House, giving me some of her tips which even now, many years later, we're still following. For example, she wrote that she tried to teach her children history by attempting to relive it. In Massachusetts, April 19 is a school holiday to commemorate Paul Revere's ride, and to observe it she took her children to Lexington and Concord to trace his route. History also dominated much of their conversation. We do the same thing at Merrywood; using the Senate calendar, which lists an important event each day, we talk about it at breakfast. Mrs. Kennedy also said that she told Bible stories to her children on religious holidays, and recalled one spring when she was preparing her children for Palm Sunday and Easter. She told them about Jesus, of how he rode into Jerusalem on a donkey and of how the people beside the road waved palm fronds as he went by. Then she told about the Crucifixion and the Resurrection. "When I finished telling the entire story," she wrote, "a little red-headed boy looked up and said, 'Whatever happened to the donkey?' And now that little boy is President of the United States."

Shortly after we moved to Merrywood, my parents from Wisconsin, my sister, brother-in-law, and their four children planned a reunion at Merrywood. This meant a total of fourteen people sleeping in, and on the day before they were to arrive the cook who had been hired didn't show up. At one point the maid was out and I had three children on my hands, a niece, a nephew and Janie, when I was assigned to a news conference at the White House. Since I had no place to leave the children, I got special permission to take them with me. They behaved very well, but it was a little awesome for them. Fortunately Joe Schershel, the Cedar Street photographer, was covering the event, and he took their pictures on the White House steps.

Afterward the children and I took a taxi for lunch at a Georgetown restaurant. The cabdriver was a big, fat, happy man, and as we drove along Pennsylvania Avenue he waved out the window to various other cabdrivers and pedestrians, simultaneously keeping up a running conversation with us. Since he seemed to know everyone in town, I asked him if he happened to know of a good cook, a subject much on my mind since there would soon be fourteen people in the house. "It just so happens that I'm a cook myself," he answered. "I used to work on the Norfolk and Western Railroad." Anyone who has ever traveled on that railroad knows that it serves marvelous food. Then the driver turned around and gave me his calling card, saying, "My name is Winston N. Jones; I eats no meat, I just licks the bones." By now the three children were nudging me and whispering, "Hire him, Nancy, hire him. He's fun." So I asked Winston if he wanted to take on a temporary job, and that's how I found one of the best cooks in America.

116

With Edward R. Murrow and Don Hewitt, planning the 1960 inaugural coverage for CBS at the Capitol.

With Walter Cronkite at JFK's Inaugural Ball.

Setting up the Inaugural Ball coverage a few hours earlier.

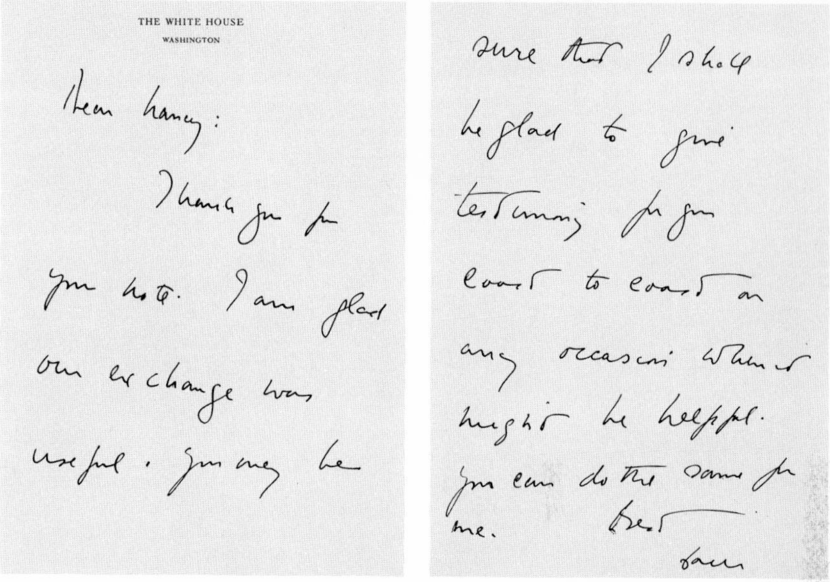

THE WHITE HOUSE
WASHINGTON

Dear Nancy:

Thank you for your note. I am glad our exchange was useful. You may be sure that I shall be glad to give testimony for you coast to coast on any occasion where it might be helpful. You can do the same for me.

Best

Jack

JFK's note, which arrived a few days later.

MARVIN LICHTNER

In the Oval Office, shortly after JFK became President.

With Dick at Merrywood in 1963.

NBC News has its first baby (Michael Dickerson).

Opposite page: Dancing with LBJ in the East Ballroom in 1965.

The Dickerson family at Merrywood in 1968. *From left to right:* Ann, Jane, CWD, Michael, NHD and Elizabeth.

With John Dickerson, age seven, Merrywood, summer 1976.

Conversation with the President, January 4, 1971, with John Chancellor (NBC), Eric Sevareid with back to camera (CBS), and Howard K. Smith (ABC).

With CWD and Henry Kissinger at a party in 1974.

With President Ford in 1975 at a state dinner at the White House.

When I arrived home that night it was a delight to see Winston's yellow cab in the back drive. (There's something very reassuring about your own yellow cab in the backyard; it gives you an immense sense of security.) When I entered the kitchen there was Winston, his black chauffeur's hat off, his tall white chef's hat on, and this was reassuring too. Dick, who had preceded me home, said that by the time he arrived, Winston had already made two apple pies. That was the only problem; Winston simply didn't know how to cook for a small group. When he made biscuits, there were always enough for the first serving on the railroad. Never mind; great Southern cooking and a warm philosophy were the exports of that kitchen.

That night I was scheduled to go to the White House, and as I went out the back door, there was Winston, his black chauffeur's hat back on, about to drive off in his taxi. I hailed him, saying, "Just a minute, I'm coming with you." So he drove me to the White House through the private gates, a first for him which he enjoyed hugely. Clearly Winston and I were made for each other, so we worked out a wonderful arrangement: in the morning he'd drive his cab, come to Merrywood in the afternoon, pick up Mike, who adored him, take him along to pick up the girls at their school in Maryland, and then return to cook dinner. We all had a lovely time of it until Winston ran into trouble with a woman friend who took a knife to him and he had to leave town precipitously.

Amazingly enough, the last time we saw Winston was on television. We were all watching the news when suddenly Winston appeared on camera. We shouted to each other as he gave his considered views on some new taxi regulations in the capital. Afterward everyone agreed that the news would be much better were Winston to appear more frequently.

Marvelous characters and friends have come to work at Merrywood, and today Cordalina and Manuel and their daughter, who are from Portugal, live with us. Without them this book couldn't be written. In the past few years we've managed to bring their two fine sons and daughters-in-law here, and I was the matron of honor at the wedding of one of them. I pray that we all live happily ever after at Merrywood.

CHAPTER 14 ⌒

LBJ never fully understood the role of the press. To him there was no historic nobility in the fourth estate; in fact, its only useful role was to be flattering or to broadcast the party line. When you were assigned to his campaign he felt that your role was to tell what was going on from his point of view—that is, to tell it as his advocate. The idea that you might report a story from a different angle than his was infuriating to him.

LBJ was also frustrated by what stories made headlines. He could see no pattern for the choice of stories that were played big, as compared to those that made only the back pages. Often he would show me a newspaper and demand to know why certain articles made the first page while others did not. Once when he was Vice President I was visiting him in his office, and he was perplexed and annoyed by the amount of coverage given the appointment of one Charles Horsky to be Advisor for National Capital Affairs. In addition to the main story, there was a full page of family pictures. "Look at that," he said. "More attention to Horsky than they give to the Vice President." He considered his staff partly to blame for the lack of space devoted to him, and of course any unfavorable story would be blamed on an aide who was "leaking to the press."

When there was inadequate coverage, the press secretary suffered; usually this was poor George Reedy, who never could satisfy Mr. Johnson. After the assassination Pierre Salinger, JFK's press secretary, continued on as White House press secretary. Three days later, when every paper in the world emblazoned Johnson in headlines, he spread all the papers out on his bed and the floor, then called Reedy in, and pointing to the coverage, said, "See! Salinger has had the job three days, and look what he's done already!" To this day George believes that LBJ never understood that even without a press secretary the coverage would have been the same. I think that he understood very well, but that he wanted to prod George into trying harder.

When LBJ became President he did not know many of the regular White House reporters, or even many of those who covered Capitol

Hill. He didn't like or trust journalists much, and he had no time for academic concepts about the independence of the fourth estate. You were either for him or against him, and he gave only lip service to the right of the press to find fault. As he said many times, "I'm the only President they've got," and he was extremely thin-skinned about any criticism. In fact, when he believed that he was doing his best for his country, he thought that any rejection of him or his policies was unpatriotic, if not treasonous.

There is always a natural antagonism between a President and the press because a Chief Executive wants action which he often feels is thwarted by the focus of publicity. Add to this Johnson's fanatic passion for secrecy (euphemistically referred to as "preserving my options") and the situation is intolerable.

When he moved into the White House, Johnson made his first mistake in press relations by showering reporters with an unprecedented flood of gifts, favors, candy and presidential jewelry. In effect, he was saying, "I'll make heroes of you all if you'll play the game my way," and there was the clear implication that he would give lavish favors to those who were sympathetic, and cut off the sources of those who weren't. This shocked a good many reporters, who in any case have a built-in propensity for outrage. Once, when Blair Clark was a CBS News correspondent, he was seated next to LBJ on a plane. During the flight, LBJ told him that Frank Stanton, the CBS president, was a good friend of his, and that if Blair wanted to stay in Stanton's good graces he should be sure to report things as they "were"—meaning not in unfavorable ways. Blair was shocked at this, and almost as shocked that I wasn't as outraged as he was. But I was used to that kind of quintessential Johnson tactic and had long ignored it. Besides, though his tactics worked in Congress and in business, they were antithetical to the press, and for the most part they failed. Indeed, as in many other areas, LBJ's lack of subtlety backfired. His blatant attempts to influence sometimes forced reporters into being overly critical just to preserve their independence.

Johnson's second mistake was in toying with the press. At a news conference he was asked if he was "thinking about" appointing Henry Cabot Lodge to be ambassador to Vietnam. He said that he was not, and this was duly reported in the papers and on the networks. Yet the next day he announced Lodge's appointment, thereby ensuring the outrage of the entire White House press corps. When

119

asked to explain, he said that he had not been "thinking about" appointing Lodge; he had already made up his mind to do it. It was the same thing he had done to me when he said that he would not run *for* Vice President, but would run *as* the vice-presidential candidate. Before he was President he could get away with this kind of sophistry, but when focused upon by the entire press corps, such behavior became a large boil that would not be lanced.

The third major mistake LBJ made was to try to manipulate press conferences by planting the questions to be asked. As much as anything, this helped to create his credibility gap. The tactic has been tried before, notably in Ike's day, with little fuss, but it hurt Johnson immeasurably. In our system, the press fulfills the role of the loyal opposition in England. There is no other way for the Chief Executive to be held to account except through the press and an open, free and unrehearsed press conference. The integrity of this confrontation depends on reporters asking questions about any issue they feel the President should be accountable for to the American people. If the public realizes that questions are planted, it becomes a sham and should be treated with the contempt it deserves, for both the government and the press lose their integrity.

One day when I phoned Bill Moyers he asked if I was going to go to the press conference later that day. When I said that I was, he suggested, "You'd be the perfect one to ask LBJ how he feels; after all, it's his birthday." I thought it a reasonable question and agreed to do it. However, the President called on Ray Scherer of NBC News before me at the conference and Ray happened to ask this same question, so naturally I never sprang to my feet, despite the fact that LBJ kept staring at me in some exasperation.

I don't know how many other plants there were that day, but in retrospect I know that I was wrong in agreeing to ask one, even if it was a valid news question. Bill Moyers was out of line in suggesting it, and I was at fault in agreeing to it. Years later Bill told me that Jim Hagerty and Pierre Salinger had done the same thing with great skill, and that it was necessary to compensate for the inadequacies of a press corps that often fails to ask the key question. I disagree. If a President has some information he feels the American people should know, he has only to make an announcement before the reporters' questions start.

*   *   *

Toward the end of 1967 Johnson's press relations could not have been worse—a line I write now with some trepidation because the first time I said it publicly I was lecturing at Baylor University in Waco, Texas, and just as I made the statement, lightning struck nearby, thunder shook the building, the lights and sound went out, and I was left in a blacked-out auditorium filled with giggling students. Later I told the President that while I knew he was powerful, I didn't know that his authority went so high; to which he replied that I should learn not to attack him in his own backyard, pointed out that an early relative had once been president of Baylor, and that the thunder was really his ancestors rolling in their graves.

As LBJ's press relations soured, he became more and more unhappy about his coverage. He would complain to reporters, he would complain to their bosses, he would swear that a handful of columnists had more power than his entire Cabinet, and when he found that he couldn't woo some of them he would berate them indiscreetly. Rowland Evans must surely have heard from several sources that the President of the United States had judged him and found him wanting, declaring that "Even on a clear day Rowly couldn't find his ass with both hands."

For their part, the press ridiculed Johnson for his Texas origins, for his accent, for the cut of his pants, for the way he tweaked his big ears and for his lack of what they considered "style." The latter attribute and his alleged lack of it maddened Johnson more than anything else. Press opposition on substance was fair ground, even though Johnson didn't think so, but ridicule based on geographic origin and other subjective criteria promulgated in candlelit Georgetown parlors by an unfriendly press was not. The acrimony between Johnson and reporters was an unhappy chapter in the history of governmental press relations.

CHAPTER 15

LBJ didn't hate the Kennedys, but he didn't like them, either. He was in awe of the admiration they inspired, and he wanted people to think that he was as extraordinary as they were. He loved his Texas hill country, was convinced that it was as fine as the Kennedys' Boston, and if others didn't think so, he was hurt. His raging inferiority complex was fueled by everything the Kennedys did. He didn't understand them, and they certainly didn't understand him. He wanted everyone to love him, but most of all he wanted the Kennedys' approval—which was, to say the least, illusive.

Lady Bird came to terms with herself and with her role as successor in the White House and never envied the Kennedys except for their physical prowess, but LBJ always wanted to be younger, more hand- some and to have a different accent. At times he almost seemed to apologize for not being a Kennedy. This feeling so obsessed him that it altered all our lives. Yet he tried to conceal it. While his book presents his version of history as he wants it remembered, it does not give the full story on such touchy matters as eliminating Bobby Kennedy as a vice-presidential candidate in 1964. LBJ's account is fascinating because it reveals that though he vetoed Bobby from the ticket, the Attorney General was still very much on his mind.

Given their past history, the animosity between the two men was not unexpected. JFK had even foreseen it, and predicted a confronta- tion between the two when they sought to fill the power vacuum after he himself left office. Though he spoke of it only rarely, and then in guarded language, it worried him.

The build-up for Bobby Kennedy was spreading, and LBJ was alarmed by it. It would have been intolerable for him to have Bobby as his appointed successor because he couldn't stomach him. Yet he wanted to do something to pacify the Kennedy clan, as well as to attract its following to his own camp, and so he came up with the idea of Sargent Shriver as Vice President. To LBJ it seemed the perfect way of putting Bobby on ice. He liked Shriver, admired his work at the Peace Corps, thought his Catholicism was a political plus, and valued his "clean image," but he had also been heard to disparage Sarge. When LBJ discussed the Shriver candidacy with Bill Moyers at dinner one night, he said gleefully, "That ought to take the steam out of Bobby." In the days that followed, both Johnson and Moyers tested the Shriver idea with a few people, and Moyers even suspects that LBJ may have discussed it with Bobby himself.

However, Moyers was told by someone who knew but whose name he won't reveal that "the Kennedy family thinks Shriver would be the most objectionable choice." If the family had a choice between a

Kennedy and an in-law, the blood relative would always win. They would never give the nod to Shriver if Bobby still had a chance, no matter how remote. It was not that the Kennedys were *against* Sarge, but that they were *pro* Bobby. As a result, Moyers reported back to LBJ that the Kennedys had vetoed Shriver, a judgment that LBJ had himself heard independently. Were it not for that family veto, Shriver would have been chosen as his running mate.

While the Shriver trial balloon was being floated past the Kennedys, only to be pricked, the build-up for Bobby was gaining momentum, and by July 1, 1964, his devotees were organizing all across the country. Ironically, it was a broadcast of mine that helped trigger the timing of the "dump Bobby" maneuver. During the week of July 19 I did an NBC radio broadcast about a Kennedy conclave at Hyannisport: Rumor had it, I reported, that Bobby and Jackie had planned their entrance at the forthcoming Democratic convention and talked about the tribute to be given the late President; that they had speculated about the predictable outpouring of pro-Kennedy emotion that would follow their arrival; and that they believed, probably correctly, what Kennedy devotees were telling them: that when the two of them appeared, the delegates would rise up and demand that Bobby be on the ticket. I stated that Kennedy aficionados were toying with a scenario that could force LBJ's hand, conceivably taking the decision away from him altogether. In retrospect such a scenario seems highly plausible, especially when one remembers that Bobby's appearance on stage at the convention evoked an eighteen-minute, emotion-packed ovation—unrestrained adulation for the memory of his brother as well as for him personally and what he stood for.

As soon as I got off the air, Liz Carpenter's office phoned for a copy of the broadcast. She sent it to the President, who read it immediately and said, "If Nancy says such a thing on the air, then Jackie and Bobby really are behind the build-up." Convinced that they were planning a power play which he would not be able to quell at the convention, he decided that the Kennedy faction should be allowed no more time in which to build a groundswell. The next week, on July 30, he announced on television that no member of his Cabinet would be considered as a running mate, a tactic that eliminated Bobby before matters got out of hand.

*   *   *

From then on LBJ encouraged a national guessing game about his choice of a running mate. Playing cat and mouse, he dangled it before everyone. A lot *thought* they were it, but no one knew. Everyone wanted to be courted and was. Senator Eugene McCarthy thought he might be chosen. Hubert Humphrey thought he was the man, but so did Senator Tom Dodd.

As the Democratic convention convened in Atlantic City, no one yet knew who LBJ's choice would be. On the afternoon of August 26, he walked around the back lawn of the White House, followed by the press corps panting in the steaming sun. They quizzed him, but he wouldn't tell them whom he'd chosen. A few hours earlier I had covered a so-called ladies' meeting in Atlantic City in the rain, noted that Muriel Humphrey was with Lady Bird and drew the logical conclusion that Humphrey would be the Johnson choice for Vice President. LBJ was watching the program back in the Oval Office, and was delighted that my deductions happened to be correct; he liked people to be smart and right. However, he wouldn't confirm my predictions or anyone else's—an infuriating game for all concerned. Suddenly, to everyone's consternation and surprise, he decided to go to Atlantic City that evening, which was twenty-four hours ahead of his scheduled arrival. His precipitous change of plans destroyed the plans of hundreds of people—not only the Secret Service, the FBI and the White House staff, but all the convention planners who had set up the schedule months in advance. But LBJ loved to surprise, and he threw the whole convention and all the networks into a tizzy.

No one knew at which airport he would arrive, when, or with whom. I was no wiser, but on learning that the President was on his way, NBC News ordered me to find him. Between Bill Moyers, Walter Jenkins, and some smiles from the Secret Service men, I learned that it might be wise to show up at the helicopter pad just outside of town. From the start of the convention there had been little action there, and the reporters staked out were both frustrated and bored. Julian Goodman shouted at Joe Feeney, a publicity man, to help me, and we commandeered a passing CBS car, arriving at the pad just as LBJ's helicopter landed. Out I went, dragging yards of heavy TV cable with me. A young production assistant chose that moment to declare his independence—or antifeminism—and refused to watch my big purse filled with mikes, TV make-up and notebooks, a combination mobile office and research library necessary because we were always on the run and rarely near an office. Loaded down with it on one arm and the cable on the other, I marched out on the field. Looking like a packhorse, I could see the humor in the situation; all that was lacking was background music, preferably the "The Battle Hymn of the Republic" or the march from *The Bridge on the River Kwai*. The crew was screaming to the master booth at NBC Control, "Switch to us, give it to us, she's got him, he's here and she's got him!"

It was like a first-night opening, with the script yet to be written and the stage being the whole country. The instant I strode out on the field, the Secret Service activated the floodlights as if on cue. By the time it dawned on everyone that the President was landing, the security men had taken over and everyone else was held back, so that I was the only mike in town. As if he were following a script, LBJ came down the helicopter stairs, walked straight up to me and said, "Hello, Nancy, I've been watching you all day and you're doing a wonderful job." Back in the plush RCA sponsors' booth, the Sarnoffs and Bob Kintner, the NBC president, let out a cheer, had another drink, and all danced in a little circle. It's helpful to get presidential endorsement, particularly when you're in such cut-throat competition. Meanwhile I was throwing questions at LBJ for the benefit of all three networks, who by now had switched from the parade in the hall to the airport. (In a way LBJ outsmarted himself. Though he was a master of television and its impact, he arrived at the precise time that his name was being put in nomination and his managers were staging an enormous demonstration for him, which was then upstaged on the screen by his dramatic arrival.)

I was pleased with that interview because the next day Jack Gould, the television critic of the *New York Times*, the guru of all the medium's critics, said, "And her questions were right on the beam." As millions watched, LBJ told me that Hubert Humphrey was his vice-presidential choice, so I asked Hubert a few questions too. Afterward *Variety* said that the interview ranked high in the history of journalistic scoops, and included me in their list of the top ten television reporters. They headlined their article "9 Guys & a Doll."

For such occasions the friendship or knowledge of the character of public officials is essential; without it I couldn't have gotten such a scoop on live television. Also, on live television, there is no time to ask pap questions. Right from the start, I knew that it would be a far better interview—"better television"—if I asked the tough ones, and any smart politician knows the same thing. However, when I switched from being a hard-news reporter on the scene to the role of analyst or syndicated columnist-of-the-air, I learned the danger of being too close or too personally fond of the source involved. Luckily for me, by the time I became a commentator, Mr. Nixon was in the White House, and since he has never been known to form close relationships, the question was moot. But when you're on live television, knowing the players without a program is essential, and knowing them well enough to get them to come to your mike rather than someone else's is almost as important as knowing what questions to ask.

For the Democrats in 1964 the election was a foregone conclusion, so the campaign lost some of its urgency and had a mood of festivity. The only soft spot of support was in the South, where Johnson's civil rights programs were unpopular. They would have been unpopular in any event, but since a Southern President had initiated them, they were even more unpalatable, and Johnson was freely referred to as a traitor. Therefore it was decided that Lady Bird, whose Southern accent was incomparable, should cover the South, and a special train of campaign whistle stops was planned.

It was a good idea, masterly executed by Lady Bird. At each stop she would make a speech from the observation platform, always accompanied by the wives of the congressmen in the area, or by congressmen and the senators of the state themselves. In this way she helped them get votes, they helped her, and together they presented an image of Democrats as one big happy family, which was not always the case. Hale Boggs, the popular congressman from Louisiana, who was traveling on the train, would introduce Lady Bird, and the farther south we got, the more Southern his accent became and the more frequently his speeches would be spotted with references to grits, black-eyed peas and other regional dishes. For those of us who weren't brought up on grits, the descriptions of those Southern specialties were nothing short of fascinating. Local dignitaries would be invited to the lounge in Lady Bird's special car. She always did her homework, so was well prepared with questions for each, and for

126

them it was a real ego trip to have the wife of the President listen to them so attentively.

There were only a few bad moments, and these Lady Bird handled with extraordinary grace. In South Carolina the crowd was hostile, and though the advance men had done their best, they couldn't keep the anti–civil rights hecklers away. Chanting loudly, the demonstrators refused to let Mrs. Johnson speak, but with great self-discipline, she stood serenely before them. When she tried a second and third time, they still wouldn't let her talk. Finally, speaking into the mike, she raised her voice as loud as she could and said, "You've had your turn, now let me have mine!" It was a very good example of how to handle an unfriendly crowd, and they listened to her. If there was any chance of winning those people over, Lady Bird did it.

Any campaign trip induces a kind of camaraderie among those participating in it, including the candidate, his aides, the transportation people and the press, and this certainly was true of Lady Bird's train, on which we reporters traveled for several nights. Of course there were no showers on board, but at one stop Liz Carpenter made arrangements for a communal bath, and the share-your-shower accommodations produced an even closer rapport.

I had a marvelous time on that journey because I was working with a first-rate camera crew. No one who hasn't watched them in action can know how hard camera men work when they're out of a studio. On this assignment they had to carry heavy equipment, get off the train while it was still moving, run around to the front of the train, get in position to take pictures of Mrs. Johnson, film her and unload the cameras before the train pulled out. At the same time they had to locate the runner who had been sent to the whistle stop to pick up the film and speed it to the nearest plane so that it could be flown to a major city to be processed before the competition got on the air.

This particular crew was especially helpful to me, and we all worked hard and were pleased with ourselves and the results. But it became a bond between us to complain about the stupidity of the production staffs back in the studios. Somewhere along the line one producer got the idea that we should situate ourselves on the observation platform, and as the moving train chugged down the track, film the open and close—that is, the speaker's introduction and conclusion for each story. Someone had decided that it would be "good television" for me to stand on the platform, with the scenery fading into the distance, and tell the poignant story of a Southern wife returning to her homeland in support of her husband. The logistics took some ingenuity; the platform swayed vigorously from side to side, and besides, it wasn't deep enough for the proper camera angle, so I had to lean way out over the rail. It was an athletic feat to keep upright, let alone avoid falling off as the train raced down the tracks. Also, we had a great deal of trouble with the microphones because they picked up only the track noise and not me. By the time the sound engineer had solved the problem, the train was slowing for another stop and the Secret Service was pushing us away. We had to start all over again, trying to get the shot between stops—made even more complicated because we had to get special permission each time to go through Lady Bird's private quarters to get out on the platform. I did several openings and closings from the wildly swaying observation deck, and finally one of them was used on the air. Afterward the show switched back to the studio, where David Brinkley was shown doubled up in laughter; all he could say was "The Perils of Pauline," and there I was, killing myself for NBC in a contemporary Mack Sennett comedy.

The whistle-stop tour was followed with interest by newspapers and television, and soon turned into a soap opera. Often the people who came down to meet the train had been watching our progress on their home screens, so I was given the same kind of deference that is given anybody—criminal, athlete or weatherman—who appears on television regularly. Just by being on the spot one is accorded the status of celebrity; as a result, from time to time the Johnson people would haul me out as an exhibit for visiting VIP's and I would use the opportunity to get their political views, which were always interesting and sometimes even helpful.

At about this time the *Saturday Evening Post* did a cover story on the Johnson campaign, and there was a big feature on me called "The Princess of the Press Corps." It was the kind of article that is nice for one's ego but not healthy for one's relationship with other reporters. In addition, there was the factor that by now more glamour was attached to network reporters than to the writing press. Also, the demands and economics of the two media exacerbated rivalries. TV deadlines are different from newspapers because television correspondents have to get their film to a city where it can be developed by show time, compared to writing for a morning paper, to which copy is sent by wire. It's heady stuff to hire a plane, fly into a strange city, be met by people from the local NBC affiliate, roar into town with a police escort, get the film developed and edited, and then appear on the air in the nick of time.

All of which is what I was doing as Lady Bird went through Alabama. I had chartered a plane to New Orleans, had been on the air, and was waiting at the New Orleans depot when her train pulled in. Also waiting was President Johnson, who had just arrived from a triumphant appearance in Louisville, where, he made a point of telling me, more people had turned out to see him than had ever showed up for anything, including the Kentucky Derby. Ebullient, he gave me a big kiss, and was anxious for all the gossip from the train.

Then we heard the whistle blowing down the track. True to form, the people in my crew were first off the train; while it was still moving, they ran ahead of it, and in a remarkable display of physical prowess set up at the end of the line and tossed me a mike, so that we were shooting our final chapter of the serial just as the train rolled to a stop. LBJ climbed aboard, surrounded by all those "Ladies for Lyndon" in their red-white-and-blue outfits waving their straw hats and pennants, and gave Lady Bird a big kiss as if on cue while I did the wrap-up on her saga through the South. The timing all around was impeccable; we ran out of film, but not before we recorded the last scene of this uniquely American campaign hoopla.

Having finished the Lady Bird assignment, I was through for the night, but I decided to stay to listen to LBJ's speech. I'm glad I did, because it was the best I ever heard him give. It was not only the highlight of his campaign, it was one of his finest hours. After you cover a campaign long enough you get bored; every speech is repetitious at least in part, because candidates can't write a new speech every day, so you recognize—sometimes even memorize involuntarily —various passages. But that night Johnson was different, both in manner and delivery. He had been briefed repeatedly on the extreme racial volatility of Louisiana, and had been told not to mention civil rights by his advisers, particularly by his old friend who was on the platform, Senator Ellender of Louisiana. As LBJ spoke, I watched the senator's face grow grumpier and grumpier.

While Johnson made an emotional appeal for racial equality, saying that prosperity must know no Mason-Dixon line, and that opportunity must know no color line, Ellender was listing to the other side, trying to put as much space as possible between himself and the President. Exhilarated by the record crowds of the last few days, LBJ was almost messianic as he warmed to his subject, a preacher who could not turn back. Afterward he was justifiably proud of himself, and he said to me, "I really gave it to them, didn't I?" Then he added, "They'd better not claim any more that I say one thing in the North and something else in the South."

At this moment Johnson was way ahead in the polls, and it could be argued that it was safe for him to lecture the South on racism that night. Even so, in the first half of the sixties, prejudice was high throughout the country, and it took courage as well as a special instinct for the President to know that the time was right for him to go to the South and lecture the people there on racism. His total dedication to equality, combined with an exquisite sense of timing prompted the only criticism I ever heard him make of President Kennedy. During the civil rights march on Washington in August 1963, LBJ thought that Kennedy should have seized that opportunity to help the black cause and gone to the Lincoln Memorial to speak to the crowd, instead of "sitting in the White House."

Johnson liked to tell you that he was the Majority Leader when the civil rights bill passed in the Senate. Now, as a Southern President, he knew that he was in a unique position to rectify some of the racial wrongs over the years, and he savored the opportunity and embraced it.

Only Johnson knows why he pretended in later life that he did not want to be President. Frequently he had talked with me about how he could capture the nomination, the tactics he would employ, how he was wooing various national committeemen, and how popular he was in certain areas (usually he mentioned big cities, for he was proudest of his following there, especially if they were in the East).

After LBJ had succeeded to the Presidency and the 1964 campaign was approaching, we were invited to a little dinner at the White House on the third floor. During that evening it was impossible to talk of anything else but the forthcoming campaign. Columnist Joe Alsop tried to change the subject occasionally, but with no success, and Lady Bird fared no better; LBJ was only exasperated by their interruptions. Soon he picked up a large loose-leaf notebook about four inches thick which gave a rundown on each state and his chances of carrying it, and made us listen as he went through it page by page. Inexorably he went over every facet of the forthcoming campaign, including elaborate polls on every conceivable issue to help him plan his strategy. Later LBJ gave me as an exclusive a copy of a major poll he had had commissioned to test his running strength with a number of potential vice-presidential candidates. The conclusion of the poll was that he could run with a monkey and it would make no difference.

Although LBJ had kept Bobby off the ticket in 1964, the Kennedys still bedeviled him even on election night when he was racking up one of the biggest majorities in a landslide incomparable to any in election history. As he stood watching the returns on television Bobby Kennedy, who had run for the Senate after he was barred from the Vice Presidency, appeared on camera to make his victory speech. LBJ had campaigned for Bobby both in New York City and throughout the state, and felt he had done much more than could be expected of him. Also, Bobby's victory margin was enhanced by—indeed, was perhaps solely due to—LBJ's overwhelming landslide. Yet Kennedy's victory statement—a long one in which he carefully thanked many people, including members of his family and previously unknown ward politicians—did not so much as whisper the President's name.

Watching the performance miles away in a little Texas hotel room, LBJ was transfixed, oblivious of those around him. Speaking softly to himself, he asked, "I wonder why he doesn't mention me?" And he repeated it a few more times. It was one of LBJ's greatest triumphs, a moment in which he had the country at his feet, yet it was marred for him because the Kennedys were not acclaiming him, let alone giving him credit.

In his book, LBJ mentions none of this. Instead, he writes that of the thousands of words written and spoken about the size and nature of his victory, those he liked the best were made three years later—in a speech by Senator Robert F. Kennedy to New York State Democrats on June 2, 1967:

> "In 1964 [President Johnson] won the greatest popular victory in modern times . . . He has gained huge popularity, but he has never failed to spend it in the pursuit of his beliefs or in the interest of his country.

He has led us to build schools and clinics and homes and hospitals, to clean the water and to clear the air, to rebuild the city and to recapture the beauty of the countryside, to educate children and to heal the sick and comfort the oppressed on a scale unmatched in our history."

Election night of 1964 was highly revealing of Johnson in other ways. Phil Potter of the Baltimore *Sun* and I were the only reporters who had been there four years previously, when LBJ was elected Vice President, so we were invited into the inner sanctum to watch the returns with a handful of his old friends—an invitation which naturally infuriated the hundred other reporters left outside. It was typical of LBJ to remember, in time of glory, those who, like Phil and me, had been around when he wasn't so important—and never mind that it had been an assignment editor who was really responsible.

As we stood looking at the television screen I thought of Walter Jenkins, who had done so much to establish the victory but who could not be there because he had recently been arrested on morals charges. I said to LBJ, "The only person missing I really wish was here is Walter." At this LBJ asked me if I felt that someone had been out to "get" Walter, and he indicated that he thought there was. Then he said, "A man has the kind of problem that Walter had if he has a domineering mother, a wife who is a problem, or a boss who demands too much—and Walter had all three." After an extended pause he said angrily, "Don't you worry about Walter. I'll take care of him, just the way I took care of John Connally"—a comment that would have greatly irritated the then governor of Texas, a man who liked to think he'd made it on his own.

On January 4, 1965, Johnson made his first State of the Union address after having been elected in his own right. He gave it at night —something that hadn't been done since FDR—and afterward he came to a party Dick and I gave for him at the F Street Club. It was a very special gathering that included both reporters and other friends, many of whom came directly from the Capitol after the speech.

Flying in from California for the speech was Lloyd Hand, an instant celebrity because that day he had been appointed Chief of Protocol. Lloyd was an old friend from campaign days and relatively unknown to Washington, so people wanted to meet him. The French ambassador, Hervé Alphand, and his wife had just returned from Paris that day and were there. Gerald Ford and his wife, Betty, whom I had known longer than I had known all the Democrats there, came. That day he had unseated Charlie Halleck to become the new GOP Minority Leader and was now a power to be reckoned with, an emerging Republican at a time when the party was in the doldrums, still staggering to re-establish itself after the stunning Goldwater defeat. Washington *Post* publisher Katharine Graham had been invited and her office called to ask if she could bring an escort. Of course I said yes, and asked his name. It was Adlai Stevenson, which made her the envy of many of the women present.

That night LBJ was jubilant. The assassination was beginning to recede in the national conscience, and he was emerging as his own man, and enjoying it to the hilt. He had used his extraordinary influence in Congress to win approval of his War on Poverty, and he was convinced that we were on the threshold of a new day for America and all its citizens.

Ten days later, just before the inauguration, I had a miscarriage, which is always a depressing experience. The Johnsons sent flowers to Georgetown Hospital, and if your flowers come with a label that says, "From the White House Florist," you can be sure that you will receive deferential treatment from every nurse on the floor. NBC was also considerate, and since I was going to help cover the event, let me hire my former assistant, M'Liz Beardsley, to help me do research at the hospital about inaugurations.

Almost in one motion I was out of bed and started reporting the story. Dick and I had been invited to the special church services that morning, when no television cameras were permitted, and later I went on the air to report the details, particularly the quaint prayer of the preacher, who called on the Almighty to look with favor "on thy servant, Lyndon, and thy servant, Hubert."

Though the networks and Capitol officials had imposed stern restrictions on reporters permitted inside the Rotunda, so that none would have an advantage, the Capitol Hill policemen were still my friends, and it was thanks to them that I was the only reporter in the corridor giving the color as the President and his honor reception committee walked by. Because of my recent hospitalization LBJ stopped to say, "Hello, Nancy," and ask how I was, all on live television. Having set the pattern, he was emulated by most of the senators and congressmen who accompanied him out to the podium, which gave NBC an added fillip to its coverage. It was hardly earth-shaking, but it enraged the other networks, and during the inaugural address I was ejected from my spot in the corridor!

At the Inaugural Ball that night, NBC continued to be solicitous of my health, and Julian Goodman, by then the NBC president, came up to the broadcast booth to thank me for being there. I couldn't have felt better, all dressed up in a new dress that had a turtleneck. (My trademark on the air was a turtleneck blouse with a suit because Murrow had warned me that it was enough of a shock to have a woman give the news, and that I shouldn't wear frilly clothes that might suggest frivolity. Mollie Parnis, the designer, has good sense about such things, and produced a white dress made totally of beads—with a turtleneck.)

One goal of Inaugural Ball coverage is to get as many VIP's as possible on the air, and I had some expert assistance from David Merrick, the Broadway producer. David is an old friend of Dick's, and though he has the reputation of being the devil incarnate, I find him both amusing and benign. A few months earlier, at the Republican convention in San Francisco, Goldwater supporters had taken the title tune from Merrick's hit *Hello, Dolly!* and were blasting "Hello, Barry!"—with special lyrics—through loudspeakers all over the city. Merrick was furious because he's a Democrat and did not agree with anything that Barry Goldwater stood for. But he is also a great publicist and saw an opportunity, so he sent me a message from New York to say that he was going to sue Barry Goldwater and the Republican National Committee. Whereupon I wrote a little piece for the NBC hotline (an internal wire for convention reporters), which so struck David Brinkley's fancy that he used it on prime time that night. Needless to say, back in New York City the "abominable showman" grinned wickedly from ear to ear. Later David gave "Hello, Dolly!" to President Johnson during the Democratic convention in Atlantic City, and a special version of "Hello, Lyndon!" was performed by Carol Channing. Now, pleased by all that coverage, David was anxious to reciprocate, and offered his services as floorman on the night of the Inaugural Ball. As my runner, New York's biggest and busiest producer did a superb job. Almost everything David does eventually leads to some publicity for himself, but I didn't mind because it was good for the show when I interviewed him, with the band playing "Hello, Lyndon!," just as the newly inaugurated President made his entrance. All in all, it was a very nice party.

CHAPTER 16 ⌒

Lady Bird Johnson wanted her life to have a purpose, she wanted to learn, and she wanted to make the opportunity of living in the White House meaningful. Though she grew up in comfortable circumstances in the rural South, as a child she was not surrounded by the sophisticated accouterments of the Eastern seaboard or the very rich. One night when she and the President dropped me off at Merrywood after a dinner party, it was endearing to see how pleased she was to be able to identify an Aubusson rug and a Palladian window. Everywhere she went she studied the history and landmarks of each place beforehand and made a point of seeing them, whether it was the klongs of Bangkok or the site of Custer's last stand.

Lady Bird made a receiving line an experience rather than a perfunctory greeting. The Johnson receiving lines were probably the slowest in history because the President and Lady Bird always had something to say to everybody. When she visited the White House before LBJ became President, it meant so much to her that she wanted it to be the same for those who came there while she was First Lady. On the day of a reception or dinner she would go to the beauty parlor; while her hair was being done she would study the guest list and phone her office continuously with questions about guests so that later she could talk intelligently with them.

From the first, Lady Bird's voice and accent were against her. The twang peculiar to the rural area of East Texas of her youth was generally considered by the Eastern establishment—quite wrongly— indicative of an uneducated woman. Even her name, Lady Bird, was against her. Once, after she and LBJ were official delegates to the Jamaica independence ceremony, she told me that she naturally signed the official guest book as "Lady Bird Johnson." Equally naturally, the British followed their custom, and while no one called him "Lord Johnson," they all addressed her as "Lady Bird." She said if

135

she had her life to live over, she would get rid of her nickname and have a "nose job." Her long nose does not photograph well, and in person she is immeasurably better-looking than in her pictures.

When the Johnsons moved into the White House, Lady Bird immediately charted her own course of action, and within a few weeks I accompanied her to the Pennsylvania coal country to inspect what she called the "pockets of poverty." Afterward she gave me her first exclusive interview as First Lady for a Sunday-afternoon program on NBC. It was an example of trying to do too many things too soon, but the network was pushing me, I was pushing her, and she agreed. It was a coup to get that first interview; Jackie had given only one on television, and there was great competition among the networks to be the first with Mrs. Johnson. Unfortunately, the make-up person didn't have enough light and did a miserable job. I put a mike on Lady Bird, and as we left the powder room, with me carrying the long black cord that emerged from her hem, she said she felt just like a dog on a leash—which, she joked, was symbolic of her life during the past few weeks.

A few days later the Johnsons watched the program from Camp David. Afterward LBJ leaned over, patted her hand and said, "I guess television just isn't our medium." But one failure was not enough to deter either of them, and they never stopped trying to improve their performances, though she was more successful than he.

It was widely predicted that, like Eleanor Roosevelt, Lady Bird would be an extra pair of eyes and ears for her husband, and she was. Moreover, he listened to her and respected her views, and she was a constant observer and reporter for him. For example, I once told Jack Valenti that I thought Defense Secretary McNamara was souring on the President's Vietnam policy. Shortly thereafter I was upstairs at the White House when Mrs. Johnson took me off to her little private office and asked me about it; she wanted to hear it firsthand.

Lady Bird's great accomplishment was that she could carve her own role in life and still be the helpful and soothing wife of a restless volcano. She kept LBJ human and acted as a counterbalance. Her choice of beautification as her pet project shows how perceptive she was; beautification was probably the only subject that LBJ would have let her handle without jealousy. He really wanted to run everything, but somehow in his mind beautification was more properly a woman's pursuit. Not that he didn't join in and help even there; in fact, he simply couldn't stay away. And he loved to joke that he could never settle down for a little afternoon nap without the whole White House becoming noisy while Laurance Rockefeller and a group of ladies planned ways to keep America beautiful. But whenever appropriations were lagging or laws for Lady Bird's projects were floundering, such as antibillboard provisions or prohibitions against used-car dumps along federal highways, LBJ would personally phone key legislators to ask their help.

To be her own woman, and simultaneously be a wife, mother, hostess and First Lady took incredible wisdom and stamina. When I was marveling about this one day to Luci, she answered, "What else would you expect of Lyndon Johnson's wife?" He wanted his three women to be the best-dressed, smartest, most intelligent, best-mannered, most chic—in fact, the most of everything. But even Lady Bird did not have time to do everything. As one of her top aides explained it to me, at one point she had made a conscious decision that she would be a wife first and a mother second. Since she didn't have as much time for the girls as she would have liked during their early years, she tried hard to compensate later.

LBJ loved and respected Lady Bird, and he was proud of her. But this does not mean he did not admire other women. He did, particularly pretty women, and all those who reminded him of his mother, which added up to a considerable number of us. Lady Bird understood this, and always instructed the social secretaries to seat an attractive woman on each side of him at dinner. But while Lyndon Johnson aspired to many things in life, not even he thought of himself as a national sex symbol—an image evoked by the posthumous stories about his sexual prowess when a spate of women claimed to have had affairs with him. I'm skeptical of some of those reports, which often were wildly exaggerated. For instance, one woman's whole career was built on her supposed association with LBJ, when in point of fact the time she spent in the presence of the President is logged as one hour and forty-five minutes. Unless you were prepared for the "Johnson Treatment" it could be overwhelming—especially at the White House, where a President's choice of favorites is emulated by his staff. It's very heady stuff to be told by a President that he needs you, and LBJ could make it sound as if he were incapable of running the world without your specific presence.

But it wasn't just in Washington that this ego-boosting took place.

At his ranch when he wanted to lose steam and was cavorting about in his car looking for deer, he could give anyone, man or woman, a big build-up, and if you weren't used to that sort of thing—and who is?—you could feel like a king or queen. What was endearing about it was that he'd give the same treatment to Cousin Oriole, his elderly deaf cousin who lived on the ranch, as to a beautiful or merely interesting young woman. It was all just one more example of his overblown rhetoric, and anyone who didn't know how to cope with such attention was apt to take it for meaning more than it did.

(Not only in sex and politics was Johnson prone to exaggeration. One day his hand was bandaged and I asked him what the problem was. Looking like his own beagle, he answered woefully, "Cancer." "My God," I said. "I'm terribly sorry." Just then our conversation was interrupted, but before I went on the air to announce that the Vice President of the United States had cancer I checked with his office. No cancer; he'd had a small wart removed.)

The most publicized Johnson relationship was announced posthumously by Doris Kearns, a White House Fellow from Harvard who had worked on his book with him. She told interviewers that in his last years LBJ wanted to marry her, a point that Johnson loyalists vigorously deny. She may have been one more victim of the Johnson Treatment. He could say "I need you" and be sincere, but it didn't mean that he wanted to jump in bed with you at that moment.

Like other powerful men, LBJ liked to feel that he had a call on you. Right after Dick and I were married he invited us to a Saturday-night party, but I sent word back that we were spending the night with the three girls. LBJ got on the phone, raised the devil, said he needed me (us), wanted me (us), and that it was a sorry state of affairs when baby-sitting took precedence over the Vice President of the United States. Often what he really wanted was nothing more than a playmate. His ego needed such nurturing and his energies were so inexhaustible that it was beyond the ability of any one person to handle. Lady Bird tolerated—in fact, welcomed—such companions, who usually were nothing more than an adoring audience. (Not that he wanted a bunch of bunnies for company. He thought that women could be smart and have as much sense as men, and he didn't tolerate dummies of either sex.)

Lady Bird was secure in the knowledge that LBJ's love for her superseded any sexual desire, or even sexual relationship. In her realm she had no peer; she knew it, he knew it, and so did everybody else. Which is not to say that she approved possible other relationships. The only time anyone broached the subject with her in public was during a television interview with Barbara Walters on the *Today* show, when she answered that her husband was a people lover, that women were people, and that she thought she could learn a great deal from those ladies. Perhaps it was her own philosophy that was reflected one day in private when she first learned about the love affair between Lucy Mercer and FDR. She said she was sorry that Mrs. Roosevelt had made so much of it because, as Lady Bird put it, "It was only a fly on the wedding cake."

According to the audience mail sent to NBC, there was considerable speculation about LBJ and me—a direct result of his calling me by my first name and of my interviewing him so frequently at crucial moments during conventions. I hereby end the speculation: I loved being with LBJ, but sex had nothing to do with it. I enjoyed him because power is fascinating. It was immensely flattering to be sought after and respected by him. Besides, he could be tremendously charming, witty and downright funny. There really is no way to describe the way he would talk, explain, cajole and tell stories. As Scotty Reston of the *New York Times* once wrote, a recording was the only way to capture the essence of the man. (His daughter Lynda tried to get him to let her tape his raconteuring, but he wouldn't do it.) He liked to tease and flirt, and when he wanted to be funny, he could tell a story better than anyone. Indeed, he was such a superb mimic, often brutally so, that he would have done well on the stage.

Johnson was fascinated by my love life, would bluntly ask about any man he saw me with—as well as many he didn't see me with—and would offer unsolicited comments and advice which were amusing and often perceptive. But though he might talk about sex, it was mostly just that—talk. In fact, he only really propositioned me once. I use the word "propositioned" in the old-fashioned way, since he was rather old-fashioned about it. It was after a long exhausting day on the campaign trail in Chicago, and he'd had a few drinks. We were all staying at the airport motel, and he was wandering around in his pajamas when he found me in my room. It wasn't very romantic; he kept pacing back and forth in his bare feet, waving his arms, and I had curlers in my hair. No hearts-and-flowers scene. It became even less romantic shortly thereafter when there was a knock on the door.

This time it was Bill Moyers. Lady Bird had sent the former divinity student out to retrieve her husband, whose pajama-clad figure was by then strutting all around my room. LBJ was astonished to see Bill, but not really angry. He just muttered something like "What the hell is he doing here?" and then, his audience having been increased by one, quickly returned to his diatribe. Bill discreetly shut the door and kind of hovered near it. He has a pixielike sense of humor, and I could see he was trying hard not to laugh. He had a silly look on his face which probably matched my own, but he was the essence of savoir-faire as he first gently and then more sternly suggested that everyone get some sleep—alone. I never took the proposition very seriously because Bill was there for most of it and because LBJ truly was more interested in talking politics than sex.

I have been told firsthand about LBJ's amorous pursuits; some of the stories are plausible, others simply not true. However, there are so many accounts that there will always be questions about the subject. My own belief is that the only meaningful affair that he ever had predated his Presidency, and I doubt whether anyone will ever know about it. As for me, I just never thought he was very sexy.

CHAPTER 17

Historians will long ponder whether we would have been so involved in Vietnam if Kennedy had lived. His loyalists fervently believe that we would not, because Kennedy had always said that he wouldn't—but then, so did Johnson. Still, even if one believes that Kennedy could have reversed his initial build-up, the fact remains that his staff bears some responsibility for what followed.

LBJ always felt that his own staff was inferior to JFK's, and he was determined to retain as many Kennedy aides as possible. This was his downfall. Since he was often intimidated by the "Kennedy crowd," and since he was filled with self-doubts about his own judgment in foreign affairs, it was a ready-made situation for a man like Walt Rostow to exert undue influence—certainly more influence than any man could have had in the domestic field, where Johnson was confident of himself. Eventually Rostow had as much influence on LBJ as Kissinger has had on subsequent Presidents.

One of the ironies of Vietnam is that Walt Rostow, the hawk from M.I.T., had originally been brought to Washington by Senator Fulbright, the dove who later became the most outspoken critic of the war. Fulbright had seen a Rostow piece in the *New York Times Magazine,* and asked Carl Marcy why the Senate Foreign Relations Committee didn't have such brilliant analysts. Marcy discussed it with Francis Valeo, then on the committee staff, and they suggested that experts from the Library of Congress be consulted. But Fulbright insisted on Rostow.

If LBJ had been beguiled on his first trip to Vietnam in 1961, Rostow had been even more so. Along with General Maxwell Taylor, he had been among the first to suggest to Kennedy that a U.S. military task force be sent to Vietnam to carry out combat operations in an emergency.

One run-in that I had with Rostow was enough to convince me that he was a highly nervous and excitable fellow who so lacked common sense that it was impossible not to question his judgment on everything. It was in January 1968, a time when there were constant rumors of enemy peace feelers, as well as a crescendo of demands that we try to talk directly with the North Vietnamese. Although initiatives were being urged from all quarters, especially from England and France, there seemed little hard evidence that the North Vietnamese would even listen, let alone respond. In this climate it was decided that Prince Sihanouk, the Cambodian leader who had close contacts with both the North Vietnamese and the Chinese, might be the perfect conduit. Sihanouk was trying to walk a middle road between the two sides; he was considered friendly to the Communists, but he also had invited Jacqueline Kennedy to visit the ruins of Ankor Wat, and had permitted his land to be secretly used by us for search-and-destroy missions. Therefore his services as negotiator or go-between were highly touted by people anxious to try anything to extricate us from the war, and it was a front-page story.

There was further debate over who should make the initial contact with Sihanouk, and some speculation that Mike Mansfield would be chosen because he knew the prince and corresponded with him regularly. However, through contacts on Capitol Hill, I found out that Chester Bowles, then our ambassador to India, had been chosen instead. It was a respectable scoop, and we were going to lead off the

NBC evening news with it. Since I didn't get the story until late in the afternoon, there was no time to find out more details. For instance, was Bowles chosen because he was already on the spot in India or because Sihanouk felt that Bowles was close to the Kennedys? (He was not, but it was thought that Sihanouk may have believed he was.)

In an effort to answer some of these questions, I phoned Walt Rostow just before air time, told him that I knew about Bowles's role, that we were leading the news with it, and could he give me some background and pertinent data to flesh out the story?

There followed an incredible conversation. First Rostow said that if I could only see what was on his desk, I certainly wouldn't use the story. When I asked what it was, he said that he couldn't tell me. I pointed out that the announcement was to be made shortly in any case, and I couldn't see why I shouldn't go ahead with my scoop. To this Rostow answered, "In my entire life in Washington I have never asked a reporter not to use a story, but I am respectfully asking you now." He added that in my business he knew that "nice guys finish last," but "for the good of the country, please don't broadcast this one." I replied that although I was a reporter, I liked to think that I was as patriotic as anyone, and that I certainly did not want to imperil the security of the United States. He kept repeating, "If only you could see what's on my desk!" and was so agitated that I decided I'd better kill the story.

I had phoned Rostow from the office of Irv Margolis, a dynamic young man who was in charge of NBC's local Washington news. He had heard the conversation and suggested that I check with Reuven Frank, the NBC News president in New York, since it's a highly unusual step to withhold news at government request. Certainly I had never been confronted by the situation before. After telling Frank about Rostow's request and his use of phrases like "our boys are dying in Vietnam," Reuven concurred and the story was cut.

That night the early editions of the Washington *Post* came out with banner headlines that Bowles was going to Cambodia to see Sihanouk in a major peace initiative. I was furious, not only because I had worked on the story for weeks and was scooped on it, but because by this time I was so opposed to the war that I had wanted to be in on the announcement of the initiative.

My visit the next morning to Rostow's White House office was not rewarding. When asked again what had been so important on his desk that I couldn't use the story while the *Post* had it in banner headlines, Rostow said, "Let me show you these captured enemy documents." The documents had absolutely nothing to do with Sihanouk. At that time captured enemy documents were a dime a dozen, and were handed out at every opportunity by the Administration to try to con reporters into painting a rosier view of the war. (Subsequently it was charged that such enemy documents were doctored by our own people to suit their purposes.)

I was flabbergasted, and repeated my question: What is so important? This time around Rostow showed me a routine State Department wire asking that the announcement of the Bowles trip be held up for a few hours because Sihanouk had not yet decided on the dinner menu for the meeting. At first I thought he was kidding. I couldn't believe him. Helplessly I held up the wire, pointed to the headlines in the morning *Post* and asked again how the scoop could possibly jeopardize the security of the United States. It didn't make sense then and it still doesn't.

Rostow kept jumping around his little office like a grasshopper, flitting from one phone call to the next. It was a comical scene, and I might have laughed at it and at myself for getting so upset if I had not been so fed up with the man and with the surrealistic smile on his face. Also, I kept thinking that only hours before, Rostow had been talking about ". . . boys dying in Viet Nam."

Afterward nobody at NBC said much about the incident, but I felt pretty stupid. To top it all off, it turned out that Sihanouk wasn't much of a peace negotiator and that nothing came of the initiative. Later at a convention of radio and television news directors I mentioned this episode as an example of governmental attempts to manage the news. When Rostow was asked about it, he said that he couldn't remember it.

This incident was not an aberration on the part of Rostow; it was typical of his judgment, and of the way the war was run from Washington. Naïvely, I thought that when LBJ heard about it he would raise a fuss, as he had at other times, but I was wrong. By then he was too weary; more significant, he had relegated me, professionally at least, to being one of "them"—meaning "all those reporters who are against me on the war." My position on Vietnam had evolved from the standard patriotic support for U.S. policy to total opposition. As the years went by, it was clear that we were intruding in a civil war, fighting in the wrong place at the wrong time for a cause which our allies did not cherish as much as we, and in which our enemies were perceived to be fighting for the traditional American ideals.

Just two years after his historic landslide, Johnson began to lose popularity in the polls. The war was going badly, the country was restless, LBJ was bogged down in a quagmire, and frustration was the national mood. More and more citizens were beginning to think Vietnam was a madness, and it became apparent that those who made policy were bereft of ideas. As Johnson and the Kennedy holdovers steadily escalated the war, the sense of outrage throughout the country also increased. But it was an ineffectual rage because it lacked a single spokesman.

As always, I was looking for a story, so in October 1967 I called Senator Eugene McCarthy, who always was good copy because he was provocative. I had known him since he came to the House, when he used to wile away his time in the press gallery making acerbic remarks on a variety of subjects. His offbeat observations were an amusing relief in the political arena, where wit and humor are rare. When I called him he said that something was bothering him, and that he'd like to talk about it in his office.

It's well known that McCarthy can't say yes or no. His every comment is cloaked in ambiguity, which to his supporters suggests great wisdom, and to others connotes confusion. But now, contrary to his usual vagueness, he was clearly concerned that Johnson and the Pentagon were going to continue to escalate the war, and he was determined to do something about it. When I asked him if he would spearhead a movement, he kept saying, "Someone has to do it." It was as if he were trying to talk himself into it. Johnson and those around him were out of touch with the country, he said, and had no idea of the extent of the unpopularity of the war. Antiwar sentiment was widespread, he was certain, but it could be harnessed only if the protestors could coalesce around one person who would personify the cause. Finally, he came right out with it and stated that if someone else of stature didn't lead the dissenters, he would do it himself.

A Democratic senator willing to put his neck on the block and start a "dump Johnson" move was news, but I had seen too many other good stories turned down by the producers of the Huntley-Brinkley program to offer this one to them. Instead I called the *Today* show, but they were unimpressed. It wasn't important, they said. What makes news is always open to question—it's one person's judgment against another's—but the New York City network mentality has often had a provincial attitude toward what is news throughout the country, and particularly what constitutes a good news story from Washington. The news staff of the *Today* program simply did not include a "dump Johnson" movement in their preconceived ideas of what was newsworthy in the capital, and I couldn't change their minds.

Thus frustrated, I offered the story to Irv Margolis, and he put it on the air locally in Washington. Unbeknownst to me, however, he sent a tape of it on the cable to New York, where the news director of the local NBC station also broadcast it, accurately assessing its importance. Bill McAndrew had unfailing instincts about a story, and when he heard the item, he said he wanted it to lead the next network news program—the *Today* show.

Often networks are just as inefficient as government bureaucracies. McAndrew's orders got lost until the *Today* newswriting team reported for work. Since he rarely interfered on such specifics as which story should begin a program, his order created a stir, and I was awakened at 2 a.m. by the *Today* program with a request that I lead off with the McCarthy story in the morning. Half asleep, I argued with them, pointing out coldly that they had already turned down the piece, but when they told me that McAndrew had ordered it I agreed to do it, because I would have done anything for him.

Besides, there's something about being a reporter that gets in your blood, and such a news story comes along rarely. Although I knew it was important, I had no idea that night how far the McCarthy campaign would go. By providing a figurehead for the protesters to rally around, McCarthy came to personify antiwar sentiment, and thus set in motion events which ultimately led to the downfall and resignation of President Johnson.

By March of 1968 it had become clear LBJ couldn't get out of the war and he couldn't win it. He was frustrated, and so was the nation. As he saw it, there was nothing to do except resign. He had lost the respect of the people, and while he could still convince some leaders and some small groups, the people were against him. He did not have the Churchillian ability to exhort the masses and they left him on the war in Vietnam. Thus deserted, he himself left the White House. His announcement astonished almost all of his closest associates and everyone else, including one senator who was having a drink while watching the speech on television. When LBJ said that he wouldn't be a candidate again, the senator poured his drink down the kitchen sink, deciding that either he'd had too many or that he couldn't hear properly.

Watching that speech, I was deeply sorry for LBJ. I know that he felt desperately inadequate because he had been unable to stop the war, and I also knew that it was far tougher for him to resign than to stay on. He had entered the White House thinking that he could do better than anyone else; he left knowing that only another President could end the war.

CHAPTER 18

At the time, Bobby Kennedy's murder seemed to me to be even more tragic than his brother's, because in death JFK at least left a legacy of hope, whereas Bobby was cut down before he had his full chance. Catholics sometimes have an easier time accepting tragedy because they are sustained by their religion, but this time my faith was of no help. Coming so soon after the assassination of Martin Luther King, Jr., it seemed triply senseless. I did a broadcast about the Jordanian embassy dissociating itself from Sirhan Sirhan, who was of Jordanian ancestry, but as I spoke I remember thinking that it didn't make much difference. Most of what was said on the air was meaningless. Only Art Buchwald seemed relevant as he told lovely anecdotes about his close friend, the late senator.

Once again the Kennedys, as flawed as any of us in life, seemed superhuman in facing death. Ethel Kennedy is one of the world's most joyous people, and the extraordinary courage and love she displayed at the time was a national treasure and great help to all who knew her and Senator Kennedy. Inspired by her example, I was determined to go to the funeral in New York, even though I was about to have a baby. The airline, understandably skittish about pregnant women as passengers, protested mildly, but since I'd only gained about ten pounds I convinced the agent that birth was not imminent.

The funeral was an extraordinary combination of organization and love. There is a Kennedy network that takes over in times of crises: the apex is the family office in New York, which is abetted by friends and supporters who suddenly appear from all over to man impromptu offices. They sent wires to those who should be invited, carefully keeping the seating areas for close friends apart from more casual ones and officials. The most poignant moment for me came when Andy Williams sang "The Battle Hymn of the Republic," chosen to epitomize Bobby's intensive fight for Negro rights. Looking across the aisle I saw Thurgood Marshall, the first black appointed to the Supreme Court, with tears streaming down his face.

I wanted to take the funeral train back to Washington but didn't dare to; it was hot, and we weren't sure when the baby was due. Michael, then five years old, was growing as impatient as I was with the long pregnancy. I've always thought that God could have arranged a shorter gestation for humans, a point with which Michael concurred. He kept asking me to take him swimming, and I had to keep turning him down, saying, "Wait till the new baby comes." Bored with this answer, he told me to lean over and open my mouth; then with undisguised impatience he shouted down my throat, "New baby! Hurry up and come!"

On July Fourth we went to the Bartletts' traditional party. Mrs. Longworth, who was there, was convinced I had made a mistake about the arrival date; in fact, she professed to think I wasn't having a baby at all. But though he had kept himself inconspicuous, I decided it was time for him to make an entrance. Besides, if he waited much longer, I wouldn't be able to go to the GOP convention in Florida at the end of July.

Induced labor had been an unpleasant experience and I had decided not to go through it again, but in pregnancies, as in some other areas, I believe that the mind can dominate and even instigate. In my mind, it was time for delivery, and so I did my last regularly scheduled newscast on Friday, July 5, told the office that I was going on maternity leave, had my hair done and went back to Merrywood.

Dick was on a business trip to Florida, and Ann and Jane were at camp, but Liz was home and I was counting on her to drive me to the hospital. I woke up that night at about one o'clock with the obvious signs that the baby was en route, but I could tell that I didn't need to hurry, so I began to read *All The King's Men* and had almost finished it before awakening Liz at five-thirty. She was endearing on the trip over to Georgetown, not knowing whether to go slowly and be late or to drive fast and trigger the baby's arrival by a bumpy ride. Once there, I phoned Dick, who was sound asleep in Fort Lauderdale; he kept saying drowsily, "That's nice, dear, call me when something happens." I found the remark infuriating; broadcasting up to delivery is one thing, but a phone call from the labor room seems a bit much, an opinion I managed to convey.

John Frederich arrived a few hours later, but with a proper sense of timing, not until five minutes after Dick had flown in from Florida. To the degree that Michael's birth was unpleasant, John's was a delight. Since I was older than most pregnant women, there was some cause for worry, and I had exacted a promise from Dr. Walsh that he would tell me right away if the baby was unhealthy in any way. But he arrived perfectly formed, with a head full of blond curls, screaming at full volume.

The following Monday, Robert Goralski substituted for me on my daily news show and announced the birth, which was a surprise to the viewing audience; as the camera took only waist shots, it wasn't known that I was pregnant.

Determined to avoid sibling rivalry, we had touted John Frederich —the middle name was my father's—as a new friend and playmate to Michael, and when we came home from the hospital, we arrived with presents for him from the new baby. It didn't work, though it might have if the nurse we had at first hadn't been such a pill. She wouldn't let Mike touch John, let alone play with him, and as attention naturally focused on the baby, Mike grew bored and suggested that since we'd acquired John at the hospital, we ought to send him back there. Luckily, Alma soon arrived to take care of John. She had a gentle, placid disposition, and thanks to her John is a happy, relaxed little creature who smiled at an earlier age than anyone who has ever lived.

Three weeks after the birth I was on my way to the Republican National Convention. It wasn't much of a show. Nelson Rockefeller flip-flopped in and out of the running, finally joining the race on the remarkable theory that the polls alone should determine the choice of a candidate. In fact, it was generally believed that Nixon was a loser nationally, popular only with the GOP faithful. However, just as the convention started, a Gallup poll came out declaring that Nixon was the most favored candidate, and that was the end of the contest. Congressman Mel Laird, the reigning kingmaker of modern times, gave me the scenario in advance: since Rockefeller had suggested that the polls should decide the candidate, Nixon would accept this criterion, and since the Gallup poll, which Laird calls the "granddaddy" of them all, showed that Nixon was on top, the contest was over. That's truly all there was to the convention; the rest was playacting to satisfy the carnival atmosphere of political conventions. At the time I did an analysis explaining the Laird scenario which was well received by the president of NBC News. Since then, as now, it was highly unusual to let a woman on a television network do news analysis, as opposed to spot reporting, I was immensely pleased by the compliment.

Dick had come to Miami with me, partly because he was involved in some real-estate transactions there and partly because conventions can be exciting. Tickets to them are often hard to get, but he ran into Betty Ford, so he sat with her in their box, a prime seat because Jerry was the convention chairman. While he was running the affair from the podium and I was running around the floor, Betty and Dick had a fine time and occasionally would sneak out for a drink.

My specific assignment at the convention was Spiro Agnew, then the nationally unknown Maryland governor. Months earlier I had broken the story that he was planning a "draft Rockefeller" movement against Nixon, a story considered sufficiently newsworthy to make the wires. Through this I had gotten to know him, and at the convention I was supposed to follow him everywhere he went. I didn't get on the air much because Agnew was considered only a remote possibility for running mate. He simply wasn't well enough known. But one afternoon before the voting of the delegates began, NBC got a tip that Agnew was going to play golf several miles away in Fort Lauderdale with Ohio Governor James A. Rhodes, and that the two men would decide where the so-called neutral block would cast its support. At this moment the support of the border-state governors was considered crucial; in fact, it was no longer essential because Nixon already had the nomination sewed up. But the story got a lot of play and was trumped up out of all proportion to accommodate the needs of the news media. It was also the kind of story which bolsters the egos of lesser politicians who must justify their presence at a convention and establish their role as being significant enough as kingmakers to merit future favors.

The golf match was cloaked in secrecy, and like a secret agent I hid in the back of a car so that no one would recognize me as we tailed Agnew to the Fort Lauderdale golf course, a remote spot chosen to escape the press. But the men's locker room was off bounds and I couldn't burst in on the two governors and surprise them. When they heard that I was outside, they slipped out a side door and escaped in a golf cart, taking their story and my scoop with them. Left standing on the green, I looked silly, felt silly, and found myself wondering whether the new mother of a three-week-old baby couldn't spend her time more profitably.

Since Agnew wasn't much in demand, I was, aside from the Maryland regulars, virtually the only reporter around his headquarters; only David Broder, Pulitzer Prize-winner from the Washington *Post*, had suggested that he would be Nixon's choice for Vice President. When the governor finally did get the word, I found out and tried desperately to get it on the air, but communications with headquarters had broken down and NBC News lost a chance to be first with the story. Communications are always tricky at a convention, but in this instance the arrogance and perhaps fatigue of some of my associates were also responsible. As the only major female correspondent covering the convention, I was beginning to suffer the backlash of women's lib. So far I had prospered fairly well in a man's world, but now that network executives were beginning to suffer from the birth pains of the movement, I bore the consequences of their male chauvinism and suddenly found myself relegated to second-class stories and position. In addition, a couple of them simply didn't think that I was very good at my job.

A network is such a highly competitive arena that working relationships are constantly exacerbated. I am impatient by nature and rarely hide my disgust at incompetence, so when I screamed into the intercom for the network control center with my Agnew scoop during the middle of the nightly news, I was put on hold. Naturally, I was furious, and the senator who had gone to considerable trouble to give me the story first never could understand how I got scooped.

I was always controversial at the networks. Aside from being the only female in my position, I irked some people. I was raising five children, working a full day and often at night and on Sundays, and I simply did not have time to waste. As a result I could be excessively abrupt, even arrogant, which naturally prompted retribution, and may have been the cause of the breakdown of communications that night in Florida. Agnew won, but NBC lost and so did I.

Like Michael, John had to wait so long for his baptism that my mother suggested that soon he would be able to walk down the aisle on his own. His godfather is Edward Bennett Williams, the brilliant criminal lawyer and president of the Redskins football team. In the courtroom or in his office Ed often paces the floor, and that afternoon he was vigorously pacing the back of Holy Trinity Church in Georgetown. Later I found out why: he was awaiting final word on his deal to hire Vince Lombardi as the new coach of the Redskins. It was a banner day for the Redskins as well as for the newest Dickerson; at the party to celebrate John's belated baptism his godfather showed up with a Redskins contract naming John the quarterback twenty years hence. John has already gone into training to prepare for the job.

CHAPTER 19 ⌒

The Democratic convention in Chicago in 1968 was a dark chapter in American political history. It's dreadful to be so outraged and so scared at the same time. I was caught in a collision between the police and the antiwar demonstrators, and was naïvely incredulous that people would push me or each other around so brutally. Equally surprising was the stench of tear gas; I had never realized that it smelled so bad, and it permeated the Hilton Hotel for days.

I've lost my notes of that convention, but looking back on it, I recall a mélange of conflicting scenes. I can hear the thud of police clubs hitting human bodies. I also remember seeing some McCarthy supporters turning large hotel ashtrays into lethal weapons as they hurled them down on policemen from the thirteenth floor. I recall

Senator Fred Harris, one of Humphrey's two campaign managers, sitting in his office out at the stockyards holding the hands of two of his children and openly weeping as they watched policemen use their clubs.

The convention documented Humphrey's inadequacies. He couldn't say where he stood on the issues, and he demonstrated a remarkable lack of political acumen. At one point he and his lieutenants so irritated the Johnson camp that there was talk of blocking him from the nomination. Maimed by the convention, his campaign floundered subsequently. He never discovered how to untie the umbilical cord that bound him to Lyndon Johnson; in fact, he never discovered his own political personality. His loyalties to LBJ were misplaced, and he found it hard to repudiate the bankrupt policies which he himself had so vigorously and publicly endorsed during the previous four years. It made no difference that he had privately written LBJ, urging withdrawal from Vietnam. This only earned him the enmity of Johnson and the lack of respect from his peers, who knew that in his heart Hubert Humphrey thought the Vietnam policy was wrong.

No one really knows why Hubert talks so much. Before he ran for the nomination in 1972, I had a long talk with him about it, and all his friends have discussed it with him, so he knows better. He pledged that he would cut short his speeches so that his campaign trains could run on time, but he never did. I well remember one hot night when Humphrey was talking on and on; the audience was growing more and more restless, and it seemed that he would never stop. At last his wife, Muriel, the marvelously gentle woman who has brought joy and balance to their lives, sent a small note up to the podium; it said, "Dear: Remember that for a speech to be immortal it need not be eternal."

Shortly after the 1968 convention we had a dinner party at Merrywood at which, as often happens in that dining room, guests jumped up to give toasts or make speeches. One of Humphrey's campaign managers, Senator Walter F. Mondale, an eloquent man, rose to his feet that evening to declare that he'd had enough. It was the first I knew that he was easing out of the campaign. He explained how tough it was, because of his personal friendship with Hubert and his long association with the Democratic party, to dissociate himself from both of them at this moment, but that he felt he had to do so

152

because of their stand on the war. After he sat down, our heretofore happy crowd was dead silent. No one knew what to say.

When Nixon squeaked through in November, the adjustment in Washington was not as traumatic as it normally would have been for a capital and bureaucracy attuned to a Democratic Administration. With the war hanging over us, we preferred to believe that any change was for the better, and the city gamely tried to discover virtues in Richard Nixon that had never been perceived before. I remember walking over to the Capitol Plaza with Wilbur Mills, then chairman of the House Ways and Means Committee and often referred to as the second most powerful man in Washington. As we looked at the wooden bleachers built for the forthcoming inauguration, Wilbur said, "You know, I'm not a Nixon hater, I never have been. I think the fellow might do all right." Even Walter Lippmann had come out for Nixon, declaring that after the flamboyance and frenetic activity of the Kennedy and Johnson administrations, the country was suffering from a hangover, and that Nixon was just what the doctor ordered. During the two previous administrations, three hundred and ninety new domestic social programs had been instituted. Now we were told that it was a time to cut back; the government would stop interfering with our daily lives, and there would be a new look at the war.

The transition between the Johnson and Nixon administrations was remarkably smooth, with cooperation on both sides, an example of democracy at its best. The Nixon crowd had a lot of new faces and displayed a new efficiency in its dealings with the press. There were innumerable briefings on how the inauguration and the Inaugural Ball were to be covered. In charge was Herb Klein, one of the nicest men ever to come to Washington and one of the few Nixon men of any prominence who is deservedly listed among the good guys. Taking me aside before the inauguration, he mentioned the Kennedy inauguration eight years earlier, when JFK had spent so much time talking to me in the Rotunda. "Would you like President Nixon to do the same thing?" he asked me. I said that it would be very nice indeed, but I couldn't conceal my surprise until Herb reminded me that it was at the Kennedy inauguration that I had introduced him to JFK, which was the only time he ever met the late President.

Herb must have briefed Mr. Nixon pretty well. On the morning

of the inauguration, after Johnson and Nixon had taken the traditional ride together to the Capitol in the presidential limousine,
Johnson, as was normal for him, came right over to my mike and said,
"Hello, Nancy." At the same time President-elect Nixon popped out
of the other side of the car and ran around so he could say, almost
in unison, "Hello, Nancy."

The inauguration itself was predictable: everything was very proper
—perhaps reassuring, but hardly exciting.

One of the most poignant moments of the day came at the airport,
when the Johnsons flew off to Texas. Most of the farewell was not
on television because it occurred while the inaugural parade was
passing in review before the White House, and the networks had
learned that if they switched away from a small-town marching band,
the complaints from that one town were louder than the band itself
—and that inevitably the marching group that was omitted included
the first cousin of a network vice president.

Out at the airport the farewell was emotional, full of love, friendship, joy and tears, and LBJ displayed loyalty, acerbic wit, humor and
more tears. Everyone had a little booze to stay warm on the windy
tarmac, and there was a feeling of love for one another and for the
country. Then he was standing at the top of the steps of *Air Force
One*, the last to enter, throwing kisses to everyone, prolonging the
inevitable as long as he could. Outwardly it was a happy occasion, but
inwardly we were all sad. While he made no apologies for a job he
thought he'd done as best as he could, he was frustrated that he
hadn't been able to get out of Vietnam. Surrounded by friends who
loved him, he took away with him perhaps the last personal Presidency.

The book Johnson later wrote attempts to put the best light on his
actions, which is understandable and hardly unusual, but he also
paints himself as that preacher I always thought he was trying to
emulate. The book seems defensive, self-serving and apologetic in
tone. It makes the turbulent seem calm, the chaotic seem tepid, and
his Administration like a weak drink—which it certainly never was.
When he wrote this final testament, apparently he did not dare to
be himself. An enigma to everyone around him, he often was to
himself as well. Although he was not introspective, he did have a
capacity for self-analysis, and once he said to me, "I'm just like a fox:

I can see the jugular in any man and go for it, but I always keep myself in rein. I keep myself on a leash, just like you would an animal."

I wept as the Johnsons left. By then I had separated from him completely on Vietnam, and he never forgave me for it, but I cried because I knew he had tried so hard to be right, and because he too had cried about the men we lost in Vietnam. As the big jet roared off, I remember hoping that Walter Lippmann was right when he said that the country needed a sobering influence like Richard Nixon to help us recover.

I didn't see much of LBJ after he left the White House: a few times when he visited Washington, and once when I went down for the dedication of the Johnson Library in Austin. He was in high spirits that day in May 1971, and there was a general outpouring of love and good will. It was the last time I ever saw him.

While dying is the quintessential individual experience, some are at least blessed to have a friend nearby when their spirit departs. Ironically, Johnson, who was not a private man, who loved a crowd, who freely discussed his most intimate thoughts, who shared his joy and sorrow with his friends and as large a portion of the world as he could encompass, was alone when he died.

LBJ had a premonition of death; he had invited Bobby Baker, his long-time aide, to visit him almost as if to say goodbye. He had seen the famous heart specialist Dr. Michael DeBakey, and had talked about having a pacemaker inserted but his heart wasn't considered strong enough to withstand either that or an operation for his painful diverticulitis.

After Johnson died, on January 22, 1973, they brought his body to Washington to lie in state in the Capitol Rotunda. I went up there alone to report it, not knowing that the rest of the press was leaving together at a specific time from the White House. Near Capitol Hill my cab couldn't get through because the area was cordoned off, and so I started walking up the long circular drive to the Senate. Once again the Capitol Hill policemen whom I knew so well let me through. Walking up the hill, remembering how many times I'd gone up it before to cover Senator, then Vice President, then President Johnson, I realized that this was the last time. I was so deep in my memories that I didn't notice until I'd almost reached the top that

155

I was the only person on the sidewalk. Then I saw that the rest of the press was behind barricades, and when I looked to the left I saw a line of black limousines. For some reason the official cortege was momentarily detained, and just as I glanced over Lady Bird, Lynda and Luci were all waving at me. It seemed so familiar; just as so often in the past, I was the only reporter allowed through. But though the scene was the same, this time there would be no exuberant "Hello, Nancy," and there never would be again. At that moment I couldn't help weeping a little bit for LBJ—and a little bit for me too, because of the parallel between our fortunes. When he had been at his peak, my professional career was going well. Now, on this cold January day I had just learned that several stations were going to drop my syndication because of the state of the economy.

The day of the funeral was perfect—cold but brilliantly sunny. Lady Bird was dignified, proud and splendid. President Nixon led the official mourners, and members of the establishment, including some of the hypocrites who had maligned him in life, were there in full force. In death they could not tarnish the moment which belonged to those loyalists who had stood by him through the years and knew how hard he had tried, especially on Vietnam. The day belonged to those who understood that although victory had eluded him and events had proved him wrong, he had given more than they could ask of themselves. Although they understood that trying was not enough, and that action is no substitute for wisdom or success, they knew that no man could have tried harder. It was for these people, and not for the Washington establishment, that the first line of the eulogy was intended. Marvin Watson, the Johnson friend and aide who also came from the Texas hill country, stood up and defiantly began, "He was ours and we loved him beyond all telling of it."

CHAPTER 20 ⌒⌒

When a new Administration takes over there's not only a political and legislative honeymoon, but a social one as well. This generally results in happy occasions when the President can do things and go places that his office inhibits him from enjoying later on.

In the first springtime of their Administration, the Nixons accepted an invitation from Senator and Mrs. Harry Byrd to their annual Apple Blossom luncheon in Winchester, Virginia. Dick and I were also invited and drove down, as did the other guests, but the Nixons arrived by presidential helicopter. Such an entrance is always exciting, particularly in a spot outside Washington when presidential comings and goings are not commonplace, and especially when the President is a new one and is arriving at a private party.

The Byrds had the friendliest house imaginable, of Southern architecture, with large, inviting, open rooms, and as guests entered they were embraced by the warmth of the Byrds and the graciousness of suburban life in Virginia. The family excelled in traditional Southern hospitality, so we ate and drank royally and had a happy time.

It was the first time that Pat Nixon had ever met my husband and she couldn't have been nicer. In turn, I had a long talk with the President, who gave me a detailed dissertation on personal style. He said that everything a leader does must exude confidence and convey the image that he is in charge. He cited De Gaulle as an example of a man whose mere presence exuded power. He did not think De Gaulle guilty of hauteur; rather, he found him strong and forceful, and the very qualities that made others think the man arrogant and imperious were what Nixon most admired. It was obvious that he had carefully studied De Gaulle's mannerisms, and later the Secretary of HEW, Robert Finch confirmed to me that the President indeed conscientiously tried to imitate De Gaulle.

As I reflected on this conversation later, I often wondered whether President Nixon ever did anything spontaneously. Both in word and in physical movement his responses always seemed to have been preprogramed and premeditated, as if he didn't trust his own instincts.

People are always curious to know about the differences at the White House when a new Administration moves in. Mrs. Longworth never said anything more true than this: when your crowd is in the White House, you like it just fine, but that when the other crowd is there, you criticize. Still, perhaps the tone set by the new First Family was best summarized by a society writer—obviously a Democrat—who said, "Were Calvin Coolidge to return to Washington today, he'd be known as 'The Playboy of the Potomac.'"

In commenting on his family's style, the President said that they were not "swingers," but that they "have a lot of fun." If so, it wasn't noticeable. When I asked Congressman Les Arends, the House GOP whip, what changes he thought the Nixons would bring, he said, "They'll bring back a little class." That wasn't noticeable, either.

At the end there was no entertaining at the Nixon White House, but in the beginning the family set records for the number of people invited. There were lots of movies, big musicales and receptions, but few small dinners. Reporters were never high on the Nixons' guest list, and in the last years none were invited, but I was the first woman correspondent to be asked to a Nixon state dinner, and was very pleased to be there. (I always will be. I remember that when I first came to Washington, Senator Green told me that one should never turn down a White House invitation. The subject came up because Tom Connally, chairman of the Senate Foreign Relations Committee, had first accepted a White House invitation and then canceled out an hour before the lunch; the Reverend Billy Graham was coming to see him and Connally thought his visit would be more politically advantageous than going to the White House. Green was shocked by this, and lectured me never to do the same.)

The dinner was for the Japanese Prime Minister Eisaku Sato, who had recently been re-elected. On such occasions the guests have a cocktail in the East Ballroom while awaiting the President's entrance. But the guests make entrances too; you enter on the arm of a White House aide, your husband or escort following you, as a military aide announces your name over a loudspeaker. Everyone turns around to stare at you—sometimes to see what you're wearing, often to ponder why you're there; in fact, it's the only social event where you can stare with impunity, because everyone else is staring too. I can remember Bob Hope, certainly among the best-known men in the world, looking around the room goggle-eyed and asking me who was who. Then, after the President and his wife appear, the guests are lined up by White House aides to go through the receiving line, the foreign dignitaries by protocal, the rest alphabetically. The man precedes the woman, and tells his name to the Chief of Protocal, who in turn repeats the name to the President.

As we were standing around with our drinks, a man with the most engaging face came up to me and eagerly asked, "Are you Nancy Dickerson?" When I said I was, he said, "I'm Andy Wyeth and I adore you." Andy's wife, Betsy, had caught the flu at the last moment and couldn't be there, so their son Jaime, who is also a marvelous painter, came in her stead. Andy shouted across the room, "Jaime, come here and see who I've found!" It was the beginning of one of the most delightful times I've ever had at the White House.

Sitting next to Henry Kissinger at dinner, I told him about my practice of signing menu cards, and he inscribed mine. On my left was Jaime, who also signed my card, but Tricia Nixon quick-wittedly asked him not for his autograph but for a picture. He took out his pen and on the back of her card sketched a picture of her and of himself leaning over to kiss her hand.

Those official White House dinners often have endless toasts, and this one was no exception; Sato's remarks went on long enough to qualify him as the Hubert Humphrey of Japan. When I asked for a translation of the Japanese, Dr. Kissinger whispered back, "He's saying that all American reporters are 'effete snobs'!"

The Japanese visitors were still suffering from jet lag, and as the toast dragged on, the Japanese foreign minister dozed off, listing practically onto Mrs. Nixon's shoulders. He would awaken with a start, catch himself and sit bolt upright until he fell asleep again. Unfortunately, he never quite toppled all the way, so I lost a bet to Dr. Kissinger.

The food at the White House is usually good, for the same chef, or at least the same kitchen staff, carries over from one Administration to another. But it looks even better than it tastes because it is served on historic, beautiful china surrounded by the famous Biddle vermeil candlesticks and epergnes filled with glorious flowers.

The two Wyeth men had come to Washington not anticipating a very good time, so Andy had made a date with an art critic for later in the evening. But we all had so much fun dancing after dinner that it was long past one o'clock when he finally walked into the Hay-Adams Hotel for his interview. But besides dancing, Andy took Jaime and me on a tour of the paintings in the formal rooms. What a way to learn about White House portraits! Andy told us that another painter, Ike, had once given him the same tour, and that Ike did not like the stern picture of Woodrow Wilson reading a book and looking down over his glasses because, as Ike said, every time he looked at it he thought that Wilson was about to correct his grammar.

Later Andy Wyeth invited Dick and me to his Brandywine house and showed us his own paintings and the countryside in which he painted them. We went to visit his niece, Ann, and her husband, Frolic Weymouth, who is also a distinguished artist; driving in a vintage carriage, with four splendid horses to pull us and a trumpeteer sounding his horn through the Pennsylvania countryside, we sat bundled up in blankets drinking Jack Daniel's out of paper cups. I recommend such company and transportation as one of the better ways to spend a Saturday afternoon in winter.

Although the Nixon White House was stuffy, one of the swinging-est parties ever held there was during his Administration. Given for the late Duke Ellington, whose father had worked as a White House butler, it went on long into the night, and people walking past 1600 Pennsylvania Avenue could hear the music wafting out until the early hours. Leonard Garment, the counsel to President Nixon who turned out to be one of the few white hats in the Watergate mess because he advised full disclosure, played the clarinet with the Ellington band, and some of Mr. Ellington's relatives joined in too. It's ironic that President Nixon, who did not count blacks among his constituency, should have had more of them to a formal dinner than any of his predecessors. But one dinner does not change a policy, and most blacks felt their hopes and dreams were never recognized by the Nixon White House.

CHAPTER 21 ⌒

In 1969 Nixon made his first round-the-world trip as President. It was timed to coincide with the splashdown of the astronauts; afterward he was going to India, Pakistan and perhaps Vietnam.

Essentially, there are only two ways to travel: to be a young, single, unattached woman, or to go with the President of the United States —and of the two, the latter is the best. Whenever you cover a President's trip you start from the White House in a big Army bus which delivers you to the tarmac at Andrews Air Force Base. It's off the bus and onto the plane, with no waiting for tickets or a seat assignment. Such treatment can spoil you, and when you're a mere civilian you find yourself growing impatient at having to stand in line. Also, there are no luggage problems on a presidential trip: you take your suitcase to the White House and that's the last you have to worry about it. When you reach your destination, you're working and there's no time to claim a suitcase. Often it's hours before you get to your hotel, but when you do, bone-tired, the White House trans-portation-office staff has put your bag in your room. Then, when you get up the next morning after two or three hours' sleep, there's no need to call a bellboy: the transportation people are there again to pick up your suitcase.

At each stop the press plane lands about twenty minutes before the President so that reporters can be in position to report the arrival ceremonies. Usually the host country has everything in readiness and officials are standing there waiting, so when the press gets off the plane instead of the President, the arrival committee looks up in such anticipation that sometimes you think that they're waiting there for you. This has a strange and not altogether beneficial effect. After VIP treatment around the world, reporters have a tendency to act as if they themselves were the visiting potentates.

But while the deference is enjoyable, traveling with the President is also an endurance test—and it's not just a question of stamina, but also of frustration. Often you are in a time zone that is so different from the New York broadcasting schedule that you have to get up in the middle of the night to go on the air. Thus, even when the schedule has allowed for a couple of hours rest, during this period you are generally running all over a strange town trying to make a broad-cast that will reach New York in time. Fortunately, it's easier now with satellites.

When Nixon decided to make this trip, in July 1969, he wanted Mrs. Nixon to come along and to be featured on television; as a result, some White House people went to NBC and asked that a special program be done about her. It's tough for a network to turn down such a request; if they do, they may not get the future cooperation from the President's office that is essential for survival. Besides, most news directors would consider the First Lady's journey news. In addition, the White House held out another carrot: Mrs. Nixon's first televised interview. Clearly, all this was government pressure on a network; at the same time, any news director would have to admit

161

that a first exclusive interview, as well as pictures of the First Lady in Vietnam, was a legitimate story. NBC would have covered her in any event, but as a result of the pressure, the network received kid-glove treatment and the President got a special called "Mrs. Nixon's Journey."

Generally I don't like to be assigned "women's news," but in retrospect I prefer having covered Pat Nixon's efforts on this trip; in the long run they had more meaning than the disastrous policy her husband was cementing at the same time.

While traveling with Presidents can be exciting, they usually don't choose the best season to go. For political reasons it always seems that the best time to visit the Far East is the rainy season. But as hot as it was, I never saw Mrs. Nixon complain. The work of her staff in those early days was so disorganized that she was put through unnecessary rigors; yet she cheerfully did everything required of her. I was used to the efficiency of Mrs. Johnson's staff, which handled her travels with as much or even more professionalism than the President's, but there was no such orchestration for Mrs. Nixon. Her aides were jockeying for position, and it became a challenge to cope with their infighting.

From the West Coast the Nixons went in his and her airplanes because he was flying to the splashdown to welcome back the astronauts aboard a Navy ship, on which women weren't allowed. The two planes left at about the same time, and as the President veered off toward the east, it was a thrill to look out the window and see *Air Force One* dip its wings to us in Mrs. Nixon's plane in a salute.

In Hawaii we waited for the splashdown at the Kahala Hilton, one of the best hotels in the world. Of course Mrs. Nixon had the best suite, which overlooks both the ocean ringed by palms and the special pool in which two dolphins perform tricks. Half a dozen of us sat in her room, watching the splashdown on television and relaxing with a drink. After the astronauts landed safely, Nixon, who like his predecessors was trying to associate himself with their spectacular, boarded the ship amid a backdrop of thousands of uniformed men standing at attention. Suddenly one of Mrs. Nixon's aides shouted that we should stand up, which we all obediently did. There didn't seem to be any alternative and I suppose we feared to appear unpatriotic. Admittedly it was a moment of great national pride, but we did look like a bunch of dopes standing at attention before the television set. Mrs. Nixon even had her right hand over her heart.

On to Guam. I doubt that any advance man had arranged Mrs. Nixon's visit to a training center for the mentally retarded in Guam, but she plunged right in. The first person she tried to shake hands with had no hand. Mrs. Nixon never flinched; she shook the stump of his elbow, and if she was surprised, she never showed it, displaying good human instincts despite the chaos of a scrambling entourage of reporters and television crews around her. In Indonesia she went not just to one hospital, which would have been sufficient, but to several, always in excruciating heat. In Thailand she did the same, and she also went to a snake farm there with Queen Sirikit. Everywhere the queen went, so too went her lady-in-waiting. Since I was in precisely the same relationship to Mrs. Nixon, trailing her everywhere with my mike, I began to feel like *her* lady-in-waiting. The Thai officials also began to treat me that way, a memory I don't like to dwell on. Luckily, it didn't last long; the queen went off in her carriage, a custom-built, cream-colored Mercedes lined in gold silk, and I went back to the press bus.

In Bangkok the rumors were confirmed: there was to be a presidential visit to Vietnam, which had not been announced before for security reasons. There was only limited space for reporters on the flight, but press secretary Ronald Ziegler made sure that my crew and I were on board. They wanted pictures of the First Lady in the war zone because they thought it would be good television, and they were right.

Saigon was hotter than I thought it possible to be. While Nixon conferred with President Nguyen Van Thieu, Mrs. Nixon flew to an orphanage outside of Saigon run by Catholic sisters for the children of Vietnamese mothers and American soldiers. Those adorable little children sang, danced and presented flowers to Mrs. Nixon, who always does well in such situations. She communicates easily with children, and of course they were delighted that she'd come, because it was a special day with treats and cookies.

It was not only hot in Vietnam, it rained constantly. Consequently, I always looked like a dripping duck, a point that television viewers always mentioned first when they wrote in. But Carol Laise, an ambassador in her own right who is also the wife of Ellsworth Bunker, then American ambassador to Vietnam, almost made up for the weather during our visit to the orphanage. As I jumped around telling the camera crew what to do, trying to hold the mike low enough to pick up the voices of the children and Mrs. Nixon's responses, being pushed on all sides by other reporters, Secret Service agents, children and untold supernumeraries, Ambassador Laise carried not only my raincoat but even some of our equipment, and was enormously helpful.

With an abundance of guards, we bounced back to Thieu's palace in Saigon in Marine helicopters. This may be the most efficient and safest way to get around in a war zone, but it is also the most uncomfortable and noisiest. Since you can't talk in a helicopter, it was only after we landed that our pilot said wistfully, "I wish I were going back home with you."

In India we were met by Ambassador Kenneth Keating, an interesting reunion for the Nixons and me, since I had met them originally through Ken. Pat and I laughed about his preference for the heat of India; we didn't understand how anybody could enjoy it. Our press plane had to wait in the sun on the tarmac for a couple of hours during the official ceremonies, and inside, it was even hotter than Saigon.

Mrs. Gandhi and President Nixon didn't hit it off well. She wasn't his kind of person and he wasn't hers. But despite the coolness of their personal relations, there was the usual pomp and circumstance accorded a visiting chief of state. India may be a poverty-stricken country, but it certainly puts on a rich welcoming ceremony, and Nixon clearly enjoyed it. We drove into town preceded by scarlet-coated outriders on magnificent horses that clattered over the red stone road leading to the government palace, a grand leftover from the days of the Empire, where the Nixons were to stay. Nixon was so impressed with all the panoply that when he returned to Washington he ordered new uniforms for the White House guards. When they appeared in their new white coats with thick leather belts and visor hats, they were promptly ridiculed as extras in a Gilbert and Sullivan operetta. So much fun was made of their uniforms—they emphasized the potbellies of the White House police, who were then directed to diet—that they were never worn again, and no one can tell you where they are now or how much we taxpayers paid for that folly.

164

Outside of Delhi, Mrs. Nixon visited a village center that taught people how to make handicrafts for export. As the word of her presence spread, a crowd gathered. There's nothing quite like an Indian crowd. Within instants there are hundreds of people, and they are so used to being jammed together that they surge in by habit. The situation was clearly about to get out of hand, and there weren't enough Secret Service agents or advance men; they hadn't anticipated a mob, and began to call urgently on their walkie-talkies for re-enforcements while the natives swarmed forward to see and touch Mrs. Nixon. It was a frightening, unpredictable moment, but Mrs. Nixon was calm throughout. Finally the Secret Service pushed enough bodies away to be able to open the car door and we got out of there. As soon as we did, just as quickly as the crowd had appeared, it vanished.

There is so little time on official visits that it's difficult to see anything except what the host country wants you to. Still, some of what our Western eyes were shown had the wrong effect. In New Delhi we were taken to a day-care center for infants whose mothers were working. Tiny, listless babies lay on straw mats with big open sores and flies all over them. The center was their best and they were proud of it, but I was horrified.

In Pakistan it was just as hot and almost as crowded, but away from the city there was one marvelous garden party at the presidential palace. Special plush velvet chairs, a holdover from colonial days, were set out on a green lawn, a startling contrast to most of dusty Karachi, and Mrs. Nixon was placed on a Victorian sofa that was flanked by two air conditioners. I've never seen an air conditioner outside before, but they were better than fans and provided a little cool breeze until they broke down. Performing for the distinguished guests was the dance troupe of the Pakistani army. Costumed in voluminous bloomers, red hats and vests, boots and long-sleeved white lace shirts in the incredible heat, they put on a remarkable show of continuous movement in a high-spirited dance. Some of the participants were young men who were beautiful to behold. It was whispered that they were recruited specifically for the army, in which homosexuality is said to be a tradition, a sensitive subject which no Pakistani would discuss with me. Later, as we left the presidential palace, I saw the dancers almost hidden behind a clump of trees.

165

Some were lying prostrate on the ground, their red hats off, white pantaloons limp; others were gathered around a large earthen jug of water, and as each took his turn at the ladle it looked like a scene from Kipling.

On to Rumania for two days, the last stop. With Nixon's penchant for notable firsts, there were a lot of press releases about the first trip of an American President to Communist Rumania. His entrance into Bucharest on August 2 was triumphant, as if he were a visiting emperor in ancient times. Such demonstrations are always staged in Communist countries, but this one far surpassed what the government had expected. It was a genuine emotional tribute to the United States and to the President who personified the dream of America. Nixon was ecstatic.

The hotel lobby in Bucharest, filled with American reporters waiting to do wrap-up pieces on the Nixon adventure to the East, looked like the Crillon in Paris. The three networks had sent dozens of men to televise the Nixon tour, and the atmosphere was one of a holiday.

While Communist countries like to tout themselves as the "peoples' government," what their people don't know is how well their leaders live and entertain. The Nixons' guesthouse in Bucharest had everything that could be associated with capitalistic extravagance. My crew and I were among the few allowed to see it because we were going to film our interview with Mrs. Nixon there. Outside were beautifully landscaped parks and fountains; inside there were more fountains, large drawing rooms and even a dining room and kitchen for servants that had every modern convenience, all in impeccable taste worthy of the cover of *Architectural Digest.* The glass walls of the house overlooked endless vistas that had been cut through the woods, and the bedroom assigned to the President was designed for a giant; I've never seen a bigger bed. The bathroom was even more spectacular, with a little swimming pool, gigantic showers with sprays coming out at every angle, an enormous sauna, a Jacuzzi and the biggest bathtub in the world. In my travels I've seen quite a few palatial residences, but never one like this.

As was the custom in every place we visited, the host country gave a formal state dinner in honor of the Nixons, and they returned the hospitality the following day—on this occasion at lunch, using American china, glasses, wines and foods flown in especially from the States.

The guesthouse dining room was large enough to seat one hundred and fifty persons.

The crew and I did a dry run for the interview, which was to take place the next day, squeezed into the schedule before the luncheon. The next morning, when we set out for the guesthouse, I found out exactly how a Communist government rules at such times: there were roadblocks everywhere. President Nixon and President Nicolas Ceausescu were meeting downtown that morning, and soldiers or agents were at every corner, their guns out. No passage, no access. The freedom as we had entered the city had been deceptive; for that brief period citizens had been allowed to express themselves, but within hours, restrictions were back to normal. The Rumanians we saw looked sullen and afraid, and we were virtual prisoners in a two-block area around the hotel.

I had anticipated the governmental obstruction that is normal in Communist capitals, and had taken the precaution of having a Nixon aide with us, but he was no help. By walkie-talkie we were in communication with American officials all over Bucharest, but there was simply no passage; we couldn't move. Some Secret Service agents tried to help, but even they couldn't talk the Rumanian guards into giving us access to the guesthouse.

By this point I was getting anxious, for Mrs. Nixon had only a limited amount of time before the luncheon. In desperation I convinced our Secret Service agents to phone President Nixon's guard. It took a while, but when we finally got through to the President, the roadblocks were miraculously opened and we raced to the guesthouse at a hundred miles an hour trying to make up the time lost behind the barricades.

But when we arrived, the site for the interview was wrong because of the unexpected sunlight, the electricity did not work without converters, and my panic increased. Unless you've been on a television remote, it's difficult to understand the number of potential difficulties, particularly in a foreign country. I had gone around the world in less than two weeks to do this exclusive interview with Mrs. Nixon, and suddenly it was all going down the drain. Pat was patient throughout as we traipsed from one area to another, repeating the previous day's careful labors to find the right background. "It's got to look like Rumania, for Chrissake," one of the cameramen kept saying.

By the time we'd satisfied the demands of lighting, background, electricity and other problems, I was exhausted. I had changed the décor of the guesthouse, had ordered Rumanians around, and was trying to placate Mrs. Nixon's aides, who were worrying about her schedule and about the kinds of questions I would ask during the interview. The crew was proficient and professional, but its previous experience had been in the controlled conditions of a New York studio—quite a different set of circumstances from doing a remote in a foreign country for which there is no set script. In addition, I had to ad-lib questions that would sound intelligent and have news value days later. Thus, it was no wonder that by the time the interview actually began I was frazzled, wet and in need of nothing so much as a shower and a good hairdresser. I was not good, the interview was not good, and Mrs. Nixon was not good. In fact, she was inarticulate, tired and uncomfortable, and she looked it.

It is part of the great mythology of network operations in New York that all First Ladies are amateur actresses and automatically eloquent, but it is not true. Sometimes they're even shy. As the interview droned on, I was slowly dying. Pat seemed to have no thoughts or opinions of her own, or else she was scared to voice them. The only revealing piece of information in the entire interview came when I asked her if she and the President shared any private jokes when they were alone together. "Yes," she said, "the first thing we do is say hello to the four corners"—meaning an acknowledgment of the probable presence of electronic bugs. The next day the White House staff pleaded with me not to use this, saying that it could only affect adversely our relations with other countries. In retrospect, it's interesting that even then both the Nixons were preoccupied with bugs and tapes.

Midway through the interview I switched course and asked Mrs. Nixon questions *only* about the specific sights and events on the trip that I knew we had pictures of. In this way, when we returned to New York we were able to use a sound track of her voice, which is a pleasant one, and superimpose it on our pictures, which were terrific. It was a Herculean task, but it was worth it because it produced the effect of Mrs. Nixon giving a running commentary, and as a result the show turned out better than could be expected.

The program was broadcast a week later, and as soon as we were off the air, both Pat and the President telephoned, so that I was talking with her on one line while he waited on another. She thanked me and said that throughout the show, "Dick kept pounding the table in front of him saying, 'That's right! That's right! That's the way you are, and that's the way they should see you.' " She added, "I don't know why he thought it was so different; I was just doing what I always do, in the same way."

CHAPTER 22

After his round-the-world journey, Nixon continued his misguided Vietnam policy throughout the fall of 1969. In the spring of 1970, on April 30, he went on television to announce the American incursion into Cambodia to destroy the enemy sanctuaries. The announcement came as a shock to the American people. The public in general, the doves and the liberals in particular, thought the expansion of the war a reversal of the Vietnamization plan to get the United States out of Southeast Asia. Buying time for a more orderly withdrawal of U.S. troops made no sense to antiwar groups. They felt tricked; Nixon had said he would wind down the war, and instead he was escalating it. Moreover, the decision was made in such secrecy that even Secretary of State William Rogers didn't know what was going on, a fact that led to charges of one-man rule and speculations about dissension among Nixon advisers.

The way the President phrased it in his address, listeners got the idea that there was a specific enemy headquarters, well stocked with ammunition and orchestrating enemy activity, that was similar to the Pentagon command. In reality the enemy sanctuaries were as stable as a floating crap game. The difference between what was suggested and what existed in fact created a large credibility gap, and the President's opponents had already started to say that it was no longer the Democrats' war, but Nixon's.

William Safire, Nixon's speech writer and sympathetic biographer, writes: "In retrospect the Cambodian decision was the turning point of the war . . . part of Vietnamization . . . not an escalation of the war," and goes on to say that the incursion was not only daring and surprising, but successful both in the short and long run. I disagree:

in even further retrospect, the decision seems not to have been successful at all; if it was supposed to buy time for us, as advertised, today it seems clear that we could have left a lot sooner than we did, and—in view of the subsequent status of both Cambodia and Vietnam—with no less than we did, and perhaps more.

Both Nixon's speech and the incursion itself were seen by antiwar groups as a way to revitalize their dying cause, and they planned a massive march on Washington. As preparations were being made for hundreds of thousands of young people from all over the country to descend on the capital, Nixon made matters worse by calling the student protesters "bums." While he may not have meant to include all campus activists, that's the way it came out, either because of the way he said it or the way it was reported. Then, in a tragedy that exacerbated the pitch and intensity of feeling everywhere, the National Guard at Kent State University killed four students during antiwar demonstrations. The whole country seemed on a binge of masochistic self-destruction.

Next, Interior Secretary Walter Hickel wrote to Nixon. Trying to initiate some kind of dialogue, he told the President that he ought to talk to more people, specifically his Cabinet officers, and should open up a line of communication with young people. For his pains he was later fired.

Coming as it did four years before Nixon's resignation, Hickel's letter pinpointed the weakness that was as responsible as any for Nixon's fall: his exclusivity, his unwillingness to talk with more than a few people, his penchant for being a loner, his search for solitude while he made massive decisions which could have been improved by consultation and cross-fertilization of ideas.

During the period leading up to the Cambodian decision, John Ehrlichman had worried about the President's image among young people, and had pressed his chief to try to alter it. Not that he disagreed with the incursion; rather, he thought it was presented poorly from the standpoint of the young. It was a classic example of the Nixon White House mentality: there was more concern over image, appearance, press relations and public relations than over the substance of the act. (Incidentally, Ehrlichman was the only person I ever talked to at the White House who had any concern for young people other than during a campaign, at which time it became prudent to mobilize young Republicans to get out the vote.)

As soon as Nixon announced the invasion, the war protesters started to swarm toward Washington. They were arriving as he called them "bums," and were gathering at Peace Headquarters while the Kent State shootings dominated the headlines. In this agitated atmosphere four distinguished university presidents came for a talk in an attempt to cool things down, and were told by Mr. Nixon that he would try to lower the rhetoric of his Administration. With this in mind, the President culminated the week of tragedy and dissent by holding a news conference on Friday night, May 8, 1970. The press corps was troubled too, and some reporters were among those outraged by what they considered a betrayal.

I had been covering Peace Headquarters on Vermont Avenue and was highly sympathetic to the protesters' cause. I saw in them and their efforts a continuation of my summer as a United Nations student delegate when I'd been their age. They were carrying the banner that we'd raised in the peace seminars of postwar Europe. They were profoundly disillusioned, and determined to see that their views made some impact. Worse, they were angry at themselves because they felt they had allowed themselves to be hoodwinked into thinking that Vietnamization and gradual withdrawal were working, if only we gave these tactics a chance. The Cambodian decision served to reinforce their well-developed proclivities for cynical disbelief—and also reactivated their peace movement, which had been languishing.

As the press walked up the White House drive to the news conference, we could see the marchers gathering outside the wrought-iron fence, and during the conference itself they staged a candlelight march, each candle representing an American killed in Vietnam. It was beautiful but heartbreaking to see the thousands of candles flickering in a serpentine pattern around the White House and down Pennsylvania Avenue. But the curtains at the White House were drawn, and I doubt whether Nixon or any of his family peeked out to look at the procession.

Early in the news conference, in which Nixon handled himself very coolly in the face of hostile questions, he called on me. With the peace marchers outside and his comment about "bums" and the killings at Kent State in mind, I asked him why it was that, though he had promised to tone down his criticism of those who disagreed with him, on this very night Vice President Agnew was scheduled to

171

make a speech in which his advance text quoted him as saying that "every debate has its cadre of Jeremiahs, embittered older intellectuals, and choleric young people."

Obviously angry, the President glared at me, and I had the strange feeling that he would have liked to slap me. I stared right back as he said that from the beginning, people had been trying to find ways to split the President and his Vice President, implying that I was guilty of such mischief; then, changing his mood abruptly, both facially and in tone, his eyes danced and he righteously declared that he certainly wouldn't want to censor *anyone* in his Administration, expecially not Interior Secretary Hickel. As he said this I had another crazy thought: that he was flirting with me, a concept I find incredible even now. I was appalled. I've never had that instinct before or since, but I distinctly remember the strength and immediacy of my reaction.

As I walked down the circular drive after the conference and observed the silent crowds of protesters, they did not look like hippies; rather, they seemed to be nice Midwestern kids, and many of the protesters were middle-aged. I remember thinking that it was exactly twenty-five years after V-E Day, which was both my late father's and Truman's birthday. As I drove home in the splendor that is Washington's springtime, with the dogwood and other flowering trees in bloom, the marchers were bivouacking for the night in little groups along the Mall. It certainly was a peaceful demonstration, especially in contrast to the bombs and shooting in Vietnam. The visitors didn't look like "choleric young people," and on that balmy night the rainy season in Southeast Asia seemed remote, and the bombings even more so.

It was after ten when I got home and I was exhausted. I kissed a few sleeping children's faces, Dick and I had a nightcap and talked about the children in Vietnam and how lucky we were to be able to go the night through without a bombing, and then we went to bed.

At about a quarter past one the phone rang. One of the girls picked it up and buzzed us on the intercom. Dick grumbled and answered, obviously irritated at being awakened. We have an unlisted number just so some kook can't phone us in the middle of the night after seeing me on a television show. Dick said, "*Who* at the White House is calling Mrs. Dickerson?" Pause. As he handed me the phone he said, "She says it's the President."

It was my turn to be irritated; I took the phone and asked, "Who's calling Mrs. Dickerson?" to which the operator responded, "This is Nancy Hanschman, isn't it?" Now I knew it really was the President and not a practical joker; both Nixon and LBJ often used my maiden name absent-mindedly.

The conversation started with "This is Dick." I used to call him "Dick," but of course not since he'd become President. I was momentarily confused, since my husband, also nicknamed Dick, was hovering over me and I wasn't quite awake, but I came alert quickly when Nixon started talking about the news conference. He thanked me for asking him the question: ". . . toughest question that was asked me and I appreciated it—gives me a chance to answer it and put it on the record . . . Always like tough questions, really makes me look better . . ." Then he startled me because he sounded just like LBJ as he said, "I don't know what's the matter with the goddamn press. I'm the best thing they've got—I'm the only President they have."

By this time my husband had gone for a drink of water and the Dick on the phone was back on the subject of the news conference. By now I was warming to my subject, pacing back and forth in my bare feet in a heated conversation, giving lots of advice—after all, what else do you do in the dead of the night when a President awakens you on the phone?

Referring to the marchers, Nixon said, "I really love those kids, I really do."

"It certainly didn't come through in your news conference," I answered.

"But I do! I love those kids, and I understand what bothers them and what they're trying to say."

"Well, you didn't say that on television, and in watching your news conference they certainly couldn't have got that idea. In fact," I continued, "the best thing about your whole news conference was when you said you were going to go out and see them."

"Oh, sure, I told Haldeman and Ehrlichman to bring them all in here . . . 'Bring them all in here,' I said. I told them both I'd love to see the kids."

"That's not the way you put it in your news conference," I reminded him. "You said *you* were going to go out and see *them*, not bring them in. And why not? Why don't you go out and talk with them? It probably would do you both good, and it certainly couldn't do any harm." Nixon answered that it *was* a good idea, and later on,

173

shortly after our conversation, that's precisely what he did.

At the end of our long telephone talk, the President said, "Well, I'll see you in church tomorrow."

I asked, "What do you mean?" By now my husband had returned and was sitting on the other side of the room, shaking his head in disbelief at me, as if I were the one who had initiated the call.

"Aren't you coming to church?" the President asked. He meant the White House religious services.

"I haven't been invited."

"Oh! I can take care of that"—this said with the bravado and pride in his power that would have been more fitting if he were announcing his ability to bomb Hanoi. The reading of the line was astonishing; it was almost like a small boy bragging about his physical prowess. There was an enormous contrast between the uncertain, questioning way he talked about the war, and his assurance when he was on the safer ground of invitations to the White House.

Nixon emphasized that he wanted Dick and me to bring all the children. I reminded him that there were a good number of them, as well as one fiancé, and he magnanimously included them all. With a final "Now don't forget," he hung up.

I sat down on the side of the bed and said, "That man has not been drinking, but I would feel better if he had been."

People have often speculated about what prompted the President to go out to the Lincoln Memorial in the early hours of the morning. Well, it was our conversation. I certainly didn't expect him to go out then and there, and would not have urged it. He was exhausted from a week of hammer blows, and in any case there was no hurry; the major demonstration wasn't scheduled until the next day. But he could no more sleep than could the protesters on the Mall, so before dawn that Saturday morning, in the crisp spring air, he slipped out of the White House and made his way through the quiet but restless crowds to the Lincoln Memorial to mingle with the protesters. It was a disaster. While he talked about foreign affairs with some of the students, mostly his conversation was about college football.

The reporting of those conversations has been haphazard, but the fact remains that those marchers were there for a cause they deeply believed in, and they saw no connection between it and their college football teams. Even if the football angle was overreported, it was a mistake for Nixon to bring up the subject at all. I do know that he was deeply agitated, and if he talked to the students the way he talked to me, they had reason to be taken aback, and even a little scared. But they were on such different wavelengths that they were aware only of disagreement over policy, so perhaps they didn't notice a dislocation of personality. Also, none of them had met him before, hence couldn't tell that he was behaving in a peculiar way. At any rate, whatever the reason, no such innuendos were made; instead, the emphasis was on his lack of judgment in discussing sports at such a time.

By Saturday morning, Nixon's aides had caught up with him having breakfast at the Mayflower Hotel, and once it was known that he had been making phone calls and been out all night, I did a television spot for the NBC evening news in which I stressed his concern for the students, as he had described it on the phone.

Every man will act differently under pressure, but there are parameters of behavior beyond which a President ought never to go. I think that Nixon crossed the line that night. I realized then what Haldeman meant when he said years later that Nixon was "weird"; it was eerie to see him fluctuate between a flare-up of anger at a news conference and unctuous solicitude immediately thereafter. Because of his fast and mercurial changes of mood when he telephoned me, I know what Nancy Kissinger meant when she said that he was "unstable." Indeed, I felt just as Senator William Saxbe did later when Nixon ordered the Christmas bombing of Cambodia; Saxbe said, "The man has taken leave of his senses."

I had no desire to initiate scary speculation about "The Day the President Went Mad," but I was disturbed by the way Nixon talked and by his manner. When I mentioned my concern the next day to Frank Jordan, the NBC News bureau chief, he gave me a patronizing little smile that suggested that I might need more rest. In retrospect, perhaps I should have said more about my fears; a warning signal from the people he called that night would have made us more alert to the bizarre behavior which became even more obvious during the period before his resignation. On the other hand, such speculation in that week of turmoil and trauma in May might only have been harmful. Besides, at that time if I had aired my concern publicly— that President Nixon was mentally erratic—it probably would have been considered one more attempt by the Washington press to "get Nixon."

*   *   *

Later in the day I started getting phone calls reminding me about the church service. Lucy Winchester, the White House social secretary, called to say that Mr. Nixon particularly wanted us to be there, Ziegler conveyed the same message, and by the third call I began to wonder if I had said anything the previous night that suggested I needed religious revival. I had every intention of going. An invitation to the White House services had become a new status symbol almost akin to an invitation to a state dinner. Even if it had not been, I was curious to see what the service would be like.

With a traditional Catholic background and a firm belief in the separation of church and state, I was prejudiced against the idea of religious services in the White House, but philosophical principles aside, I see nothing wrong with a little moralizing among friends at home on a Sunday morning; in fact, it seems to me the best thing you can do on that day. I didn't fault the religious nature of the meeting, except that it wasn't as good for Mr. Nixon as it was for the rest of us. It would have been far better for him to go to God than trying to bring God into the White House. It was all part of his pattern of withdrawal—one more manifestation of holing up within the confines of the White House and shutting off contact with any potential dissent. Indeed, by the time of Watergate, Nixon had become so isolated that services were no longer held even there, and when he occasionally did venture to church outside, he found the clergy saying the same things in their sermons as his critics, a circumstance that did not encourage him to hurry back the next Sunday.

All the Dickersons except John, who was too young, dressed in their church clothes the next day. The East Room was jammed, but they had saved seats for us. Rows of chairs were placed in a semicircle facing a lectern, a boys' choir was on the right, and the proceedings began with a brief welcoming speech by the President. The choir sang a few songs, and then the preacher for the day was introduced.

It had become a great honor to be asked to sing or preach at the White House, and since politics enters into everything connected with a presidential invitation, senators and congressmen used to plague the White House to wangle an invitation for their favorite hometown clergyman to hold services there. It's one of many harmless favors a President can bestow, a benign payoff which shows the folks back home the prestige and importance of their elected representative.

On this occasion the preacher, who came from the Midwest, was introduced with due credit to his senator sitting in the front row, and a sketch of his background was offered to the congregation; he had fought bravely for religious freedom in eastern Europe, had been tortured, and had escaped to the United States. But while his credentials were impeccable, no one had bothered to check his voice. He had such a thick Slavic accent that he sounded like a stage caricature. In addition, it was Mother's Day, a phrase he lovingly pronounced in resonant tones as "Mudder's Day." Every sentence featured Mudder in one way or another, and this started the Dickersons giggling. On the back of my program I wrote, "A mudder runs well on a rainy track," and passed it down our row; somehow we all thought this hilarious, especially as the preacher was warming to his subject, and Mudder, intoned with great reverence, was becoming ever more prominent in his message. Treasury Secretary George Shultz and his wife were sitting in back of us and they could see all of us smiling at each other, trying to hold back the laughter and behave properly.

Laughter is contagious, and it spread all around us, fueled by the sermon itself, which was positively ghoulish. It featured one story about a mudder whose son was in jail, and when she went to visit him he bit her ear off to punish her for not having raised him better. For some reason the mudder didn't mind. Then there was another mudder whose son was getting married and whose fiancée asked for only one gift: the heart of his mudder cut out and presented to her, the fiancée, on a silver platter. As can be imagined, Michael Dickerson, aged six, was riveted by these poor mudders' misadventures, but finally and mercifully God in Heaven took pity on his children in the East Room that Sunday morning, and the good preacher stopped.

Afterward the President offered everyone coffee, juice and pastry, but I had a queasy stomach as a result of the sermon and ate little. Still, it was a pleasant gathering, similar to any church social, and everyone was very nice to me—almost as if they were afraid that I might say something derogatory about the President's phone call.

When we went through the customary receiving line, the President never mentioned his call. He looked rested and so ruddy-faced that we wondered whether he had been under a sun lamp. I knew he must have had some sleep, because the public President that

177

Sunday morning was a far cry from the beleaguered man I had spoken with thirty hours before. He didn't look me in the eye, but complimented me on my jewelry, my dress, my children, and was trying to be charming with endless small talk. I could not believe that I was hearing such glib trivia from the same man who had so recently been desperately seeking reassurance on the phone for his war policy.

On the way home I assured Mike that no boy in his right mind ever bites his mudder's ear off.

CHAPTER 23

As had happened so many times in the past, national events affected our personal lives. The Glenn shot had determined our wedding date; Mike's birth was arranged so that the gynecologist could keep a White House appointment; a miscarriage at an inauguration; John's birth just in time for a political convention. Now, in the fall of 1969 and spring of 1970, when the country was in travail, we were having our own turmoil at Merrywood.

Dick had been president of Liberty Equities, a company that had a tremendous success, but in the summer of 1969, when interest rates soared and the stock market plummeted, his company, like many others at that time, suffered severe financial difficulties. It was about to go under, but Dick felt morally responsible and spent the next year and a half working at no salary to make sure that the company survived. Ironically, for legal reasons we could not sell either our stock or Merrywood, so while we were still worth a great deal of money, we were also cash-poor. This meant that while Dick was rebuilding a professional career and reorganizing our finances, I was supporting the seven of us and a staff of servants. We cut back to one housekeeper, who was essential because I left for the office each morning at seven-fifteen—sometimes earlier, when I did the *Today* show—and there were breakfasts to be made and children's lunches to be packed. We also needed help on weekends because I was often working then too. Times were difficult, but Dick never complained, and I didn't either. We'd had a terrific run, and if luck was bad for a while, so be it. We were even considering selling the furniture when

NBC decided to cut out its "strip shows"—that is, the five-minute news programs scheduled three times a day—because it could make more money on soap operas than on news. I had been the anchorman for six years on one daily news strip, and when it was canceled my salary suffered. Without that prestigious assignment, I was only one member of a pack of reporters that vied with one another for assignments and beats. I was back where I started: trying to scoop my male colleagues to get on the air.

A couple of years earlier I had convinced NBC to promote a syndication service for its affiliates. I envisioned syndication as offering a fuller diet of features and background to the news that local stations didn't get on the half-hour nightly news program and which they couldn't afford to pay for individually. At first I was the only reporter giving top priority to syndication; in effect, it was my baby. But when it began to pay good money to those whose stories were used, once again there was competition among all of us.

My particular goal was to try to find something to do on a regular basis that wouldn't duplicate the work of every other reporter. The problem was exacerbated by the fact that I was earning more than any male NBC correspondent in Washington except David Brinkley, but with the loss of the strip show I was doing work for which someone else could be hired for half or a third of what I was getting. In addition, I wanted to do news analysis, but so does every other news correspondent, and there's only one to a network. Even that wasn't the biggest handicap: a *female* network news correspondent doing analysis was perhaps an even bigger jump than my becoming the first woman correspondent.

While news judgment is always open to argument and any two editors at any given moment can legitimately disagree about the most important story of the evening, NBC News just didn't seem to care. A network news department is only as good as its flagship show, the half-hour nightly news. At that time, the great combination of Huntley and Brinkley was breaking up, and while the show's staff included many first-rate men, the overall production was in disarray and they missed stories. For example, I had a scoop on the government's banning of cyclamates, which affected the life of every American who drank soft drinks, but I couldn't get it on NBC television. I did manage to insert it in an NBC radio program which was monitored by the wire services. Ironically, the wires picked it up and put out a news bulletin—as a result of which Walter Cronkite headlined it on CBS. I was discouraged and embarrassed when I tried to explain what had happened to the Cabinet officer who had leaked the story to me. When he asked, "Why didn't they think it was news?," I had no answer.

In the early seventies the women's movement was just beginning to surface, and men who heretofore had always treated me as a reporter suddenly became self-conscious about "women's lib." When I anchored a program to commemorate the fiftieth anniversary of the women's suffrage amendment, it had a weird effect on my colleagues; they even giggled about it. Among the network hierarchy I also suffered a women's lib backlash; suddenly men felt their masculinity threatened. Their roles were in upheaval, and I represented part of an overall challenge which was assaulting them in all facets of their lives. It was a new role for me as well, because up to then I had generally been treated as a reporter rather than as a woman.

For all these reasons NBC and I decided to part company, which meant that both Dick and I were out of work. But I left full of hope; I was planning to write a book and to form my own company to syndicate my own "column-on-the-air" which I called "Inside Washington." These pieces were part news, part analysis, and were designed to be inserted in the body of a news program, thus giving the local station its own independent voice in Washington, over and above a network's stories. My theory was that television of the future would develop independence and courage, and offer controversial views. I envisioned the medium having the maturity and courage to emulate newspapers' editorial pages, and to hire columnists of the air, no matter how inimical to the politics or philosophy of the station owner.

How wrong I was! Most television stations are not as interested in the public's right-to-know as they are in their financial statements. For the most part, stations are quite content to let the networks take the flack from irate listeners who disagree with what they hear or see. Why bother to offer opposing views and thus stir up the hornet's nest of viewers and advertisers? Therefore syndication became viable financially only because I combed the market coast-to-coast, and found enough stations that really did want to offer their viewers an independent voice and were willing to take a chance on their audience's acceptance of a woman commentator. The Orion stations, with headquarters in Louisville, signed on, although it was a financial loss for them. WGN, the Chicago *Tribune* station, was one of my best; known for its conservative stand, it never once questioned what I said. I was put on the station's ten o'clock nightly news, and within a few months WGN placed an ad in *Variety* saying that my analyses had improved their ratings by four points. Baltimore had the most courage of all: station WMAR ran my analyses right before the Redskin football games!

I think that doing three columns a week on the air or in a newspaper is the hardest job in journalism. You don't get an assignment; you have to figure one out for yourself, then pursue it and hope to discover an angle that no one else has expounded. Dick set up the business end of syndication with a superb failproof system for delivery and billing, and a marvelous assistant, Francine Proulx, who is now the executive head of American Women in Radio and Television, did the rest of the work. We taped three columns a week, sent them across the country, and in the beginning, made a very good living out of it.

I didn't mind the hard work, even though it meant putting Merrywood off limits on Sundays, much to the dismay of some of my children, so that I could concentrate. But getting three columns ready for Monday that would be newsworthy, yet that would also hold up for several days in case a station couldn't run them early in the week, was a challenge, to say the least. I had been used to writing for immediate broadcast, since television is not a medium that digests anything more than an hour old, let alone analysis that is a week out of date. A few other reporters were trying the same thing but didn't make a go of it, generally because their inserts were too long—that is, over a minute. It is a fact of television life that the audience doesn't listen to a "talking head" for more than forty-five or sixty seconds, so I forced myself to write as if I were creating a math equation. I'd type out a story, then cut it in half, or even by two-thirds, reducing it to its lowest possible denominator, always remembering Murrow's advice not to tell everything I knew. What was hardest was to part with a favorite phrase, but either you learn to do it or to part with your audience.

But while the editorial part of syndication was a challenge and a delight, the business end was not. In the early seventies, television was suffering an economic crisis just like every other business, and the first sacrifice to be made at a station was the luxury of an independent

181

voice from Washington. Whenever this happened, I had to scramble around to find another news director who didn't feel that he was losing control, or that his ego was in question if he allowed his audience to hear a woman give another view from Washington. Eventually the obstacles became too great, particularly because Dick was finding some ventures he could follow profitably and didn't have enough time to devote to syndication. Consequently, I joined *Newsweek*, which at the time had a separate television-syndication division. But this proved to be a mistake, because it turned out that I was in the news business, while they were in the feature business—the "back of the book," as they called it. They wanted television spots on the "evergreens," as they were known, meaning stories that would hold up for weeks or even longer. (The most famous evergreen was done by Chet Huntley on "The Demise of the Fedora." The subject matter remains timeless.)

For *Newsweek* I did one piece a week—an analysis, original report or interview—and then, though it seemed right on the nose, would have to wait a week or two for it to be aired. It drove me crazy, so the magazine and I parted company amicably.

In the meanwhile, the Dickersons survived on special programs that I produced and syndicated—shows as diverse as one on the women's movement, and one featuring Secretary of the Treasury John Connally explaining Nixon's economic policy. The latter program was a chance to see again that vivid and controversial man.

The Nixon crowd was lackluster. With a few exceptions, they all looked and sounded alike, so it was no wonder that John Connally captivated Nixon. As Harry Dent, a political adviser, said, "The President's in love with him." He was everything that Nixon longed to be: tough, tall, handsome, confident and self-assured.

Daniel "Pat" Moynihan believed that the Nixon men collectively suffered from a massive inferiority complex; they thought that they read all the wrong books and wore the wrong clothes. Connally had no such self-doubts. He thought that he was the best and acted that way, and Nixon envied him for it.

When word spread that Connally was a presidential favorite, his star rose even higher. His picture was on magazine covers, and television shows featured him. Naturally he inspired jealousy among other Cabinet members whose names were hardly known. Their grumpiness was reflected by Martha Mitchell's remark, "If he's so great, why don't they make him Pope?" But he convinced even his skeptics by his brilliant televised defense of the new economic program, quite a trick since it was a 180-degree switch from the President's previous policy. In private Connally also stood up for Nixon, which was never popular to do in Washington.

Later, when Connally was indicted and acquitted in connection with a Watergate-related scandal, both his friends and enemies in Washington thought that it was wrong to have prosecuted him on the evidence at hand. As Mel Laird said, "He got a bum go."

I had first met Connally when I was working on the staff of the Senate Foreign Relations Committee. One afternoon he took me out for drinks with a Texan named Sid Richardson. The fame of Texas oil tycoons had not reached Wauwatosa, and I naïvely asked Mr. Richardson what he did for a living. When Mr. Richardson died, Connally was the executor of his will, of which he got a percentage, and this made him a very rich man.

Though he was in the Nixon Cabinet, Connally was also a good friend of Robert Strauss, the chairman of the Democratic National Committee and a fellow Texan. In Connally's first weeks as Secretary of the Treasury, I arranged to have lunch with him at the Sans Souci on a Thursday. Later his office called to switch it to Friday, and Strauss, with whom I had planned to lunch that day, obligingly switched dates.

Friday is always a big day at the Sans Souci, but especially on this particular date when the annual conference of newspaper editors was being held. Many of them, as well as the usual big names in Washington, were at the restaurant. Connally was late, and I was embarrassed to be sitting alone at the table. Then he entered—he never walks in; he makes an entrance—and was ceremoniously escorted by the headwaiter to my table as everyone watched. Several men rose to shake his hand, and every eye in the restaurant was on him, which suited him just fine.

Within seconds a man came over to the table and delivered a letter to me. In Washington, this is guaranteed to garner even more attention than if one asks for a telephone to be brought to the table. I was self-conscious, and Connally was a bit annoyed at my upstaging of his entrance. When I ripped open the envelope, a large hotel-room key dropped out. Also enclosed was this note from Robert Strauss:

Dear Nancy—

You asked for some pointers to help you through a "boring" lunch with John Connally, as you put it.

a) He's reticent & shy;

b) Lacks confidence;

c) Is without vanity;

d) Is pure in heart & mind (if he has either);

e) Despite the above, he is basically a nice, pleasant, jolly, plump older man.

See you at the regular place after lunch.

Bob

By 1971 I had also become a regular on the lecture circuit. I was on the road so much that sometimes I felt like a traveling salesman; I went everywhere, telling business and women's groups what Washington was like. Judging by the size of the audiences and the number of my speaking dates, people "out there" thirsted to know what was going on in the capital.

Lecturing is good for a reporter because the question period gives an invaluable insight into what is bothering citizens, a view virtually unheard in Washington. Lecturing is also good for the ego. There is nothing like a standing ovation to convince you that you should have been on the stage all along. Certainly it beats a television floor producer's hurrying you off the set so that he can switch to the sports news.

My prolonged absences did not make it easy for John, Mike and Janie, the three children still at home, but there was no alternative. Besides, Dick spent more time with the children than he would have normally, and this was good for all of them. Still, our life was exceedingly tough for a few years, but we never let it get us down. Dick was resilient, and eventually was successful in everything from shipping to oil and coal to real estate. In between, he had some fun starting a restaurant, producing a Broadway musical, and originating Washington's first swinging private club. As the saying goes, "I've been rich and I've been poor, and rich is better." It was a good lesson.

*   *   *

In 1970 Liz got married to C. Gregory Earls, and two years later Ann married Norman Harrower III. Janie was an attendant in each, adding a special joy with her smile, and Mike was ring bearer for Liz, and John for Ann.

The wedding receptions were held at Merrywood, which is a beautiful spot for such occasions. In fact, Merrywood and its spacious, well-proportioned rooms and magnificent grounds are a perfect background for almost anything! It is a "people" house, particularly a children's house. Nothing is off limits for them, provided their shoes are clean and they don't track in mud. And they've had some pleasant parties here, ranging from college weekends to a room full of little boys in sleeping bags on the floor.

Our best party of the year is on Christmas Eve and is planned around the children. The tradition started just after we were married. I remembered that Eleanor Roosevelt had said that some of her most joyous moments were with the orphans who spent Christmas with her family, and thinking that it would be a good experience for the girls and for us too, I called St. Ann's Orphanage, the previous beneficiary of my airline-insurance policies. (I've always been afraid to fly, so out of superstition I would buy insurance on each flight and send the policies back to St. Ann's. Whenever the weather was turbulent on a trip I would wonder whether the plane would crash so that the orphans would benefit, or whether I would be allowed to live so that I could fulfill all the good work I was so fervently promising to do at that moment.)

St. Ann's said that there was one little boy, the only child left in the orphanage for the holiday, who could come for Christmas. The girls and I thought it would be a nice surprise for Dick, so we planned it together. When they went to pick up Jimmy, he appeared with a small box of Kleenex and a very runny nose. He was scared stiff. He wouldn't talk and he didn't cry. He just stared at us. We had bought toys for him and a red suit, but nothing worked. He wouldn't eat, either. We had a crib ready for him and put him to bed in new pajamas. We considered it a major victory when he accepted a drink of water, but still he never said a word.

In the middle of the night Dick was awakened by a tugging at his pajama sleeve. It was Jimmy, and he was talking constantly, with a considerable vocabulary for a baby. That little boy had climbed out of his crib in a strange house, toddled through two sets of doors and a room to find us, and seemed as happy as any two-year-old could be. By the next morning he was quite at home, and on Christmas Eve we had a big party for him with all the children bringing presents. Gifts didn't impress him much, but the children did; suddenly he blossomed. With all those children around, it was just like the orphanage and he became a social lion.

We had a lovely time with Jimmy, but I kept dreading the hour when he had to return to the orphanage. We wanted to keep him forever, but there were obstructions and we couldn't have adopted him. When the time came for him to leave, it was uncanny. Although we had never mentioned it to him, that dear creature sensed it, and he found his little shiny black suitcase and was sitting next to it on the steps, ready to go back. By the time we reached the orphanage I felt terrible. But there's a happy ending; his aunt and uncle, who had adopted his brother and sister, also adopted Jimmy.

Now every year we have a party in memory of Jimmy and the joy he brought, and those families who have no relatives nearby to visit for the holidays are invited. We have a magician, but before he does his act, each younger child performs. Sometimes an entire family puts on a skit. That's what Senator Mondale and his family do, and one Christmas Eve they arrived with all the props for their number, including elaborate costumes they had made. John Dickerson was enthralled, for his only previous experience with costumes had been Halloween, when he wore a purple Batman suit and a black mask. In the excitement of greeting other arriving guests, I lost track of John. Later, when all were in their seats, I opened the program by proudly announcing that the first number would be by the youngest child, John Dickerson. When he walked out, I was stunned to see our own Christmas angel wearing his purple Batman suit. Sublimely satisfied with himself and his attire, he proceeded to sing "I Wish You a Merry Christmas."

Aside from the family parties, we've had some dinners that were interesting because of the guests. At the beginning there was some amount of publicity about these affairs. Being a reporter myself, I thought I had no right to exclude those from my own profession who wanted to cover the story. But that changed after Liz's graduation dance, a gala affair. I told a reporter from *Look* that she could report it, but only as part of a bigger story she had proposed on how to combine the role of working, full-time career woman with that of mother. We had a firm understanding because I didn't want to exploit Liz's party, but the reporter broke her word. The story appeared as a straight society piece, capitalizing on the guests and their celebrity status. Ever since we've shied away from publicity; I'd rather report the political news than be part of the social columns.

As life styles have changed and become more simple, so too has entertaining. Black-tie and white-tie functions, with formal settings and service, have gradually given way to the informal buffet. Extravagant gowns and diamonds are too much bother for today's pace, and household help is scarce and expensive. As life styles and entertaining have changed, so too has the reporting of these functions in Washington. The current trend is to disparage all parties as frivolous and wasteful. There seems to be a contest about who can make the most unflattering remarks on how leisure hours are spent, and I wonder why hostesses seek such publicity.

Washington entertaining exists on two levels. Anyone with enough money and the desire can get together a crowd of a hundred or more, because there are enough freeloaders around who will go to anything. Besides, the social scene in the capital is often indistinguishable from the business scene. Washington has social climbers just like any other city, but here they are more properly identified as power climbers. The big functions are often for a political cause, or are a charitable event to raise money. This includes parties to promote books, openings and cultural events, as well as those in which a hostess is paying back everyone she owes—or sometimes is doing it just for fun. Such parties are public in the sense that they are reported in the papers. In fact, their sponsors or hosts eagerly court space to further their cause, whatever it is. Also this kind of publicity can make or break a benefit.

On quite another level there are smaller parties that occasionally affect the course of national events. There are few of these, and they are not covered by society reporters because such hostesses consider their presence inhibiting. Also their presence has come to be interpreted as a hostess' desire for personal publicity. This is not to denigrate such reporters; indeed, their pieces are often more insightful than the editorials—and certainly they're read more. President Kennedy used to say that if he wanted to find out what was really going on in Washington, he read the women's section, because he already knew what would be on the front page.

While small, intimate, power-brokering parties are more prominent in political novels than in reality, they do exist, and in contrast
to society columnists, political journalists are frequently invited to
them. In fact, reporters often are the most sought-after guests in
Washington, unlike other world capitals where the press does not
enjoy such status. I remember a party that Dick and I gave for Mayor
John Lindsay and his wife, Mary, on a lovely evening in May 1970.
The dogwood were flourishing and the newly planted geraniums were
in their first bloom. The Lindsays were late because of a harrowing
day: he had been hung in effigy by striking union workers in New
York, and other events forced them to take a later plane, so they
arrived after several of the guests.

Marie and Coach Vince Lombardi came, and he made an immediate hit with John Dickerson. Vince had a way with children, and
during the cocktail hour, everywhere he went, two-year-old John went
too, clutching the coach's hand. Phyllis and Bennett Cerf also flew
down from New York, as did Punch Sulzberger, and Mrs. Longworth
came to watch, as she said, "beleaguered Merrywood." Henry Kissinger was there; so were senators, including both Frank Church and
John S. Cooper. It was little more than a week after the Cambodian
invasion; the country was in turmoil, and Congress was embroiled in
a major debate on the Cooper-Church amendment to curtail U.S.
participation in Vietnam.

At the dinner Dick made a welcoming toast and the mayor responded. Then Dr. Kissinger rose and talked pointedly about the
need for compassion toward our national leaders, a subject he has
dwelled on frequently in the ensuing years, at first on behalf of the
President and later for more personal reasons. He said that we had
assassinated one President, picked at his successor until he was
hounded out of office, and now were doing the same thing to Nixon.
He concluded by saying, "What I ask for the President, even from
his enemies, is an act of love."

As soon as he sat down, Hugh Scott, the Senate Republican leader,
jumped to his feet. Chafing from neglect and bruised because he was
carrying Nixon's banner without much White House support, Scott
sternly suggested that the President and Kissinger had better consult
more with Congress, especially on Vietnam. Unless the White House
paid more attention to Congress, he warned, Nixon's policies would

be doomed. There was a stony silence after he sat down. The evening seemed to be getting out of hand. Then, as an author of the pending bill, Senator Church rose to speak for himself and Senator Cooper. Standing only a few feet away from Kissinger, he looked him straight in the eye and said that unless the President cut our involvement in Vietnam, what we would need was not an act of love, but an act of Congress.

There were gasps. The atmosphere was getting uncomfortable. I looked over at Congressman James Symington, who often had lightened that room with his special humor, but he shook his head, indicating that he didn't want to get into the fray. I felt that something should be done to smooth things over, so while I rarely speak at my own dinners, I stood and said that since we had heard from the executive and legislative branches, perhaps the fourth estate should be recognized. I called on Eric Sevareid, and there were a few boos in recognition of my cop-out. Eric was furious but he carried it off well, and afterward I led the way back to the drawing room and coffee.

I have never been to another Washington dinner party with such a tense atmosphere. While conversation is fascinating and often lively on such evenings I've never seen it so heated. Although Scott and Kissinger talked alone together for a while after dinner, it didn't help; the dichotomy on the war had simply grown too big.

In the *New York Times* the next Sunday, May 24, Tom Wicker wrote about the Cambodian incursion:

> It is really no wonder, then, that the Church-Cooper amendment is believed to command a majority in the Senate: even Mr. Nixon's opposition to the amendment, in the face of his own pledges, raises questions about his real intentions in Cambodia.
>
> The situation was sharply illuminated at a dinner the other night when a high Administration official described the Presidency as the unifying force of the nation. He said that Americans recently had seen one President destroyed by assassination and another by lost credibility, and implored his audience not to let a third be destroyed for lack of support, even if it now required "an act of compassion, and act of love" by his critics.
>
> Whereupon a leading Senator coolly replied: "What many of us think is required is an act of Congress."

189

Agreement between Nixon and Congress was doomed, and eventually the Cooper-Church amendment was passed, as well as a War Powers Act further curtailing the President's powers to embark on undeclared wars.

Almost three years later, in April 1973, when Watergate was coming to a boil, Sevareid referred on the evening news to the Nixon men who had been accused of wrongdoing. He said:

> "Most of the political figures accused of betraying their trust have not even been indicted or tried yet, but Mr. Kissinger is already suggesting general compassion for them. Nobody is suggesting that they be treated as the President said ordinary criminals should be treated— without pity. But one thing at a time. Their guilt has not yet been established, let alone their right to compassion.
>
> "Mr. Kissinger adopted the same stance of nobility during the uproar over our invasion of Cambodia three years ago. The President's travail, he said then at a Washington dinner party, should be met by not only understanding, but loving understanding, whereupon Senator Frank Church arose and said that what was required was not an act of love but an act of Congress.
>
> "What is required today is an act of housecleaning, involving not only the White House but the Department of Justice. Hence all the speculation here of a new Attorney General to direct the cleanup."

Kissinger's concept of compassion for leaders, himself included, has become well known. As he sees it, we self-inflict lethal wounds when we chastise ourselves publicly, to our detriment and to the benefit of others. But prior to our party I did not know how deep his conviction was, nor did I dream that what he describes as compassion would later be expanded into a policy to excuse government secrecy and even mistakes.

CHAPTER 24 ⌇

Ever since the broadcast of "Mrs. Nixon's Journey" the President had wanted to do a program like it with me. Right after the telecast on August 10, 1969, he had phoned and been ecstatic; there's no other word for it. He had missed nothing, had liked everything, and it had given him an idea: he thought the dedication of the National Redwoods Park in California in a few weeks would make great television. He had it all figured out: Lady Bird was to be honored, and my television cameras would follow her and Pat through the forests; then he'd sit down under a redwood tree with former President Johnson, and I could sit between them and interview them both. With his omnipresent concern for "firsts," Nixon pointed out that this would be the first television interview with a President and a former President simultaneously. Why not? It sounded like a good idea to me. Then the would-be producer signed off, suggesting that I work out the details with Ron Ziegler.

Such presidential specials are considered highly important by network news departments, but I couldn't find anyone at NBC to talk to about this potential coup. Finally I reached President Julian Goodman, who was slightly incredulous at the production envisioned by Nixon, and reacted as if he'd thought I'd had hallucinations. In turn, I questioned his news judgment. After all, I had just been around the world with the Nixons and had seen hundreds of thousands of people clamoring for a view of the President—not the least anxious of which were the network news correspondents, every one of whom would have given his eyeteeth for such a scoop.

When I told Ron Ziegler about the proposed show the next day, he was equally incredulous, but tried to pretend that he knew something about it. He had visions of the flak he'd get from other White House correspondents if I landed such an exclusive, and was no more enthusiastic about the project than the NBC hierarchy.

Producer Nixon's scenario never materialized; Ziegler kept putting me off, and the LBJ visit to the redwoods dedication came and went without benefit of his scenario on television. I was irritated because my exclusive had been aborted, so I came up with the idea of interviewing the President at Camp David. I had lunch with Ziegler and we agreed on a format similar to Jackie's tour of the White House. Nixon and I would walk around the grounds, where reporters hadn't been permitted before, and a camera would precede us on a motorized truck with large boom mikes which would pick up his guided tour of the presidential hideaway. To keep the audience from getting dizzy following us, we would stop at some point and I would interview him, with no limitations of any kind, and of course no knowledge beforehand of what the questions would be. Agreed! As I paid the bill and we left the restaurant, Ron said, "The only thing we have to do now is set the time." I urged spring, when the mountain trees would be flowering, but spring of 1970 came and went. Then I urged fall, so that we could show the autumn leaves of the Maryland countryside, but soon we were into winter. I was not only irritated but embarrassed; I was beginning to look silly to my male superiors at NBC, and it didn't help that there was little enthusiasm for the production from the regular White House correspondents.

Finally I called on Leonard Garment, that long-suffering hero of the arts, and complained that I was getting the runaround. Still nothing happened. It was only after I left NBC News that Nixon stopped me on the way out of a news conference to ask what I thought of the "show plan." He was surprised that I knew nothing about it and said that I'd be hearing soon. When I phoned him, Director of Communications Herb Klein also knew nothing about it and said he'd call me back—which shows how far out of the strategy and policy-making decisions he was by this time. The next day he told me that the idea was for me to interview the President live, for an hour, the program to be carried simultaneously by all three networks, which had already been approached on the subject.

Of course I had no objections, since I was then free lancing and such a spectacular would help launch my syndicated news service. Klein explained to the networks that Nixon was keeping a long-standing commitment to me, but while they had no objection to my appearing, they all wanted their own men on as well. (Many years later Bill Leonard, a top CBS News executive, told me frankly that at CBS they feared I wouldn't ask tough enough questions. Not that I had a reputation for being a patsy—quite the contrary—but they became skeptical when the White House specifically requested me. It was a fear they no longer had after the program.)

Eventually someone came up with the idea of the three networks each providing their own man and of my participating on behalf of the Public Broadcasting System. For years Public Broadcasting had been trying to establish its credentials as a bona-fide network in these presidential specials but had gotten nowhere; each time it had applied for entry into the exclusive club, it had been turned down. Therefore PBS President John Macy was astonished when he received a White

House call saying that his station could participate, provided that they chose me as their correspondent.

Macy didn't object to me; in fact, we were good friends. But he did object to the Administration trying to push PBS around or influence it. There had been a great deal of pressure from the White House on PBS's budgets, as well as threats that unless its programs became "more responsive to public demand"—meaning more pro-Nixon—its financial support would be slashed altogether. This was all part of the "enemies" list and the hate-the-media mentality of the White House in those days. Macy made a hurried trip to see Herb Klein, received assurances that no White House pressure would be put on his network or on any correspondent it chose, and then phoned me to ask me to represent PBS on the show. He emphasized that their correspondent was to be hindered in no way, and that my questions should be on anything I thought newsworthy, with no holds barred. (In all fairness, no one at the White House or connected with Nixon in any way ever tried to contact me about the show.)

Macy, a former professor and a nice and dedicated man, was puzzled; in view of my friendship with the Johnsons, he said, he wouldn't have been as surprised if the request had come from LBJ. But he agreed to pay my fee, and offered the help and services of Jim Karyan, later the president of PBS News and Public Affairs. Karyan was delighted, not so much with me as with the precedent that had been set. In the past he felt that his news operation had been discriminated against by being excluded from such programs, and he believed strongly that PBS deserved to be there as the fourth network. But the last time he had complained to the White House, he had been outraged to be told that his group couldn't participate because it had had no nationally known correspondent since Paul Niven's death.

I loved the idea of taking Paul's place. He had always gone into a think tank before any major interview, reading everything he could find on the subject. In fact, this is what he was doing when he died; holed up with a dozen books, he fell asleep while reading, and a fire from his ever-present cigarette, which was always dripping ashes down his ample front, burned out his house.

I told Karyan that we'd do this one for Paul, so we had a marathon think session, holed up with old newspaper clips, interrupted only by

New Year's Eve when we shared champagne in paper cups with the researchers.

The production of any presidential interview aired on all four networks is a complicated matter. There are always disputes and different theories about who should participate, and in the early days of these affairs the White House generally selected the correspondents they would allow to do such an interview. At first it was the stars, the anchormen, who did the questioning. Later the networks thought that reporters on the scene, those assigned to the White House, were more familiar with the subject matter, and they were chosen. Still later it was decided that a man on the White House beat would have to show too much deference to his subject, or by pursuing a tough subject too vigorously, would imperil future access to White House sources.

To interview a President is the most prestigious job a network correspondent can have, and it is an honor not wasted on a new boy. In addition, it's a tough assignment. No one wants to make a fool of himself in front of fifty-five million people, with the President as witness. This time the commercial networks chose three big stars: Eric Sevareid for CBS, John Chancellor for NBC and Howard K. Smith for ABC. Each of us, with our bureau chiefs acting as seconds in a duel, met in Ron Ziegler's office to work out the details with the White House personnel. There was an argument about the format because the three men had interviewed Nixon six months earlier in Los Angeles and had been criticized for lack of substance. They felt that this was partially because of the inhibiting format, and wanted no more of it. I argued strongly for a procedure in which each of us would have fifteen consecutive minutes, without interruption from the others. Sevareid and I each felt that with this format we could bore in and get answers to some meaningful questions. But Howard and John had other ideas, and in the end the White House would agree to nothing and wanted to hear nothing; Ron Ziegler said, "The President wants no part of any prearranged format because he doesn't want the White House to be accused of managing the news." That was that, so the four of us, with our seconds, retreated to lunch to decide among ourselves what to do.

There are no better correspondents than Sevareid, Chancellor and Smith, and I know of no finer men in our profession. Eric had long helped me, and had been both my mentor and idol; Chancellor and

I had gone on an NBC trip together, and I considered him my best friend at the network; Howard K. had been dear to me when we both worked at CBS, and he and his wife, Benny, had sent me congratulatory flowers after I had covered my first convention. Since the three of them had gone through this exercise before, I asked for advice. Sevareid said, "Wear something warm." Painfully rubbing the back of his neck, he added, "They keep the place so cold that I still have bursitis from the last time."

Nixon was a "sweater," as they say in show business, and to keep him from perspiring the room was kept as cold as possible. He entered only at the last minute so that he wouldn't have to sit under the hot lights, which could melt his make-up, for any longer than necessary. In fact, they told me that he had been so late for the Los Angeles interview that the three of them began to speculate about what would happen if he didn't show up and they had to rap for an hour among themselves. Then they regaled me with an account of how the President had finally appeared, just before they went on the air, with his fly unzipped. As the announcer in the outer hall was giving the names of the correspondents, Nixon rushed in, the engineer put on his mike, and with the three correspondents staring in horror, producer Bill Small of CBS walked over and softly told the President that his fly was open. While the announcer outside was solemnly intoning, "Ladies and gentlemen, the President of the United States," Richard Nixon was zipping up his pants.

Over lunch we agreed to draw straws. The opening question would be asked by Correspondent #1, who turned out to be Chancellor; #2, Howard, would ask the next question, and twenty minutes into the program would switch the topic from domestic affairs to foreign policy; #3, which was me, would switch the focus to general questioning; and #4, Sevareid, would do the sign off. The only other prearrangement was that we agreed to tell one another over the weekend what our opening question would be. (There were several phone calls, as everyone changed his question from hour to hour.)

On the day of the broadcast Karyan wisely let me stew all by myself. By then I knew every position Nixon had taken on anything since entering the White House; I was a walking encyclopedia on the man. Two hours before the broadcast in prime time on the evening of January 4, 1971, I went to the Hay-Adams, a block from the White House, where I met Evind Bjerke, the greatest hairdresser I've ever known, and Irv Carlton, the best make-up man I'd ever seen. These two men were dear friends who had been with me through election nights, conventions, inaugurations, inaugural balls and in little lean-tos outside the White House for presidential weddings. But nothing had been so traumatic as this, and the two of them, sensitive to the pressure, tried alternately to joke to make me feel better, or to be quiet so I could get my thoughts in order. It had already been announced that Nixon had spent the last three days preparing for the upcoming confrontation—which was true of the four correspondents as well.

My faithful second, Karyan, sat biting his fingernails while my hair and make-up were being done, and I couldn't have had three better friends pulling for me. But then we turned on the television so I could get the latest news. That was a mistake. A "commentary on the media" followed the news, and some insufferable idiot appeared to say that for the momentous presidential interview soon to be aired, Public Broadcasting should not have chosen Nancy Dickerson be-cause she lacked "authority." His dreadful pomposities went on for two minutes, and I felt sorry for my three companions. They were helpless, but I knew they would gladly have strangled the man if they could. Finally I turned off the set and said, "Let's go."

A limousine was waiting outside—not an extravagance, since it was a bitter night with a strong winter wind and snow flurries. We entered the White House grounds through the diplomatic entrance, and in a few minutes I was entering the "ready room" feeling like Sidney Carton on his way to the guillotine.

But if misery loves company, I had it. There were my three col-leagues all being made up, and if I was nervous, you should have seen the others. Howard was sitting in the corner on a sofa going over his cards, muttering to himself, hardly able to say hello. Sevareid was pacing back and forth telling funny stories, and when I asked him if he was nervous, he snapped back, "Good God! You ought to know I never tell jokes."

In the ladies' room—or was it the men's room?—I ran head-on into John Chancellor. There we were outside the same booth, stand-ing before the same mirror, and suddenly I could see the humor of it all. I was nervous because I was going on with the three of them, and was scared I wouldn't be as good as they, while they were worried about going on with Nixon, something that didn't bother me at all, since I had known him for fifteen years. Besides, I've never had any compunction about asking Presidents questions, since that's what my job has been.

In the library it was so cold that I had to put on my coat. But with Sevareid's warning about the temperature in mind, I was wearing some thick white lace stockings which I thought chic, and Nixon commented on them before we went on the air. You can be sure we all glanced at his fly when he entered; then the floor man was shouting, "Stand by, quiet in the room," and Eric Sevareid, that dear and gentle man, leaned across in front of everyone and said, "Nancy, you look absolutely ravishing tonight." And we were off.

Nixon was prepared, so were we, and the program was a respectable example of the press playing the role of the opposition in the political process. Later one of the President's three speech writers told me that though none of us had revealed any of our questions to anyone else —except to one another on the first question—the White House staff had anticipated every query, and they sat there nodding their heads as Nixon reeled off their suggested answers. The only exception came when I told the President that his leadership had not been perceived by the young, the blacks and the poor, and asked when he was going to give us "the lift of a driving dream" which he had promised in his campaign. He answered that the dream would come as soon as he got over the nightmares he had inherited—an ironic response when one reflects that when *he* stepped down, his successor would say, "Our long national nightmare is over."

I also pointed out that while he had enunciated his support for various programs such as welfare reform, the people and Congress didn't think he really meant it; they did not perceive him to actually favor what he had endorsed. Although these two questions came at different intervals in the program, I was trying to point out his incapacity to lead because he didn't trust people and they in turn didn't trust him. A day later the *New York Times* editorialized:

> In short, there has nowhere in these first two years of the Nixon presidency been the "lift of a driving dream" of which he spoke in 1968 and about which one of his interviewers pertinently reminded him. President Nixon cannot be faulted for his failure to provide inspiration because the ability to inspire is not given to every leader, not even every President. But he can be held responsible for making his words and his

actions coincide and for deploying behind his programs the powers of the Presidency which are his. These are the tests of confidence. By these more modest but still demanding standards he is likely to be judged over the next years.

As soon as we were off the air, the first thing Nixon said was, "Why didn't one of you ask me about Red China?" It had been on my list but there hadn't been time after I asked him about a possible summit with the Russians. I knew China was of prime importance to him; in his first interview after the inauguration, with Theodore White, he had mentioned his desire to re-establish relations, and he had also brought it up during his meanderings at the Lincoln Memorial on the night of the Cambodian incursion. Nixon was well aware that as a recognized Cold Warrior he could make the gesture toward China more easily than a liberal—who of course would have been criticized by many of the President's followers. Shortly thereafter Nixon revealed the Kissinger trip to Peking. We lost a good story for lack of time.

After the program, photographers rushed in to take our pictures. Nixon seemed uncomfortable while this was going on, and soon hurried nervously away. It was almost as if he were afraid of us. At other times, White House staffmen had even suggested that I phone him after a television appearance to give him my impressions because, just like everyone else, he wanted to be reassured, but unlike everyone else, he didn't have a coterie of friends who felt close enough to phone and tell him.

It's one of the few times I can remember that a politician didn't stick around for the rehash. The breed exists, thrives and grows by talk and communication; it's the way they get elected, whether as sheriff or as senator. Nixon, however, never enjoyed that essential of politics. It's extraordinary that he ever became President without possessing that essential ingredient, and it explains how he lost touch with reality in his White House years.

When Karyan came in, he put his chunky arm around me and said, "You're really a pro"—the highest accolade—but I was not amused when Bill Small, the CBS producer, chauvinistically indicated that he was amazed at how well I'd done. (NBC was more gracious. Later Reuven Frank wrote me that he thought that John Chancellor and I had asked the best questions.)

At his Cabinet meeting the next day Nixon received a standing ovation, and as he walked in he asked Secretary of State Rogers, "Do you suppose we froze Nancy's ass off last night?" They had.

Shortly thereafter I saw Jim Hagerty, Ike's press secretary and later an ABC vice president, who said, "The White House sure went to great lengths to keep its promises to you, didn't they?" They had.

CHAPTER 25 ⬲

The second Nixon inauguration was cold, damp and without joy. Having won a historic landslide, the President acted as if he had just squeaked through. Such a victory would have swelled anyone else's ego, but it only seemed to make Nixon more insecure.

Nixon was always a loner, the male Greta Garbo of the White House, always uncomfortable, never at ease. Once I talked to William P. Rogers about the difficulty of having even a dinner-party conversation with Dick, as we called him in the fifties. "I know," Bill replied, "I have the same trouble, and I'm supposed to be his best friend."

In an interview John Ehrlichman once explained the Nixon personality by saying, "He's a brief man, in the legal sense of that word." Nixon liked everything to be presented on paper and written succinctly. At the time, Ehrlichman had his hands full trying to minimize the discontent of some Nixon appointees who were restless because they never saw their boss. "The trouble is," he said, "these men came to Washington expecting to put their feet up on the President's desk and talk things over, but it just doesn't happen that way." It certainly didn't. Nixon was the most remote President possible, a prisoner not so much of his position as of his own personality. His former law partner and White House aide, Leonard Garment, once explained it to me by saying that the President just didn't "enjoy rapping." When I pointed out that a dialogue is an essential of the decision-making process, Garment shook his head and said, "But he doesn't like it. That's the way he is."

Pat Hillings, Nixon's friend and a former California congressman who had come to Washington with him, once described the President as "a funny kind of guy, not palsy or anything." Nixon didn't have many friends, he admitted—"only Bebe Rebozo, because no one else will do what Bebe does." According to Hillings, "Bebe will sit in a room all alone with him for hours, saying nothing, while Nixon writes away on that long yellow pad he's always got. It would drive me nuts." Richard Nixon never was one of the boys, never enjoyed the smoke-filled rooms which sustained the Irish around Kennedy or the loyalists around Johnson. Such an atmosphere bored him.

Unfortunately for him and for all of us, Watergate also bored him. He simply wasn't interested in the details of such a folly; he found it an irritating inconvenience, and so he just ordered it away, by whatever means necessary. Which is what his staff did, and which is how the coverup started. He set the tone; they followed. Reclusiveness was integral to his personality, and one of the major flaws that led to his downfall. The two men who had known him long enough to level with him, Bob Finch and Herb Klein, lost their influence by being systematically cut off by Haldeman, the autocrat who functioned like the Prussian general his crew haircut made him resemble. Haldeman was Nixon's door to the outside and it rarely opened; it was virtually impossible to reach the President except through him. Only a few old friends could circumvent him by calling Nixon's long-time secretary, Rose Mary Woods. From the date of the break-in until the day he resigned, Nixon was a President in isolation, cut off from reality.

Two months after Watergate the GOP convention met in Miami Beach for what can best be described as a coronation for Nixon and Agnew. They were jubilantly received by an adoring audience, the adulation reinforced by slick movies which made the candidates' every deed an heroic adventure. Away from the convention hall, there was the usual extracurricular amusement attendant at political conventions. Germaine Greer, the feminist, lounged around the lobby in jeans and a cut-off top, revealing the longest torso extant, holding forth on her theory that the Kennedys were male chauvinists and that the family should be promoting the one member "who really has the balls—Eunice." Then there was Sammy Davis Jr. hugging Richard Nixon. I was so astonished that I thought it was someone in blackface imitating Sammy, or someone impersonating Nixon, or both. And I was delighted to be able to introduce Pat Oliphant, the cartoonist, to Tricia Nixon. Oliphant, a marvelous free spirit, up to then had professed to believe that Tricia was only a figment of the imagination of the GOP National Committee. He mumbled something when introduced, and then accused me of jeopardizing his political integrity.

Other incidents at the convention showed how hardened the Administration's hatred toward the press had become. My brother-in-law from Milwaukee, Ernest Philipp, was there as an alternate delegate, and I proudly introduced him to the Ehrlichmans and their daughter, who apparently could not believe that a reporter might have Republican relatives, let alone *official* Republican relatives. The Ehrlichmans were sitting in front of a large section of young people who were wildly applauding everything they heard. As they roared their well-orchestrated chants, Ehrlichman scowled and said, "That's the real story of this convention—the devoted young people who've come here spontaneously, sometimes at great hardship, to support Nixon. They've come despite what all of you say about how the Democrats have pre-empted the youth vote for McGovern. But," he lamented, "that's the story the networks won't tell."

I replied that it would be impossible for the networks to avoid the phenomenon, since the shouts were drowning out the proceedings. "Oh, they'll find a way," sneered the Ehrlichman's pretty, teen-aged daughter. The intensity of their hatred for reporters and networks radiated from the whole family.

While Ehrlichman claimed that those young people represented a spontaneous outpouring of affection for Nixon, the fact was that their expenses had been partly paid for by a GOP committee, and that their chants were well directed by a cheerleader. The Nixon people had manipulated a phony display; it was obvious that they planned to drown out convention coverage and to force the networks to show that young people liked Nixon because they didn't think that they could get the story on the air in any other way. Packing the hall is an old political trick used by both parties, but this was different because it was not one candidate's supporters against those of another, but the Nixon people against the press.

Six weeks before the Republicans anointed Nixon and Agnew, the Democrats had put up Senator George McGovern in a convention distinguished only for its ineptness. While the much-touted "new"

201

politicians who had seized power through the democratic process were a special breed of concerned citizens, they lost their souls on the way to Miami Beach. It was shocking when a crippled George Wallace spoke from the podium. While I do not believe that Wallace has the qualifications to be governor of Alabama, let alone a presidential candidate, I was appalled at the comments and the general attitude of the audience. There were boos and hisses, as if they were jeering his infirmity. As for the concerns of women, also much balleyhooed, they were pre-emptorily cast aside. And the amateurs running the McGovern campaign showed how well they qualified for that status when they managed to arrange for McGovern's acceptance speech to be televised when it was prime time only outside the continental limits of the United States.

The hope and promise of the McGovern camp were epitomized by Gary Hart, the young campaign manager who later became a Colorado senator. I interviewed him regularly during the campaign, and he never wavered from his conviction that there was a new cry throughout the land. But the devotion of an army of dedicated followers foundered on the fuzzy thinking displayed in McGovern's speeches and the debilitating choice of Senator Eagleton as a running mate, an episode from which the campaign never recovered.

On Election Day I joined Gary and some of his staff to toss a football in the parking lot behind headquarters. That's what the Kennedys used to do, but for the McGovern crowd it was a symbolic gesture of their pathetic attempt to recapture Camelot and the Kennedy dream. It was a dream that never happened.

After the conventions Watergate simmered along, failing to impregnate the national consciousness because it presented unacceptable alternatives. It was clear from the incredible revelations unfolding daily that the President of the United States either was incompetent, since he kept denying knowledge of most of what went on around him, or else was involved in criminal acts. Neither of these possibilities was palatable to the American people. As George Orwell once wrote about Victorian England, there is no censor so effective as readers themselves because there is only a certain amount that people will accept. During the fall of 1972 Americans simply did not want to accept the truth about Watergate. On the lecture circuit I found that audiences could not bring themselves to accept the fact that their President was intimately involved in Watergate. It gored too many of their sacred cows.

Though reporters are trained to be cynics, it *was* difficult even for the press corps to believe that the Nixon people could be such wholesale liars. At a football game one Sunday afternoon Jeb Magruder, the associate campaign manager, told me about hundreds of thousands of dollars in the campaign safe. When I called to check the story with him the next day, he changed it and also claimed that he had been speaking off the record. Then he changed the story *again*, and while I knew that he was lying, I dismissed him as an insignificant figure on the committee.

Toward the end of the campaign, when Henry Kissinger made his famous declaration that "Peace is at hand," I thought he meant it, and was jubilant. Although I knew that we could have gotten out of the war three years earlier with the very same deal, I was so swept up by the good news that I phoned John Ehrlichman and told him that I thought we should seize the opportunity to repair our tarnished honor and regain our lost prestige throughout the world. I said that as one citizen who could help, I thought it my duty to offer my services, and in a burst of patriotic fervor, solemnly offered to take a job in the Administration to tell the American story—perhaps as head of the Voice of America, an area in which I'd had some experience and a job that I'd been sounded out about before. I shouldn't have bothered; my enthusiasm was matched only by Ehrlichman's lack of it. For my pains he made some crack about how long it had taken me to see the light. I hung up thinking, My God! I was only trying to help. Luckily for me, I never heard from Ehrlichman about my offer to help reinstate U.S. prestige. In a few weeks they started the Christmas bombing, and I quickly wrote him that I had changed my mind. Not only did I disagree, I wouldn't have known how to explain their folly. I still don't.

Naïvely, I thought that because I had known the Nixons so long, I was exempt from their blanket hatred of the press, but I was wrong. I also didn't realize how much Mrs. Nixon disliked me. Though I missed the honor of making the President's enemies list, I believe that she had a private one of her own. For some reason that I still can't fathom, she became angry with me during a private luncheon at the F Street Club and demanded to know what I thought I had to say that was important enough to qualify me for the lecture circuit.

I told her that sometimes I even talked about her. From then on I was out, ignominiously scratched from the White House Christmas-card list. Since First Families send out thousands of cards, it's a real trick to be excluded. And Mike wasn't invited to any more White House Christmas parties, which was fine with him; he was jaded at the age of eight!

CHAPTER 26

The date of the Watergate break-in was June 17, 1972, but the ambiance which permitted it began the day that Richard Nixon walked into 1600 Pennsylvania Avenue. His own arrogance of power had encouraged the autocrats on his staff, and by April of 1973 Haldeman and Ehrlichman were out, Nixon was deeply involved in the cover-up of Watergate, and his remaining staff was in disarray, with no idea what was going on. Within days General Alexander Haig was put in charge, and in the summer two old Nixon friends, Melvin Laird and Bryce Harlow, were pressed to come back to help. Neither of them wanted to, but as Bryce later described it, it was as if the two of them were standing next to a swimming pool and one was pushed and the other fell in with him.

On his first day back, Harlow went to a senior staff meeting at which routine matters were discussed. There was no mention of Watergate, so as they started to break up, he asked what the Watergate "game plan" was. There was a shocked silence; it was as if there were a rule against mentioning it. Harlow, an old pro whose government service goes back to the days of FDR, was appalled; looking at Fred Buzhardt and Leonard Garment, Nixon's White House lawyers, he asked why they weren't out in San Clemente with the President, where they could do some good. At this there was a shaking of heads. There was no point; they couldn't get in to see Nixon. At that meeting in July 1973, at the height of the scandal, there was no policy on how to handle Watergate, and the top staff of the White House was not even discussing it.

At the prodding of the other senior staff members, Harlow agreed to go to San Clemente and talk to the President about setting up a Watergate counterattack. Earlier, however, Laird had become aware of the vacuum and had flown to San Clemente to lay out a bold new course for Nixon to follow. The President became livid and told Laird never to mention Watergate to him again. In light of this, Al Haig called Harlow to say that he didn't think the trip to California was necessary; knowing Nixon's previous reaction, he wanted to save Harlow the trip. That was the end; it closed the door on any possible salvaging of the situation by the President's admitting that he was partly at fault. Nixon had no friends who could or would level with him, and the two men he had begged to return to help him could not even mention the subject to him. Thereafter Nixon became even more remote—"taut," as Harlow described it—increasingly dominated by his effort to live the lie.

At this point the Agnew scandal surfaced as he was publicly accused of tax evasion on payoffs made by Maryland contractors. Harlow went to the President and said that he would like to resign "to help Ted, because he needs me more than you do." At that time Nixon, Haig and Buzhardt were the only ones at the White House who knew the full story of Agnew, and the President said that Harlow had better be briefed by the other two before he made a decision. On the basis of the evidence, there was no question about Agnew's exit; it was only a matter of the least painful way to bring it about, and Harlow was one of the few people the Vice President would listen to. Meanwhile Laird was openly lobbying against Agnew, calling his old friends in the Congress and telling them to withhold their support until they learned the facts. One of those he called was Les Arends, who said to me, "I wouldn't have minded his calling, but it made me angry that he thought I'd be such a damn fool to sound off before I knew what I was talking about."

At the same time I was doing righteously indignant stories filmed on the White House lawn in which I said that in all my years in Washington I'd never seen such backbiting, and that the White House was undermining the Vice President without the guts to do it publicly. I made no excuses for Agnew, whom I considered to be an oaf, nor for his policies, which I hated; I just thought that he was being railroaded, and if Nixon wanted to dump him, he ought to do it openly. The Agnew staff was convinced that their boss was innocent, and kept putting out stories that the White House was trying

205

to throw him out because he was a big enough trophy to be a sop so that the press would take the heat off the President on Watergate.

Agnew *was* convincing. When the first rumors broke he held a news conference, answering every question, and it was widely felt that if only Nixon would be as candid the country could put Watergate behind it. I didn't know whether to believe Agnew or not. For years I had heard rumors, none of them proved, about his questionable activities. But Barry Goldwater did believe him. Agnew had called on him and convinced him of his innocence, because he was still determined to fight all the way through an impeachment trial and was desperate for support. As the dominant voice of conservatism in the GOP, Goldwater was a formidable ally. He telephoned Harlow at the White House, said that he'd had a bellyful of "this stuff about Ted," that the Vice President was being mistreated, that "some guys were trying their damnedest to railroad him out of office," and that he wasn't going to allow such harassment to continue. He was flying to Phoenix within the hour, but when he returned he was going to talk to the press and put a stop to this nonsense. On this note he hung up. Knowing the Goldwater personality, Harlow commandeered Buzhardt and an Army jet, overtook Goldwater's commercial flight and was at the Phoenix airport when Barry arrived. Harlow realized that unless Goldwater had all the evidence, he might well blow his stack before returning to Washington, thus giving Agnew the support he needed. After Goldwater heard the facts, he kept quiet.

It was Nixon who orchestrated Agnew's departure. It took skill because Agnew was hanging on tightly and seemed determined to bluff it through. While Nixon directly but secretly supervised the pressure, the Vice President kept fighting publicly, and I kept doing pieces from the White House lawn in which I made odious comparisons between the White House cover-up and Agnew's openness. It's obvious now that Agnew was just trying to get a better deal in the plea bargaining. Nixon was afraid that if the pressure wasn't handled adroitly, Agnew would balk and refuse to resign, and insist on an impeachment trial, which Nixon found intolerable. It's ironic that Nixon was planning the strategy of Agnew's departure with the same delicacy as others would manipulate his own resignation within the year.

On Saturday, October 7, when Agnew made his impassioned plea before a group of Republican women in California, they believed him, for they pounded the tables in support. Peter Malatesta was there with other staff members, and none of them doubted their boss's innocence. (Peter also says that Agnew himself was never convinced of his own guilt; yet, contrarily, he was terrified of going to jail.)

The next day Dick and I gave a party at Merrywood for the John Murchisons of Texas, who had come up for the Redskins-Cowboy game. Malatesta was also there, back from California, and said that Agnew was being made a scapegoat by the White House. Judge John Sirica was also at the party and ten-year-old Michael Dickerson, who was fascinated by the judge's hawklike blue eyes, declared the next morning at breakfast that if he ever did anything wrong, he hoped he wouldn't have to go before Judge Sirica. Smart boy!

Two days later, on October 10, Agnew resigned. His announcement shocked the reporters in the courtroom, who had not expected it. I had not anticipated it either. I simply had not believed that a man could lie so much for so long. Certainly not from the White House steps. No wonder we reporters are cynics.

Nixon's celebrated selection of a vice-presidential successor was a charade. He went through the motion of accepting nominations of names for the post in sealed envelopes from various sources, but he paid no attention to the suggestions. It was a farce, one more public-relations ploy to dupe the public into thinking he was being democratic. The device was also calculated to make congressional leaders feel important, and that they were making a contribution to a historic decision. Wrong. Nixon's preference was John Connally, and he was the man he intended to name, regardless of any suggestions, sealed or otherwise. Although today Connally doesn't come right out and say that Nixon offered the nomination to him, he leaves the impression that he understood he was to be chosen. However, at decision time Melvin Laird, a modern Machiavelli, intervened. He knew nothing of Connally's pending problems with the Special Watergate Prosecutor, and was not against him; rather, he was pro-Ford. The two men had sat next to each other for sixteen years on the House Armed Services Committee and were close friends.

Laird is a formidable advocate, but when he suggested Jerry Ford, their old friend from the Chowder and Marching Club, the President was noncommittal. He had made up his mind to choose Connally, who is, as Laird puts it, "the most admired politician in Nixon's life."

Then Laird called Ford and asked him if he would take the job. Jerry said that he wanted to talk it over with Betty first, and Laird replied that he had to know right away. At eleven-thirty that night Ford phoned back to say that he'd accept the post if it was offered to him.

At one point during the maneuvering, Congressman Barber Conable of New York phoned Laird to say that he was organizing House Republicans to pass a resolution calling on Nixon to appoint Ford. Acting as Ford's manager by now, Laird vetoed the idea of a House GOP endorsement. He knew that Nixon was in such a disturbed mood that such pressure might boomerang. Again he talked to the President and pointed out the obvious: in the current climate any Nixon nominee would have a brutal time being confirmed by a hostile Congress, and this was especially true of the renegade Connally, who is unpopular with some congressional Democrats. Laird arranged for the Democratic congressional leaders, House Speaker Carl Albert and Senate Majority Leader Mike Mansfield, to talk to Nixon, and they endorsed this analysis. It was clear to Nixon that he didn't need one more massive problem, so Laird managed to convince him that to minimize his troubles, he should choose a popular member of Congress. This meant only one man: the House GOP leader, Jerry Ford, who credits Laird with his selection. Thus Laird engineered the Ford nomination on the basis that a restive Congress would go along. Otherwise Nixon would have chosen Connally.

Nixon's elaborate ceremony to announce Ford as successor to Agnew was distinguished by bad taste: red-coated Marines played violins in the White House foyer while the President appeared before a star-studded audience in the East Room, all on live television. He acted as if he were presiding over a joyous festival rather than the first resignation in history of an American Vice President. In effect, violins were playing while Washington burned. Nixon's instincts had failed him again; he was insensitive to what he was doing and did not understand that the citizens of his country were profoundly concerned about their government. Outside, there was no fighting in the streets, but the mood was one of growing skepticism and silent distrust. Inside, the President announced that there was champagne for everyone, but the taste was sour.

After Ford was designated, I did one of the first interviews with Betty Ford. She was determined to maintain their "life as always."

She told me that she had been cooking Jerry's favorite pot roast when Nixon phoned. He had used the private number, which had no extension, so he had to call back on another line because Jerry wanted Betty to hear too.

The Fords' open-door policy was a refreshing change. Jerry had already agreed to a one-hour special on their home life, and while I was there Mrs. Ford received several more requests for television interviews. The Siamese cat was the only ham in the family; it kept wanting to get into the picture. Susan Ford was also there, a strong personality who was cool about the new events in her life and very much in charge. She and her mother were delighted by a phone call telling them that while the future Vice President was on the West Coast to keep a speaking date, he had stopped in at the University of Idaho where his son Jack went to school. Several students crowded around to congratulate Ford, who was shaking hands and thanking them, when one of them said, "Hey, Dad! Don't you recognize me?" Since his father last saw him, young Ford had grown a beard.

A week later there was another White House show, this one distinguished by bad judgment, which has since become known as the Saturday Night Massacre. For the preceding five days the President had been under pressure because of two crises: first, the U.S. policy in the Mideast which resulted in the U.S. airlift to Israel; second, the demand for the Watergate tapes which Special Prosecutor Archibald Cox said were essential to his inquiry. Negotiations went on between Cox, Attorney General Elliot L. Richardson and the White House, and compromises were suggested. There was an elaborate White House plan, in which Senator John Stennis, the conscience of the Senate, was asked to listen to summaries of the tapes and decide which ones should be released. Supposedly this was agreed to, and Bryce Harlow was given the job of telling Cabinet members about it before the plan was announced publicly. When Harlow phoned Richardson as a matter of routine, he assumed that of all the members of the Cabinet, Richardson would know the most, since he had supposedly helped arrange the compromise. Wrong. Richardson told Harlow, "I've never been treated so shabbily before in my life." Bryce didn't know what Richardson was talking about and told General Haig, who didn't understand either. In the meanwhile, Cox heard the

White House statement revealing the Stennis plan, issued one of his own saying that the President was refusing to comply with the Supreme Court's decree, and called a news conference for the next day.

Saturday, October 20, was a gloriously sunny fall day, especially along the banks of the Potomac, with the leaves twirling around in a feisty breeze. Peter Malatesta, who lived a quarter mile up the river from us and was still in a state of shock over Agnew's resignation, had come to play tennis. Afterward we went inside to watch the Cox news conference. Once again events seemed so improbable that it was hard to grasp that they weren't fiction. When Cox said that he couldn't follow the President's orders, it was obvious that he would be fired. Little did we know that only four or five houses upriver, Elliot Richardson had anticipated this scenario and for the past two days had been writing and rewriting his resignation statement. At that moment, however, he was at the Justice Department watching the news conference, and when Haig phoned Richardson and told him that *he* was the one who must fire Cox, he refused and resigned. Bill Ruckelshaus, the Deputy Attorney General, also refused and resigned. This left Solicitor General Richard Bork, the next in line, and he carried out Nixon's orders reluctantly.

While Nixon had talked of firing Cox before and knew that Richardson would have to resign, Bryce Harlow believes that the President did not really expect events to occur as they did—certainly not on that day. He feels that the crisis was underestimated because of Elliot's New England characteristic of understatement—"underwhelming," as Harlow calls it. When Richardson had expressed his reservations about the firing of Cox, the White House had not understood the intensity of his convictions.

Everyone in Washington, as in the rest of the nation, was in a state of shock except for the few in the White House who were by then running the country. They had totally failed to perceive the mood of the country and the effect that the firing, compounded by the resignations, would have. People took to the streets; horns honked in front of the White House; the networks were airing specials; the FBI was sent in to guard the Justice Department files.

I phoned Jerry Ford, who had been nominated only nine days earlier, at his home in Alexandria and asked, "Has the world gone crazy? Is Nixon insane?" He seemed just as troubled as the rest of us, and equally surprised. He told me that he had spent almost an

210

hour with Nixon that same morning, that the President had been very much in command of things, that there was no inkling of the Cox-Richardson battle, and that they had talked almost exclusively about foreign affairs. Later I found out from Harlow that Nixon had probably been relaxed when Ford was talking to him because he did not anticipate that the impending defiance of Cox and subsequent resignations would come so quickly.

While talking to Ford, I said that I wondered what Judge Sirica's reaction would be, and Ford said that he'd like to know too. I said I'd phone Sirica, find out and call him back. Ford added that he didn't know Sirica and had always wanted to meet him because he admired him. But the judge was out of town. Later I began to arrange a small dinner at Merrywood so that Ford and Sirica could meet, but by that time Nixon's impending departure was more apparent, so it didn't seem a wise idea.

The next week Nixon's lawyer appeared before Sirica and the tapes were handed over. Still, by then the damage was done; the President had failed to perceive the national mood and had underestimated the effect when he tried to put himself above the law.

Events moved on, crowding the President. A month later, in November, the Republican governors met in Memphis, where Nixon gave them a long, rambling, defensive speech, and, not for the first time, said that he was not a crook. Shortly afterward, Dick and I were driving to the Redskins football game with Virginia Governor Linwood Holton, who had been chairman of the conference. He said that he was disturbed about the President and his self-destructive impulses; Holton had, in fact, seriously considered walking out, and found himself thinking how similar Nixon was to Captain Queeg. An open man, Holton has always been accessible to the press, but after hearing the President that day he ducked reporters for the first time in his life, because he was afraid of what he might say.

He also told us that at the governors' conference they had asked for and received Nixon's assurances that there would be no more "bombshells." Yet the very same day, as Holton was en route home, he got an urgent call on his car phone from Mel Laird announcing one of the biggest bombshells of all: the 18 1/2-minute gap on one tape. Holton shook his head and said, "The man is acting strangely."

Holton wasn't the only one who wondered. There was growing concern about Nixon's mental stability; all over town people speculated in private about whether the President was crazy. But only hints of this ever reached the public, for it is not a subject that is lightly mentioned in the papers or on the air.

CHAPTER 27 ⌒

When Nixon appointed him, Jerry Ford was hardly a household word, yet just a few months later, in early 1974, the polls showed that Vice President Ford was the most popular man in either party because of his "believability," by then a rare commodity in Washington.

After he became Vice President, Jerry gave me one of his first interviews. He told me that his relationship with President Nixon was based on their friendship over the years, and that he had not hesitated to take the post even in the face of increasing distrust of the President, because he had no reason to doubt him. He explained carefully that he viewed Nixon on the totality of his record, rather than solely on the events of Watergate. He emphasized that he himself was apart from Watergate, that no one associated him with it and that he intended to keep it that way. To that end he considered his job to be outside Washington as much as in it, and said that he intended to travel throughout the country, explaining the Republican position on various issues and campaigning for GOP candidates.

I asked the Vice President whether he had ever thought when he was a child that he would be President, and he quickly answered no. Then, after a pause, he said, "But I did come here with a group of Boy Scouts when I was a kid, and when we visited the House of Representatives I remember thinking that I would like to be a member, and later I dreamed that I would."

Washington always reflects the presidential mood, and as 1974 began the city had a pervasive sense of gloom. The President was acting out a lie, and it showed. Bewildering revelations continued to assault the public mind. While citizens were bored with Watergate and in many cases couldn't grasp its complexities, there was no difficulty in understanding that our tax money had been spent for

212

heaters in his swimming pool, or on $75 pillows. Talk also continued in private about the possibility that the President was having a nervous breakdown. With the regularity of shocking revelations—taxes not paid, Bebe Rebozo's questionable handling of campaign contributions, the Howard Hughes money, and the wiretaps on his own brother, Edward Nixon—it certainly wouldn't have been surprising.

Nixon, Pat and Julie showed up for Mrs. Longworth's ninetieth birthday party in February. Outwardly he was cool and confident, a marvel of composure making small talk, and of course no one mentioned Watergate. I was intrigued to see him, for he'd been a virtual recluse for months. We talked about Aunt Laura Gross's death, and he mentioned the recent death of Murray Chotiner, saying, "I'm losing all the old friends."

While I didn't want to embarrass the President at a private party, my reportorial juices began to flow and I found myself asking him how he stood up under all the pressure. He gave a broad sweep of his hand, indicating that it was water off a duck's back. At first he was convincing, but then I realized that he was speaking as if about some other person rather than about himself. He was totally detached from the realities, and it was eerie.

Events continued to move inexorably toward impeachment. The Rodino committee was on the march and would not turn back. Haldeman, Mitchell and Ehrlichman were indicted. At the end of April, Nixon decided to release transcripts of the tapes. That was the beginning of the end, because his hard-core support had come from the middle class, the proudly old-fashioned, and it was these people, the solid citizens I grew up with in Wisconsin, who were most profoundly shocked by the tapes. They had heard vulgar talk before, of course, but it was a shock coming from Nixon, who had always been so publicly pious, and had self-righteously criticized Truman's blunt language.

I had first heard about Nixon's language during the first Eisenhower campaign; for example, after the slush fund was revealed and Ike was vacillating about dumping him, Nixon had phoned and said, "General, you either have to piss or get off the pot." Now, seeing those swear words in cold print made me uncomfortable because it seemed as if he were trying to establish his masculinity and toughness.

But the vulgarity of the language wasn't as shocking as what was said in the Oval Office, a room that generates a special sense of history which is downright intimidating. Its aura inspires reverence for the place and the office, if not for the man occupying it. To me, talking about cover-ups and hush money there seemed virtually heretical, so I was astonished at the emergence of a Jesuit priest as Nixon's most vigorous apologist. "Nixon's Jesuit," as he was called, was Father John McLaughlin. He had run for the Senate in Rhode Island, was defeated by Democratic Senator John O. Pastore, and now was working in the White House as a speech writer. Thinking that it was a good story to have a Jesuit priest as a White House speech writer, I had interviewed him a couple of years earlier. He had arrived for lunch in a very good-looking salt-and-pepper summer suit. He was good-looking too, and almost the first thing he said was that I shouldn't call him "Father. Please call me Doctor." I didn't like this, and wondered what the nuns in Dubuque would think. Such priestly worldliness was unfamiliar to my unsophisticated experience in the Church.

"Doctor" McLaughlin then gave me a long argument about the bloodbath that would occur if we left Vietnam in the lurch. He had been there and talked with other Catholic priests, he said, and he predicted that all the South Vietnamese who fought with us would be murdered—"a long night of a thousand swords," as he put it. The bloodbath theory was an integral part of the Nixon folklore on the war, and I'm afraid I fell for it. I was still bitter about it when Dr. McLaughlin emerged as the new moral authority at the White House and went on national television with a resounding defense of the President. Overnight he was in demand as *the* White House spokesman, so *Newsweek*'s syndication service asked me to interview him. Other reporters were there as we moved in to his office with our cameras, and even before we had left, word came down from the White House communications office that the initial response to his televised defense had been good. The President rewarded his sole defender with an invitation to the Oval Office, which McLaughlin had rarely seen before and from which most other aides were then barred. McLaughlin loved the attention and displayed his clippings and notices at the slightest provocation. During my interview with him he stoutly defended the tapes and said that the swear words were just Nixon's way of working off steam, but he had to agree when I reminded him that one of the commandments forbid using the Lord's name in vain.

While we reloaded our film McLaughlin made a phone call, and began the conversation by saying, "Lyndon, how are we doing?" The two cameramen were as astonished as I, because we didn't know of anyone else named Lyndon except the late President. One of them whispered, "Just how far does that phone line go?" The other whispered back, "It's not a question of how far, but in what direction? Up or down?" McLaughlin may have mentioned another name, but you'll never convince us of that.

Dr. McLaughlin has since left the Jesuits to get married, and has rescinded his statement that Richard Nixon was the "greatest moral leader of the last third of this century."

While the Watergate drama was unfolding in the courts, in the Special Prosecutor's office, in the press and in the official impeachment proceedings, Congressman Peter Rodino, chairman of the House Judiciary Committee, became one of the Watergate heroes. Pushed from all sides to handle the matter differently, he did it his own way, and it was the best way. I had known Rodino from the days when I produced those two radio programs. He had been a frequent guest and always a gentleman. Well known in the Italian-American community and in Congress, he was virtually anonymous elsewhere, but now he had become the pivotal character in Richard Nixon's last days in Washington.

After it was announced that he would handle the impeachment inquiry, Rodino gave me a special interview for the *Newsweek* television syndicate. Since his staff had been ducking our requests for an appointment, the camera crew and I took our chances and traipsed over to his office. By luck we ran into him in the hall outside, accompanied by New Jersey Governor Brendan Byrne and a dozen reporters. Byrne recalled some interviews I had done with President Kennedy, and Rodino brought up some I had done with him in the past, so I seized the opportunity to suggest that we do another one right now. It worked, and everyone else waited so that we could make our deadline.

That was in January 1974, and even at that early date, Rodino was able to summarize the pattern of deliberate impartiality he intended to follow. He never varied from it, though he was urged from every quarter to move faster. It was this painstakingly methodical, slow and thorough pace of the academician, the careful, plodding research, that eventually revealed a damning pattern of culpability which led to Nixon's resignation.

While the committee plugged along in a secrecy uncustomary for Capitol Hill, President Nixon's men were briefing him on its progress as best they could. I've always wondered what went on in Nixon's mind during those last three months in office, but we'll probably never know, since former Presidents are not given to telling the whole truth when they come to write their memoirs. Besides, Nixon has so established himself as a liar that whatever he writes—even the truth —will be forever suspect. His credibility gap is forever.

In any event, the President was increasingly quick-tempered and difficult. He traveled to the Middle East, where unprecedented numbers turned out to see him, and to Russia, where Henry Kissinger had convinced Leonid Brezhnev of the continuity of the American government even in the event of impeachment. But though Nixon didn't seem to grasp that the end was near, there were cruel little hints. In California, for example, the Surf and Sand Hotel in Laguna Beach, which had provided press-conference headquarters whenever the President was in San Clemente, changed the hall back into a restaurant. Those hotel people saw the handwriting on the wall long before the Judiciary Committee hearings began.

In the six weeks before he resigned, Nixon was in the White House only five or six days. He was in San Clemente on July 24, the day the Supreme Court ruled that he had to give up the tapes and documents for which he had claimed "executive privilege." That same day the televised impeachment hearings began, one of the most dramatic moments in American history. The proceedings started with Chairman Rodino setting the tone perfectly; in a speech worthy of that solemn moment, he said, "Our judgment is not concerned with an individual, but with a system of constitutional government."

Each member followed, purposefully stating his or her fundamental beliefs, the kind of summation that you're not called on to make unless you give a lot of Fourth of July speeches. Together, by their collective decorum and stark integrity, those committee members restored a measure of respect for the House of Representatives as a whole. For years the House had been in disrepute for its inability to act with dispatch on our many national problems that screamed for solution. But television does not lie, and it showed the country thirty-eight men and women who were doing their job in Washington magnificently.

On the evening the hearings began, Michael and I went outside to play tennis and inadvertently locked ourselves out. We were so anxious to miss nothing that I broke a window to get in. For my haste, I not only activated the security system but got a deep gash in my hand, and as soon as the hearings adjourned for the night, we had to go to a hospital emergency room for ten stitches. The scar remains prominent today, and is one of many other less visible ones left by Nixon. No more tennis for six weeks.

After the House committee voted for the first article of impeachment on July 27, it seemed clear that Nixon was through, but apparently it still was not obvious to him. A few days later, when the White House released the final damning proof that the President had lied to the American people—that despite his denials, he had indeed discussed hush money and payoffs—he was still so detached from reality that even then he neither thought that he had done anything wrong nor that it was inevitable that he would have to go. Even when his Capitol Hill liaison man told him that he would get only a few votes in the House, he seemed determined to make a fight of it in the Senate, where, he said, "They're a bunch of pushovers."

On Tuesday, August 6, the Senate Republicans met for their weekly luncheon. Anything but "pushovers," they demanded that Nixon resign immediately. Vice President Ford was present, and the conversation got so strong that it was thought seemly for him to leave, which he did, with his colleagues' good wishes, while they remained to discuss what action to take that would impel Nixon to resign. Quite apart from the normal patriotic considerations of removing a criminal President, the Republicans also had partisan pride: it was their party that had been tainted by the scandal. In the end it was the Republicans who were most indignant over Nixon's crimes, especially those who had spent a lifetime building the party on a concept of honor which he had blasphemed.

On the night before it was publicly released, Senator Barry Goldwater had seen the final damning evidence. A White House aide had brought it to him in the Capitol, and he read it while walking back to his Senate office. As he described it later, "I blew my cork," and he went home and refused to answer his phone all night. At the Tuesday lunch the next day it was Goldwater, the GOP guru, the man who often had been the only Republican to speak out against the White House's handling of Watergate, who said, "Nixon has to go." He declared unequivocally that Nixon could no longer be tolerated. No one there defended the President, although one or two remained silent. Immediately after the lunch I interviewed Illinois Senator Charles Percy, who shook his head in amazement and said that he'd never thought he'd live to see the day of a GOP meeting that was so anti-Nixon.

At the White House, General Haig was trying to handle the resignation with the exquisite delicacy it demanded. Since the President's mind was in a volatile state, Haig feared that he might insist on enduring a long and divisive Senate trial. In the name of justice, it would have had to be long to ensure fairness, but this would also ensure a hiatus in government that might be highly perilous in an atomic world that was in the middle of an oil embargo. Besides, Haig knew better than anyone that for months the United States government had been virtually without a Chief Executive while Nixon grappled with Watergate.

On Wednesday, August 7, Goldwater had lunch with his former campaign manager, Dean Burch, who was now a Nixon aide, and General Haig, who asked him to tell the President the straight facts; Goldwater, whose loyalty and aggressive honesty have never been questioned, was the only person Nixon would "take it from" in his unstable mental condition. Goldwater asked Senator John Stennis, the Mississippi Democrat often called the conscience of the Senate, to go with him, but Stennis refused, "unless it is absolutely necessary" —a wise decision because it kept the Democrats and purely partisan politics out of it. Instead, Goldwater was accompanied by the Senate Republican leader, Hugh Scott, and the House Republican leader, John Rhodes, and together they told the President that he couldn't possibly muster the necessary votes in a Senate trial. At one point Goldwater told Nixon that conceivably he might be acquitted on the first and third articles of impeachment, but that on the second, the charge of abuse of power, he would undoubtedly be found guilty. Goldwater even said, "I'm leaning that way myself." (A year later when I asked Goldwater what it took to tell Nixon the truth in the

218

Oval Office, right to his face, he said, "I hope I never have to do it again.")

While this drama was being enacted in the White House, Washington was vibrant with rumors, some of them wild and fanciful, and when it was reported—accurately, as it turned out—that Goldwater had urged the President to resign, the senator went onto the Senate floor, denied it, and looking up toward the Senate press gallery, called the reporters there "a rotten bunch." In explaining this to me later, he said that the negotiations were so fragile that he was afraid that "Nixon's volatile mental state would change, and that he would insist on remaining in office through a long impeachment trial . . . The thing was sitting on a needle. Knowing Nixon, any overt or covert challenge to him, especially in the press, could topple him one way or another . . . and we wouldn't have known what to do next . . . Nixon was adamant and bullheaded, and he was thinking of fighting it out in the Senate and we wanted to save the country all the torture . . . We were afraid of having somebody say something to throw him off."

Long an outspoken critic of the Washington *Post,* Goldwater was highly complimentary of its actions the next day: "They played it cool and refrained from big headlines suggesting that Nixon was about to resign. Such a headline might well have pushed him the other way, considering his mental state." The senator told me that the only complimentary letter he ever wrote the *Post* was to congratulate them on their restraint on August 8.

During these last few days General Haig was running both the country and the White House. Nixon was incapable of doing either, and Goldwater feels that the country was lucky to have a man like Haig, who was sensitive to the dangers of the situation. But even Haig, Goldwater and everyone else couldn't *force* Nixon to resign, and he had told his Cabinet that he was going to continue in office. Haig had to prop him up and try to keep him in touch with reality so that he would be capable of seeing that there was only one rational decision to make.

The resignation came on Thursday night, August 8. I flew back from New York, where I was working, and went directly to the White House. In the circular driveway, the geraniums looked more beautiful than ever before in the twenty years I'd been walking up that drive, and I found myself thinking irrationally, The poor devil—he fixed up the West Wing more beautifully than any of his predecessors, and he gets no credit. Then, carrying the thought further, I saw the geraniums as just one more attempt at cosmetics while the core of the White House was rotten.

I went into the press room, which Nixon had redecorated in Williamsburg fashion, and had expanded by using the space previously occupied by the indoor swimming pool. Those had been happier days, and I imagined that now he probably wished that he could flood it, with all its occupants, back up with water. The room was a mess; old newspapers and notes were strewn everywhere. The television cameras were poised, ready to record any announcement, but none came. There was no coffee, and nothing in any of the dispensing machines, and the room was stuffy with the smell of cigarettes and cigar butts. I wondered if the White House cleaning staff was also quitting.

Nixon was working on his speech in the Executive Office Building across the street and had sent word over that when he walked back, he did not want to talk with anyone. Although the press has no access to the pathway in the rear of the White House, reporters were locked in the press room for thirty-two minutes lest one of them interrupt the President's final night walk. Later I was told that this was inadvertent, but I suspect that an overzealous staff member knew that on Nixon's last night at 1600 Pennsylvania Avenue, it would have been intolerable for him to even glimpse a reporter.

In any event, it was symbolic; Nixon left the way he came: wanting to be alone, the one facet of his complex personality that contributed more than anything else to his fall. The loner put himself not only apart from other men but above them as well, and when he put himself above the law, the people would not tolerate it.

Reporters crowded into the press room to watch the speech on television, and for once there were no wisecracks. No glee. It was a funeral, but the corpse was still breathing and talking.

Afterward the night air was damp as I walked back down the drive. Kissinger's office was lit, and inside I could see his daughter and son and Nancy Kissinger. What an insight into history for those children! I looked up to the Palladian window in the private living quarters just as Mrs. Nixon and the girls were hurriedly pulling the curtains closed. I'd never seen those curtains pulled before, not even after the Kennedy assassination. Despite the distance between us, I thought that I could see the hate in Pat's face. Certainly I could imagine it, and I didn't blame her. Again the action seemed symbolic: the final curtain going down as we, the spectators, walked out. All I felt was numb.

I was due at the Argentine embassy, and was so late that everyone else had started dinner. I mumbled an apology and sat down, but then realized when I looked at the food, which is always delicious there, that I couldn't eat.

And then there was Jerry Ford.

Nixon, whose instincts always seemed to be wrong in personal matters, was replaced by a man whose instincts are always right about such things. Often he is wrong on substance and one can disagree with his actions, but he is refreshingly natural. When he greets someone with a kiss, you know that he would do so in the same way even if millions were not seeing it on television, and he does it in a way that suggests that he is unaware that millions *are* watching. He set the tone when he was sworn in by saying, "Our long national nightmare is over," and so it was.

CHAPTER 28 〜⌒

After Nixon's resignation Washington was like a patient just released from the hospital after a long and enervating illness. The city was limp, encouraged only by the hope that we'd seen the last of a series of mind-boggling crises in our national life. For over two years we had been assaulted on all sides by a series of incredible events: the break-in, Agnew's resignation, the indictments, the payoffs, the lying, the Saturday Night Massacre, the impeachment proceedings and Nixon's departure. We were so satiated with astonishment that I thought I was incapable of further shock. I was wrong.

Toward the end of September, Dick and I had gone to a reception and had stopped on our way home for dinner at Le Bagatelle, a favorite spot with superb service and food. We ordered a fish mousse to be prepared for us, and settled back for a before-dinner drink. But before the mousse appeared, Congressman Wilbur Mills entered, obviously distraught and disoriented, looking for somebody. He has long been a friend, a brilliant legislator, a frequent source for news stories, and as chairman of the House Ways and Means Committee was often referred to as "the second most powerful man in Washington." I waved at him, and he joined us. I was surprised he was there since I had only seen him out at night once before in my life. He never went to cocktail parties or receptions; he never even accepted White House invitations, no matter who was President. Everyone knew that Wilbur Mills went home every night to his gray-haired wife, Polly, to read the tax laws, and that he never had a drink.

But now Wilbur said he'd love to have a drink while waiting for a friend of his from Argentina, who was supposed to be there with her daughter to celebrate her birthday. There ensued one of the most astonishing evenings of my life. In retrospect, I'm still ambivalent about the night: it was a tragedy, but it was also very funny. The Argentine friend never showed up, and Wilbur had a few more drinks while he launched into a running dialogue that was startling, to put it mildly. I had always thought that he had never been outside the continental limits of the United States, but he told us that he had gone to Argentina to help out Perón with his economic troubles, but that by the time he arrived Perón had died, and that he had stayed to help Mrs. Perón. In fact, said Wilbur, he had not only helped her but slept with her, both in Argentina and in Puerto Rico. I kicked Dick under the table.

More drinks came, and though we were starving, the fish mousse was served to someone else while we waited in vain for Wilbur's friend. At each new revelation I'd kick Dick under the table again, and he still claims that it took weeks for the black-and-blue marks to heal. I simply couldn't believe what I was hearing from the distinguished chairman. Intermittently, between startling pronouncements, he would discuss the tax laws with Dick, whom he declared to be brilliant, and during these periods he seemed perfectly lucid. But then there would follow another spate of unbelievable personal revelations about Isabel Perón and the bedroom.

The chef had prepared a second mousse for us, so we could wait to eat no longer, but Wilbur wouldn't join us; "just another drink," he said. Then, growing expansive, he invited us to visit "his place," as he called it. Wilbur assured Dick that we could park at his place, since "I own it." And indeed, when we arrived at the Silver Slipper, which I'd never heard of before, the people there acted as if he did own it. Loud swinging music flooded the street when we entered, and four or five scantily clad females rushed up, put their arms around the chairman and cooed, "Hello, Wilbur!" I kicked Dick again. I couldn't believe what I was seeing—the man who intimidated business tycoons and colleagues, the man before whom Presidents quaked, the man reverently known as "Mr. Chairman," was being smothered and called Wilbur by stripteasers.

The Silver Slipper is small, and its customers eat and drink at their tables while the show goes on. We got a big table, with room enough for the girls, Wilbur, Dick and me, and more drinks were ordered. I had not been drinking for a couple of hours, in part because I was afraid that what I was seeing was a result of wine. Wilbur ordered steak and champagne for all, and we were a very happy group. I really believed that he owned the place; there he was, sitting at the head of the table, just as he did in the House Committee room, acting like a chairman.

Then the show began, and the mistress of ceremonies, who weighed in at more than two hundred pounds, brought on the first act, an unmemorable striptease. All the performers had extraordinarily large breasts, obviously full of silicone. Wilbur had insisted that I be introduced from the stage, which the mistress of ceremonies did with zest and flourish, and I got a good hand from the friendly crowd. Dick got kicked again. Afterward a man came over and asked for my autograph. He said he was from Wisconsin, and I smiled, trying to pretend that I wasn't from Wisconsin. Throughout, Wilbur kept telling me what a great show the Silver Slipper had, and simultaneously kept asking the other girls where Anna was. "Send for her," he demanded. "I want the Dickersons to see her." We kept trying to leave, but he would hear none of it until we met Anna, and all the girls told us how much we would enjoy her.

At this stage I had to go to the ladies' room, and Wilbur assigned one of the girls to escort me there. It was one of my most memorable interviews; that is, *she* interviewed *me*. Her name was Mystique, pronounced Miss Teek, and she wanted to know all about my "line of work." She thought that it would be interesting, and imagined that the salary would be comparable to hers, but what really attracted her was my "hours." She was certain that my schedule was more convenient than hers, and I was inclined to agree. The interview continued

223

under and over the doors of our separate stalls in the ladies' room, and while we combed our hair Mystique finally decided that she would be either a reporter or a doctor.

When we returned to our table, Wilbur gave a raise to the mistress of ceremonies. However, he may have done this before because she wasn't much impressed by the gesture. Then Anna, the Argentine Firecracker—Miss Fanne Fox, that is—arrived. She was livid, so furious that she was literally shaking. She was ready to tear Wilbur apart, and while I tried not to stare, I heard her say, "I told you never to do this to me again." Wilbur introduced me to her, saying, "I own her." I was appalled. While the show went on, she and Wilbur had a bad argument and disappeared. We seized this chance to break loose, but when we reached the door we decided it would be wrong to leave Wilbur there alone; something might happen to him. Still thinking that the whole episode was an aberration in the chairman's life, we thought we'd take him back to Merrywood and let him sleep it off, so Dick asked the manager to find him. "Oh, don't worry," the manager said. "We're used to this. We'll take care of him."

The next day I thought I must have been having a nightmare. Except for the employees of the Silver Slipper, I was sure that few people, including reporters or congressmen, knew about Wilbur's secret life, and I never mentioned it to anyone, still hoping that it was just an aberration.

But two weeks later, in October, Wilbur went public, and headlines were emblazoned across the country, relating all the details of Chairman Mills and Annabella Batistella, the Argentine Firecracker, and of their fight and her dunking in the Tidal Basin. I was lecturing in Michigan at the time, and the audience wanted to know all about Chairman Mills. When I arrived home I was told that the *Post* had phoned eight times. I still hadn't mentioned our evening to anyone, but reporters who flocked to the Silver Slipper had heard all about our visit from the girls. (To hear the retelling, I was a regular customer. If I ever hire a publicity agent, it will be someone from the chorus line at the Silver Slipper.) When I refused to comment, it seemed as if I were repudiating Wilbur, so I did confirm what the reporters already knew—that Dick and I had been at the club with him. I didn't care about a story stating that the Dickersons had been to a striptease joint, but Wilbur Mills is a good and decent man, and it seemed cruel punishment that his misdeeds should be so glaringly publicized, especially in contrast to others who suffer no public disgrace even though their lives are far less exemplary. I write about it now only because part of our night with Wilbur is already in the public domain.

JFK used to say that life is unfair, and indeed it is unfair if history chooses to focus only on the brief period when Wilbur Mills was an alcoholic, instead of on his lifetime of outstanding service to his country.

CHAPTER 29

The switchover from one President to another is complicated, and in Ford's case the difficulties were compounded since he was the only man ever to assume the office without having won a national election. The electorate was not sure what to expect. When Nixon appointed him to succeed Agnew there was a spate of articles, but he was hardly scrutinized with the intensity focused on a candidate during a campaign. Also, much of the long congressional investigation about him went unread, since the nation's concern was riveted on Watergate.

For the press, bruised by the lies of the Nixon Administration, Ford was a gift from heaven. Both for Washington and for the nation, his openness, obvious decency and honesty were an intoxicating change. Boosted by the natural reservoir of good will that this nation reserves for its Presidents, Ford became the all-American boy made good, the Eagle Scout in the White House. In fact, the press corps went on a veritable binge of discovering qualities in him that had never before been perceived. But it didn't last long.

In his first news conference I asked the new President what he was going to do about the foundering economy, and in his second I asked him if he had made a deal with Nixon to pardon him. These two issues were to dominate his first six months in office, and were directly to blame for his slow start.

After leaving church on Sunday, September 8, President Ford announced the Nixon pardon. There was no warning. At his news conference he had said that there was no deal, and he left the clear impression that no decision was in process. In a democracy, it is necessary to marshal public opinion if you are to govern, a point that Ford either ignored or wasn't aware of. Unprepared for the pardon and jolted by it, the public became suspicious of the new President and he thereby self-imposed another handicap. It was a sign of his naïveté that he didn't anticipate the resultant furor.

On the day of the pardon I was in Philadelphia, presiding as the master of ceremonies in the first public commemoration of the Bicentennial of the Continental Congress. All of us, including several state officials, Mayor Frank Rizzo and Senator Hugh Scott, were seated on a flag-draped dais not far from Independence Hall. Thousands were waiting in the Mall and along the streets for the program and parade, and I was supposed to begin the ceremony by introducing the dignitaries. My remarks were carefully planned and timed to the second, tying the past to the present with Ford's line, "Our long national nightmare is over," and making the point that now we had a fresh chance to keep faith with our forefathers. But just before we went on, Scott got a phone call from President Ford saying that he was going to pardon Nixon. I was speechless, both literally and figuratively. Scott found it interesting that Ford still kept referring to Nixon as "the President," and he wasn't pleased with the decision either. Neither was Rizzo, the law-and-order mayor who had been one of the first Democrats to come out for Nixon and thereby felt doubly betrayed by his wrongdoing. As for me, I was furious, and not just because of the decision itself; I had to throw out large parts of my speech and ad-lib an explanation of an act which to me was clearly premature.

Most of Washington felt the same way. It was short-sighted to grant a pardon without demanding a confession in exchange. For the youth of today and for future generations, it seems to be mandatory to make the point that Nixon was brought down because he was guilty and because he put himself above the law. Without either a confession or official documentation of his criminality, I feared—and still do—that he might rise again and roam the country giving lectures on ethics in government.

But while I believe the speed and form of the pardon were wrong, Ford's instincts were right because until the ex-President was pardoned, the country would have continued to be obsessed by him. More than a year later we were still preoccupied with his legacy, his forthcoming writings, his future television appearances, his self-aggrandizing trip to China. Now, from the distance of time, and based on what I've gleaned on the lecture circuit both in Washington and the country generally, more and more people regard the pardon as Macbeth might have: "If it were done when 'tis done, then 'twere well it were done quickly."

In those first days Ford did not understand the urgency of doing something about the economy, and when I asked him what could be expected immediately, he talked only of study groups programed to find long-term solutions. For five months he seemed to flail at issues like a modern Don Quixote, forever taking off in his big new airplane. But when he returned from his winter skiing vacation in January 1975, he realized that something was wrong. The polls told him that citizens didn't think he had taken charge, and to his credit, he changed his policy completely. Whereas earlier he had issued "WIN" buttons and called for a tax hike, he now asked for a tax cut and began his State of the Union message by saying, "We are in trouble." He was talking sense to the American people and they liked it. Eric Sevareid noted at the time that we had a President again, that he had seized the initiative and had held on to the momentum.

Six months later Ford was still on the move. He enjoyed the popularity of the opinion polls, and Washington columnists, pundits and bureaucrats, displaying a packlike mentality, were saying that he would be unbeatable in the '76 election. Even the Democratic National Committee chairman, Robert Strauss, told me that if Ford did "just one thing right," the Democrats wouldn't be able to beat him. But as quickly as he had soared in the polls during the summer he was sinking in them by fall. The excesses of the FBI and the CIA were intruding on the conscience of citizens who had thought their country incapable of the obnoxious realities that gradually were revealed. The economy was feeble, New York City was on the verge of bankruptcy, and the opinion polls showed that people thought Ford was to blame. At this point he and his advisers decided that being a good guy was not enough, and on Sunday, November 2, 1975, in one grand step aimed at changing his image, he fired the darling of the conservatives, Defense Secretary James Schlesinger, and the CIA chief, William Colby, and demoted Kissinger. It was a clumsy maneuver, made more so because Ford's hand was forced by *News-*

227

week. The story had been leaked to the magazine and the editors were planning to print it far in advance of Ford's scheduled announcement. The President had had a long session with Schlesinger on Saturday, the day before, and hadn't mentioned the impending dismissal, but when *Newsweek* told the Secretary of Defense that he'd better check the White House to see whether the story was true, he was told to come over early on Sunday morning. As he entered the Oval Office he met Colby on his way out, and Colby said later that neither of them had had an inkling. All Sunday the story simmered; no one at the White House would confirm or deny it because the President was entertaining Egyptian President Anwar Sadat and didn't want to take the play away from the visit.

The next day, November 3, Rockefeller took himself out of the running for the Vice Presidency. A small group of us had had a long-standing date with him for an off-the-record lunch that day, but when I reached the hotel I found that lunch had abruptly been postponed. That evening Ford held a televised news conference, which was a debacle. The conference aimed to project the image of the President as a tough, take-charge leader. It failed. Reporters, reintroduced to truth and candor by Ford, suddenly saw a different man. To those present he appeared to be withholding information that the people had a right to know. Television conveyed the same impression, and the President thereby created his own credibility gap. It simply was not a satisfactory explanation to claim that he fired Schlesinger just because he wanted his own "guys" on his team—especially when Schlesinger had openly called a news conference to say that defense expenditures were too small. Moreover, there had been stories for months that Schlesinger was fighting Kissinger in a power struggle over détente, and as to whether the Russians had violated the SALT agreement. The episode was further muddied by speculation that Presidential Assistant Donald Rumsfeld had engineered the change so he could further his own career and become Defense Secretary. Other rumors had it that Kissinger promoted the firings, but I don't believe them. Dick and I went to the races with the Kissingers the following weekend, and Henry said that the last thing he wanted was the confusion of high-level musical chairs. His work demanded a calmer atmosphere in Washington, and other nations, bewildered by the move, were beseeching his office for an explanation.

Meanwhile, on the Thursday following Ford's news conference, the Vice President also met the press. Rockefeller was so open and forthright that by comparison Ford's image was further blemished.

The day after Rockefeller's news conference, I had a special interview with him about the Vice Presidency for this book. As I waited in his outer office I thought about his predecessors and how they had suffered in the job. For LBJ it had meant a million slights, some real, some imagined. Getting enough publicity to satisfy the Johnson ego was virtually impossible; besides, what is there for a Vice President to do? JFK was acutely aware of this problem, and did his best to keep it under control. At the fancy White House dinners, LBJ and Lady Bird were usually included, but often it was as if they were among strangers. LBJ did a good job as head of the space effort, but there simply was no way to outshine the glamorous young President and his romantic wife. And the Kennedy aides were not sympathetic; in fact, they exacerbated the situation. For his part, LBJ was trying to edge his way in while they were trying to keep him out.

But though LBJ hated being Vice President, he disliked even more having to pretend that he was happy. It was painful for him to sit around, growing more restless each day, trying to grasp power, keep busy and put up a front that he was more involved in affairs of state than he really was. He had thrived under his leadership role in the Senate, so it was doubly hard for him to be "number two." Besides, he wasn't number two; he was treated as if he were a lot lower. One night at Ethel and Bobby's, at a summer dinner outdoors, LBJ was the highest-ranking guest, but it was not on his place card but on Bobby's that Ethel wrote, "The Second Most Important Man in the World."

No man in history has been known to enjoy the Vice Presidency. Long before he himself took the job, I asked Nelson Rockefeller why he had turned it down when it had been offered him by both Nixon and Humphrey. He said that being Vice President had put Nixon on ice for eight years and almost killed him, that it had almost killed LBJ, and that in fact it did wipe out Hubert Humphrey.

The love-hate relationship between a President and Vice President produces the most exquisite poison. It is deflating for a man to know that he would not have the job were it not for the President. It's a dehumanizing role, since doglike loyalty is all that is demanded. For his part, the President consciously or subconsciously is constantly reminded of his own mortality whenever he sees his Vice President, the potential successor who can take over only at the President's death or debilitation. There is also a certain disdain that flows from a President, or any other powerful man, toward anyone whose role depends on his pleasure.

In the last year of the Kennedy Administration, there was much talk about whether or not he would "dump Johnson" as his running mate for a second term. When asked about it directly at a news conference, he was unequivocal and said, in part, "I don't know what they'll do about me, but I'm sure that the Vice President will be on the ticket if he chooses to run." A couple of weeks later at dinner I asked LBJ whether he thought Kennedy would dump him, and he brushed the question aside, saying that he'd never thought about it. But during the next course it was he who brought up the subject again, and he repeated word for word all of Kennedy's press-conference answer, adding, "That doesn't sound like I'm not going to be around, does it?"

Years later when Hubert Humphrey was having dinner at our house, I naïvely asked him whether it wasn't a relief to have as President a man who had been through the tortures of the post himself and understood what it is like, to which Humphrey replied, "There is *no* President who understands." I knew what he meant later when LBJ, Humphrey, Jack Valenti, Dick and I had an impromptu dinner at the Moyers' house. The President became expansive about those he loved and those he didn't, and then started talking about his choice for Vice President the next time around. There were rumors that Hubert would be dumped, and LBJ did nothing that night to discourage them; in fact, he encouraged them. He mentioned the need for national unity during a war, and said that it might best be achieved by naming a Republican as a running mate. He extolled the virtues of Nelson Rockefeller, declaring him to be the "right kind of Republican" to form a consensus ticket. In effect, he was warning Humphrey that he had better not stray from the fold on the Vietnam war, or he would be replaced. Humphrey was humiliated, and the more Johnson played his cruel cat-and-mouse game, the more humiliated he felt. I clenched my teeth and wondered how he could take it.

Now, on November 7, 1975, while waiting for Rockefeller, I thought that the job had not changed a jot since John Adams described it as "the most insignificant office that ever the invention of man contrived or his imagination conceived."

When Rockefeller bounced in, he was exuberant, encouraged by the reviews of his news conference, which had been excellent. When his withdrawal was first announced, I had thought it was one more case of vice-presidential blues, a public outburst that could have been avoided if time had been allowed to intervene and some project that he could sink his teeth into could be found. But I was wrong; Rockefeller had resigned for two other reasons. First, he thought he could make a more meaningful contribution if he removed himself from the mounting criticism of the Republican right wing; second, by dissociating himself from Ford's policy toward New York's financial troubles, he had positioned himself to be a presidential candidate himself.

On the first point, Rockefeller said that GOP conservatives still blamed him for Goldwater's defeat and for Nixon's defeat by Kennedy, and that he didn't want to give them a chance to blame him for Ford's potential defeat, especially if it meant that he couldn't do the job he'd set out to do. But although he was withdrawing because of right-wing sniping, he believed that Ford and his advisers had greatly exaggerated their potential threat.

As for his stand on Ford's policy toward New York, Rockefeller's eyes sparkled and his eyebrows jumped up and down when I compared him to Hubert Humphrey, theorizing that Humphrey might have been President had he dissociated himself earlier from Johnson's war policies. Rockefeller agreed, and said that his own closest adviser had advanced the same theory. He readily admitted that if he had not publicly disavowed the President's attitude toward New York's approaching bankruptcy, he would have been disowned by his own supporters and lost his own political base. Still, though at that moment he could not envision any scenario which would give him the nomination, during the interview his brother Laurence telephoned, and listening to one side of the conversation I heard the Vice President say that he wasn't a candidate, adding, "But who knows what might happen?"

As I was leaving I asked him why Ford hadn't urged him to stay on, to which Rockefeller replied, "With my record I wouldn't try to tell anyone how to win the nomination."

Rockefeller went to Washington fully aware of the unhappiness endemic to the job. He had studied his predecessors and had seen how miserable they were when condemned to inactivity or meaningless chores. That's why, he said, he had not accepted the job when both Nixon and Humphrey had offered it to him. He accepted Ford's offer only because of the circumstances of the Nixon resignation; he honestly felt that it was an opportunity to do something for his country. Moreover, he was convinced that he was different from his predecessors because he had more responsibility than they and therefore had been able to make a contribution. We were in a great period of rapid change, he pointed out, and it was challenging, fun and exciting when one could influence and shape the future. He spoke enthusiastically about his Committee on National Priorities, and of his hopes that its reports will form the basis for a meaningful debate in the campaign and thereafter. Being as rich as he is and as willing to spend millions on such a committee, he may well influence the national dialogue more in a private role than in public office. While he has been circumspect about his disagreements with Ford, it is known that he was uncomfortable in the do-nothing aura that permeated the White House at that time.

In January 1976, almost three months after he withdrew, I asked Rockefeller if he had any regrets, and he answered, "No. I wanted to be where the action was." Thinking that he had misunderstood me, I repeated the question, and he said again, "You heard me. I wanted to be where the action was."

CHAPTER 30 ⌒

After Ford's personnel shuffles, foreign countries dependent on U.S. policies were uneasy and perplexed. At home conservatives were angered, seeing their influence diminished; liberals were unhappy that Rockefeller was out; Reagan, in quintessential arrogance, said he was not appeased; and the President looked silly when, having just fired Colby, he had to rehire him until Ambassador George Bush arrived home from China to replace him. In short, the President's office was in disarray.

Still, all was chipper in the East Wing, sometimes called "The ladies' side of the White House," where the First Lady's press secretary and social secretary have their offices, an area often in friendly competition with the West Wing. The women there were also confused by the shakeup, but not so much that they couldn't bask in the reflected success of Mrs. Ford. Just as the President's stock was plummeting, the Harris poll announced that Betty Ford's was on the rise, and that she had beaten her husband in "job rating." There was a cartoon tacked to the wall making the point that President Ford could be re-elected if he didn't have to run against his wife.

While Mrs. Ford arrived at the White House billed primarily as a suburban housewife, she had become one of its most popular residents. She has received more mail than any of her predecessors, including Eleanor Roosevelt and Lady Bird Johnson. Over fifty thousand people have written her about her breast surgery, more than twenty thousand on various women's issues, including her defense of the Equal Rights Amendment, and more than thirty-five thousand on her televised opinions on premarital sex, pot and abortion. After she appeared on *60 Minutes*, CBS received more mail than on any program since Murrow's on Senator McCarthy. Ford's staff was alarmed. They honestly thought that Betty Ford was an albatross. But while they were wringing their hands over her candor, the people were registering strong approval. This came as a shock to the men's side of the White House, well known as a male-chauvinist stronghold. One presidential assistant told me that a copy of a problem analysis done for the President had been sent to Mrs. Ford in the belief that it would be helpful to her in a speech she was about to make. When higher aides learned that the paper was being routed to her, it was retrieved by a man trying to protect the President—on the theory that the less she knew, the better.

Such attitudes have not been shared by the President, and the men's side has since come to have a healthy respect for Betty Ford as a campaign asset. When I saw her shopping for shoes one day (she has fewer Secret Service agents around than Henry Kissinger, and no clerk recognized her) she told me that women all over the country had written to say how grateful they were that she had spoken frankly about matters which previously had often been forbidden conversation. As social scientists and psychologists tell us, the single most important step toward solving family crises is to be able to discuss a problem openly, to communicate. But they also tell us that most families cannot do it. However, the residents of the White House are fair game, and evidently by discussing the First Family's opinions, others found that they could talk about their own concerns. It is not too much to say that Betty Ford single-handedly triggered a national dialogue on the changing morals of the emerging generation.

When the Fords moved in, the White House suddenly became a happy place again. Encouraged by their parents, the four children established their independence and displayed an unusual ability to adjust. The life of presidential children is not easy, but the Fords' outspokenness helped them. Over the years, Betty Ford had done most of the raising of the children because their father was away a great deal. However, they invariably took family vacations together, usually skiing, and when he was home, he spent time with them. I recall vividly one night when the circus was in town. We were leaving early to avoid the rush, and there was Congressman Ford sitting in his car with the light on. While his children were inside, he was waiting outside for them working on a report.

Of course anything would have been a relief after the oppressiveness of Nixon's personal tragedy. Right from the beginning, the Fords were perfectly natural in whatever they did. They kept the dignity of the Executive Mansion without resorting to the phony grandeur of their predecessor. At a state dinner one night I complimented Mrs. Ford on the comfortable, relaxed atmosphere, and she said that they wanted the White House to be like someone's home rather than a public building. They have succeeded.

It's difficult not to become spoiled in the White House, where every conceivable service is available twenty-four hours a day, and where if anything more is desired, it's easy to send for. Old-timers around Washington think that the best preventive medicine to avoid delusions of grandeur is for the President and his family to lead more normal lives, on the basis that it's a leveling experience to run out of toothpaste and have to stand in line at the checkout counter along with everyone else. There's something to the theory; exclusivity is not the best way of keeping in touch with reality, and instinctively the Fords seem to know this. They appear at private parties more than any of their predecessors did, and seem to enjoy them. They also go to restaurants and frequently attend performances at the Kennedy Center. One night they took a group of old friends to see Pearl Bailey, and when the show was over they went backstage. The children and

234

I had also been invited back, and seven-year-old John was delighted to see the indomitable Pearl teach the President to do the hustle and to watch him dance along with the entire cast of *Hello, Dolly!* The Fords have a natural sensitivity, and were very friendly to the boys and Janie. They also know that children like to think that their parents are important, so as they were leaving, the President turned around, waved goodbye and called out, "Say hello to Dick!" The children beamed. Later, in relating the episode to his father, John said, "He has a very strong handshake—for a President."

CHAPTER 31

The 1976 presidential campaign began like all the others before it. Although the trappings were embellished with Bicentennial slogans, the starting line was still New Hampshire. And Wallace's war cry of 1972 was the precursor of the main campaign theme in 1976: Down with Washington. Most of the other candidates adapted this philosophy in one form or another. Even President Ford was running against the capital, in which he has worked for twenty-five years. The truth is that some of the best people here also feel that fresh ideas articulated by new leaders are needed. Certainly it is part of the reason the two Senate chiefs, Scott and Mansfield, and probably House Speaker Albert, are stepping down.

With so many new men and women coming to Washington after the election, it will be a far different place from when I arrived here. It already is. Coincidentally, on the same day in January 1975 that I interviewed Ford, I sat next to Elliot Richardson at dinner. Both of them reminisced about how much had happened since we all first came here, and how difficult it was to sort it all out. Even the city's life style has changed. For years, only the National Theatre saved it from cultural isolation, but now, with the Kennedy Center, Washington is emerging as a rival to New York. Also in the old days, the capital wasn't a restaurant town; people dined mostly at each other's houses. But that too has changed. There are quite a few good restaurants, and the women no longer dress in expensive but dowdy lace the way they did when this was a provincial Southern town. Now they are rather chic. And it's become a mecca for movie stars and the rich, who like to be around power generally and Henry Kissinger specifically. Sensing the new ambience, Dick started the Pisces Club, a place for dinner and dancing patterned after Annabel's in London. Although it is said that Washington is an early-to-bed town, Pisces has become a quick success, with a membership spanning the spectrum from Pearl Bailey to local socialites to Sheik Yamani. Within one week we went to small parties there that featured Marion Javits dancing with Nureyev, and Elizabeth Taylor, who had come to the capital to find an escort and publicity vehicle in the Iranian ambassador. Concomitantly the gossip columnists have flourished because where there is scandal there is gossip, and where there is gossip there is glamour.

For my part, I'm not so starry-eyed as I once was. I used to be awed by power, as if winning an election automatically anointed the victor with a certain infallability. I'm wiser now, but I still haven't lost the enthusiasm I came with. It would be easy to be disillusioned; I was greeted here by McCarthyism, and only recently we have endured Watergate. But even McCarthyism was no preparation for Nixon's indecencies and the outrage of Watergate. The sixties began with the hope of Camelot, but soon I was reporting the murders of three national leaders. It began to seem that assassination was as American as apple pie and as endemic to our country as the political coup is elsewhere. But in the same era in which we killed our leaders, simultaneously we lightened the burden of poverty for millions, improved education and pushed civil rights ahead with a bulldozer.

One of the most exciting advances has been in women's rights. When I came to Washington, there were no other women on network television news and no women's movement. It was devastating to be told not to try because you were female—or worse, to simply be ignored because you were. Later we went through a period when each station had one woman and one black, and if they could find a black woman, their tokenism was solved by one gesture. Now it's different. Each day another male-chauvinist stanchion is knocked down. Also the women themselves are different. Justice Holmes used to be quoted on how Washington was filled with brilliant men and the women they married before they came here. But that has changed drastically. Washington wives now are often as well informed as their husbands—and sometimes more so. In the case of some presidential candidates, it has been suggested that their wives would be better qualified than they are.

But though we were moving ahead at home, we lost our way in Vietnam. And before we belatedly extricated ourselves from that most unpopular of wars, we were assaulted by Watergate. With the current emphasis on the Bicentennial, we are constantly reminded of our history of corruption, but Watergate really *was* different. Richard Nixon did not steal our money so much as our sacred heritage. He decimated our self-image, leaving pernicious if not terminal aftereffects. Having been lied to about the war, disgusted citizens were turned even further away from government by Watergate. As the opinion polls in the 1976 primaries showed, many of them believed that their votes were meaningless; anyone in Washington was blanketed with the epithet of "crook." Capitalizing on this, candidates condemned the capital and thus generated even more disenchantment.

Almost as discouraging as the public's turnoff is what British journalist Jan Morris calls predatory journalism in the wake of Watergate. She feels that its excessive demands are distasteful, relentless and harmful because of the inescapable innuendo that nobody in high office is beyond suspicion. As she says, "The right to say anything about anybody is not one of the inalienable rights envisaged by the founding fathers." Fortunately, many reporters themselves are increasingly concerned about excesses. Proud of their role in exposing Watergate, they know that they must also use their freedom to guard against tyranny by the press.

As I look back over the years, I think of how despondent I was during the McCarthy era. Then I recall one of my most vivid memories: Senator John Stennis standing tall in the early morning hours to condemn McCarthy for dragging the Senate into "the slush and slime of the gutter." And when my own despair was at its nadir during the Nixon disgrace, I was heartened by the men and women called "ordinary" representatives—the members of the House Judiciary Committee—who showed they were most extraordinary as they carried out their duties with dignity. When we feared most for the future of America, these men and women restored our faith. While I have known about the drunks, the phonies and the brown envelopes stuffed with money, I have also seen the greatness of some of the people who came to the capital. This may sound idealistic, but I am an idealist "without illusions," as John Kennedy once put it. I have no illusions about the men and women who come here; I have seen their warts, their flaws, their human failings. Even so, I have profound respect for them. They have shown us that they can make the system work. Warned by Theodore Roosevelt, they know that if they step into the arena, they will be bloodied for their pains; yet they continue to come and to try. Despite the national cynicism, I have been in Washington too long to do less than applaud their arrival. Surely in Paradise they will be a rung above those who only criticize or, even worse, do nothing out of despair or disinterest.